James Francis Hogan

**The Irish in Australia**

James Francis Hogan

**The Irish in Australia**

ISBN/EAN: 9783744733755

Printed in Europe, USA, Canada, Australia, Japan

Cover: Foto ©ninafisch / pixelio.de

More available books at **www.hansebooks.com**

# IRISH IN AUSTRALIA.

## BY THE SAME AUTHOR.

# AN AUSTRALIAN CHRISTMAS COLLECTION.

*A Series of Colonial Stories, Sketches, and Literary Essays.*

203 Pages, handsomely bound in green and gold.   Price Five Shillings.

---

A VERY pleasant and entertaining book has reached us from Melbourne. The author, Mr. J. F. Hogan, is a young Irish-Australian, who, if we are to judge from the captivating style of the present work, has a brilliant future before him. Mr. Hogan is well known in the literary and Catholic circles of the Australian Colonies, and we sincerely trust that the volume before us will have the effect of making him known to the Irish people at home and in America. Under the title of "An Australian Christmas Collection," Mr. Hogan has republished a series of fugitive writings which he had previously contributed to Australian periodicals, and which have won for the author a high place in the literary world of the Southern hemisphere. Some of the papers deal with Irish and Catholic subjects. They are written in a racy and elegant style, and contain an amount of highly interesting matter relative to our co-religionists and fellow-countrymen under the Southern Cross. A few papers deal with inter-Colonial politics, and we think that home readers will find these even more entertaining than those which deal more immediately with the Irish element.

\* \* \* \* \*

We have quoted sufficiently from this charming book to show its merits. Our readers will soon hear of Mr. Hogan again, for he has in preparation a work on the "Irish in Australia," which, we are confident, will prove very interesting to the Irish people in every land. We know too little about the fortunes of our countrymen abroad. We are, unhappily, so engrossed in the mighty struggle which we are waging with wrong and oppression that we sometimes forget to think of those whom the fortunes of the strife sent forth from our shores, and anything which helps to foster that spirit of union, which is so characteristic of the Ireland of the present day, ought to be received as a boon for which we could not be too grateful. We must not forget, too, how nobly the Australian Irish have stood by us in the present struggle, and that time and distance have but strengthened their love and devotion to the land of their forefathers. In conclusion, we feel great pleasure in acknowledging how much credit is due to Mr. Hogan for devoting abilities of great promise to cement the union existing between Ireland and her exiled children in Australia.

*The Nation,* Dublin, February 19, 1887.

# THE IRISH

IN

# AUSTRALIA.

BY

JAMES FRANCIS HOGAN.

AUSTRALIAN EDITION.

EORGE ROBERTSON & CO., MELBOURNE & SYDNEY

1888.

PRINTED BY
KELLY AND CO., GATE STREET, LINCOLN'S INN FIELDS. W.C.
AND MIDDLE MILL, KINGSTON-ON-THAMES.

# PREFACE.

It is now some five years since I conceived the idea of writing a history of my fellow-countrymen in Australasia, but it was only within the last year or two that I could find sufficient time to make any material progress with the undertaking, although I had been collecting the materials for some period in advance. To all those old Irish colonists, to whom I applied for general reminiscences or specific information, and who very kindly, readily, and fully complied with my request, I am deeply indebted for a variety of interesting details concerning the events of the early days that were not otherwise obtainable. Written for the most part in Melbourne, the work was subjected to a thorough revision during my recent three weeks' voyage across the Pacific from Sydney to San Francisco, and the seven days on the Atlantic between New York and Liverpool. We are now at the close of the first century of colonisation in Australia, and the time is therefore opportune for an estimate of the influence exercised by the Irish element of the population on the remarkable growth and development of the Greater Britain of the South. Having lived in Australia from childhood, I have endeavoured, not I hope without some success, to present in this volume a faithful panorama of Irish life, Irish history, and Irish achievements in the land I know and love so well.

J. F. HOGAN.

LONDON, *October 5th*, 1887.

# CONTENTS.

| CHAP. | | PAGE |
|---|---|---|
| I.—A Survey of the South | | 1 |
| II.—Greater Britain's Metropolis | | 18 |
| III.—The Story of Burke and Wills | | 45 |
| IV.—A Birthplace of Freedom | | 57 |
| V.—A Golden City | | 88 |
| VI.—A Few Irish Centres | | 100 |
| VII.—Irish Immigrants in the Colonies | | 130 |
| VIII.—The Voyage of the "Erin-go-Bragh" | | 155 |
| IX.—The Mother of the Australias | | 179 |
| X.—Four of the Family | | 195 |
| XI.—The Church in the Colonies | | 225 |
| XII.—A Group of Statesmen | | 265 |
| XIII.—Notable Irish-Australians | | 303 |
| XIV.—Literature, Science and Art | | 328 |
| XV.—Irish-Australian Characteristics | | 341 |

# THE IRISH IN AUSTRALIA.

## CHAPTER I.

### A SURVEY OF THE SOUTH.

A NEW IRELAND IN AUSTRALIA—TWO STREAMS OF EMIGRATION—HOME RULE IN THE COLONIES—FOUR IRISH SPEAKERS—SUCCESSES OF IRISH-AUSTRALIANS IN SEVERAL SPHERES—FRATERNAL SYMPATHY WITH THE IRISH AT HOME—HISTORY OF COLONIZATION—BUCKLEY, "THE WILD WHITE MAN"—SIR RICHARD BOURKE, BEST OF COLONIAL GOVERNORS—THE AGITATION FOR HOME RULE IN VICTORIA—DISCOVERY OF GOLD—THE IRISH ARMY OF DIGGERS—COLONIAL PROGRESS.

" A NEW Ireland in America " is a familiar phrase to Celtic and Saxon ears, but a " New Ireland in Australia " will perhaps be a rather novel expression to many. Yet the words in the latter case convey the idea of an accomplished fact, equally as well as in the former. For more than thirty years two great streams of emigration have been flowing from Ireland, the larger shaping its course across the Atlantic and discharging its human freight on the shores of the Great Republic of the West, the smaller in volume turning to the South, and, after traversing half the circumference of the globe, striking against the sunny shores of Australia. As a consequence of the comparative proximity of America to the Old World, no difficulty whatever has been experienced in arriving at a true estimate of the position and prospects of the Irish transplanted to the West. Friends and foes alike have been enabled to closely follow their movements, to study their mode of life under altered conditions, to ascertain the opinion held respecting them by people of other nationalities, and to determine whether or not the virtues characteristic of the old land flourish on the soil of the new. And splendidly have the Irish-Americans as a body borne this crucial test. Not on the authority of friendly critics alone, but many foes of his faith and fatherland have been forced to acknowledge the genuine worth of the typical Irish-American. They have given, perhaps unwillingly, the most conclusive testimony to his value as a citizen, his fidelity as a husband, his devotion as a father, and though last, not least, his loyalty as a Catholic. The Irish at home are proud to know, from the mouths of independent and even hostile witnesses, that though a stormy ocean separates their exiled brethren from the land of their affections, they are still as Irish in heart and feeling as ever; they still cherish the memories of the historic past, and their aspirations for national unity and local self-government are only intensified by distance. The poor persecuted peasant, whom, with weak wife and helpless family, a brutal landlord or pitiless agent has evicted in the depth of winter from the hallowed home of his ancestors, is traced across the Atlantic, followed into a newly-settled district and there discovered—a respected resident, a good neighbour, and, very often, an independent man. The ardent young patriot, who employs his talents in the cause of his country's freedom, and pays the orthodox penalty for loving one's country "not wisely but too well" by a compulsory residence for a season amongst convicted criminals, is seen receiving a cordial welcome on landing in the Empire City, and soon his name is referred to as being the occupant of a distinguished and honourable position, won by the exercise of those abilities for which no scope existed in the land of his birth. And it has been a source of surprise to the host of individuals, whose knowledge of Ireland is confined to what they read in partisan books and newspapers, to find that the people, who when in their native land were described as senseless rioters and incorrigible landlord-shooters, are conspicuous in America for their quiet behaviour and respect for law and order. These facts have come out in the published evidence of foreign tourists in America, and are a splendid testimonial to the noble ingredients of the Irish character when developed under free and favourable conditions.

But, whilst the western Irish exodus has formed the subject of much European investigation, the southern branch of the great emigration stream has not been traced and examined with the same attention. The reasons are obvious. It is only of late years that the Australian colonies have completely recovered from the delirium of the gold fever, and have begun to assume the recognised aspect of settled communities. Hitherto, it would have been unsafe to describe the evidences of possibly fleeting appearances as facts indicative of the future, or to draw elaborate conclusions in the absence of substantial information. Besides, the immense watery gulf of thirteen thousand miles that separates the Australian colonies from the great centres of Europe, and the anticipated difficulty of reaching the scattered settlements of a continent only partially explored, damped the ardour of adventurous travellers and inquiring students. Hence the number of literary tourists in Australia has, until very recently, been comparatively small. Now, however, the case is far different. The Australian "Empire of the South" has advanced to an important position; the slow and tedious voyage of several months' duration has been superseded by the fleets of fast-going steamers, that traverse the distance between London and Melbourne in little more than a month. The various colonies are no longer isolated settlements; all the leading cities of the Australian continent are connected by railway and telegraph, and the grand idea of an "Australian Federal Union," advocated for many years with all the earnestness of an eloquent Irish-Australian statesman,\* is rapidly approaching the practical stage of accomplishment.

The Irish in Australia form a most interesting study. True to their national character, they have come to the front in all the colonies. In every colonial parliament, Irishmen will be found distinguishing themselves as political leaders. Responsible parliamentary government, or, in simpler words, Home Rule, is in operation in all the Australian colonies save one, and it is, therefore, not surprising that colonial legislatures should have a large proportion of Irishmen, when it is remembered that the choice of efficient representatives is left unreservedly in the hands of the people. As a striking proof of the signal political ability displayed by Irish leaders in Australia, it is worthy of note that, since the inception of parliamentary government in the leading colony, Victoria, all the Speakers of the Legislative Assembly have, without exception, been Irishmen. There can be no dispute about the nationality of gentlemen bearing such names as Sir Francis Murphy, Sir Charles MacMahon, Sir Charles Gavan Duffy, and the Hon. Peter Lalor, the last mentioned being the present first commoner of Victoria. And it must be borne in mind that the selection of these gentlemen

\* Sir Charles Gavan Duffy, who has made "Australian Federation" the subject of several brilliant addresses.

to fill successively so high and honourable an office, was solely on account of their recognised superiority, as, in every case, the majority of the assembly was composed of English and Scotch representatives. But it is not in politics alone that the Irish in Australia have made their mark. In colonial literature and art, not a few of the most distinguished names will be recognised as Irish; and, in humbler capacities, the great body of the Irish-Australians have done good service for their adopted land in a silent and unobtrusive manner. They were amongst the earliest pioneers in the development of the gold-mining industry; thousands of them wisely left the towns and, favoured by liberal land legislation, established homes for themselves in the bush, whilst hundreds, of scholarly attainments, found ready admission into the Government service. But, no matter what social position they may occupy, the Irish in Australia, no less than their American brethren, are thoroughly Irish and Catholic; and, if any proof of this were wanting, it is abundantly supplied by the munificent offering sent by Australia for the relief of the famine-stricken at home. When, a few years ago, the telegraph flashed the dire intelligence that the hideous pall of hunger was darkening the face of the old land, a simultaneous movement stirred the whole of the Australian continent. Local committees were everywhere organised, donations poured in from all ranks of society, and soon the magnificent sum of £94,916 16s. 8d. was raised by a population of less than four millions as a spontaneous gift of fraternal sympathy. The time has now arrived, I think, when the record of the Irish in Australia should be written, and I entertain not the slightest doubt that that record will not only be perused with patriotic interest, but treasured with national pride, wherever the sons and daughters of Hibernia have found a home. What other writers have done for the Irish in America, I propose attempting to do, in some measure, for the Irish in Australia; and, by way of introduction to the subject, a few historical and descriptive details will be serviceable.

Australia is the great island-continent of the globe. It has an area nearly equal in extent to the whole of Europe, although its population falls short of four millions. Until very recently, its interior was a *terra incognita*, but the systematic efforts of explorers have succeeded in thoroughly opening up the central regions, so that it has been found practicable to run a telegraph wire across the continent from north to south—a distance of nearly two thousand miles. The mainland of Australia is politically divided into five colonies, which, in the order of their birth, are as follow:—New South Wales, Western Australia, Victoria, South Australia, and Queensland. There are also two insular colonies—Tasmania, or, as it was known in bygone days, Van Diemen's Land, an island of about the size of Ireland lying to the south of Victoria; and New Zealand, the "Great Britain of the South," a chain of islands in the Pacific at a distance of more than a thousand miles from the mainland in a south-easterly direction.

Though New South Wales is the parent colony of the Australian group, she has been outstripped in the race of progress by one of her youngest children—Victoria, the wealthiest, most populous, and most important of the antipodean states. Thirty years ago the present colony of Victoria was only the Port Phillip district of New South Wales, the latter geographical term being at that time synonymous with the whole eastern half of the continent.

Victoria occupies the south-eastern corner of Australia, and comprises that small but rich strip of territory lying between the 34th and 39th parallels of south latitude, and the 141st and 150th degrees of east longitude, embracing an area of 88,198 square miles, or 56,446,720 acres. The noble Murray River is the northern boundary that separates young Victoria from old New South Wales; the boisterous Bass Straits lie on the south between the "tight little island" of Tasmania and the mainland, whilst on the western side, South Australia—the granary of the antipodes—displays her exuberant treasures. The first attempt to plant a settlement in this quarter of Australia was made in 1803, when Colonel Collins, a British officer, was placed in command of an expedition to found a new penal colony. Three hundred and sixty-seven male convicts were placed on board the "Ocean" transport, and, escorted by the "Calcutta" man-of-war, 18 guns and 170 men, were despatched from England in May, 1803. After a tedious voyage of six months, Colonel Collins landed his party on a point at the eastern entrance to Port Phillip Bay, the site of the present Sorrento, a fashionable sea-side resort in the summer months. Happily for the future of Victoria, the attempt to plant a penal settlement proved a complete failure, and the premier colony was spared the odium of ever having given a permanent abode to the scum of the English prisons. The reasons that induced Colonel Collins to abandon the settlement have never been satisfactorily explained, though the general opinion is that his inability to discover a permanent supply of fresh water was the principal cause. He could not have made a very diligent search for the precious fluid; for had he done so, it would have been found in abundance not many miles from his camp. However, after a stay of three months, orders were given to re-embark, and the two vessels sailed across the straits to Van Diemen's Land. In this lovely little island, on the site of its present capital—Hobart—Collins succeeded in planting his penal colony. Here he reigned as lieutenant-governor for a period of six years, until his sudden death on March 24th, 1810. Twenty-eight years afterwards, Sir John Franklin, the then governor, who afterwards perished in the frozen wastes of the Arctic, had a monument erected to his memory in the city whose foundation he laid.

For nearly thirty years after this unsuccessful attempt to colonize Port Phillip, no further effort was made to plant a colony on the southern shores of Australia. The blacks were left in undisputed possession of the province, though one effect of Colonel Collins's brief sojourn was the addition of a new chief to their ranks. During the three months that the colonel remained encamped on the shore, several prisoners succeeded in escaping into the bush, but, with the exception of one, the fugitives either perished miserably in the unknown land, or returned in an agony of starvation to the camp and begged for forgiveness. One, however, was determined to obtain his freedom at all hazards, and this man, who had been a soldier, and was transported for assaulting his superior officer, concealed himself in a cave, and managed to subsist for some time on berries and shellfish. Having observed from his hiding-place the preparations of Colonel Collins for leaving the settlement, he came forth, when the vessels were disappearing in the distance, and found himself a free man. In a weak and exhausted condition William Buckley, for such was his name, walked at random into the interior and soon came upon an encampment of aborigines, by whom he was kindly treated and subsequently adopted into the tribe. He was presented with two "lubras," or wives, and, acting in what he, no doubt, considered the most philosophical manner under the peculiar circumstances, he completely forgot the world of civilization, and, sinking to the low level of his savage companions, he led a merely animal existence for the long period of thirty-two years. This remarkable character lived to be useful in his latter days as a medium of communication between the whites and the blacks.

In 1835, Port Phillip was permanently colonised under the auspices of freemen. The leader of the successful expedition and the founder of the colony of Victoria was John Batman, a young farmer resident in Van Diemen's Land, and a man of energy, perseverance, and self-reliance. With twelve others he formed a colonising association, under whose auspices the country surrounding Port Phillip Bay was thoroughly explored, and the excellence of the soil, both for agricultural and pastoral purposes, was abundantly demonstrated. Twelve months after Batman's arrival, the incipient colony had a population of two hundred settlers, who were owners of fifteen thousand sheep. In March, 1837, the first representative of Royalty visited the new settlement in the person of Major-General Sir Richard Bourke, Governor of New South Wales. Sir Richard won his spurs in the Peninsula, and, as one of the best colonial governors, his name will appear again in these pages. He was of course an Irishman, having been born in Limerick in 1778, and in the same city he died in 1855. Bourke remained in the infant colony for a month, and during his brief stay laid out the sites of Melbourne (the metropolis), Geelong, and Williamstown. The first place was named after the then English Premier, Lord Melbourne; the second was allowed to retain its native name, whilst the third received its title from the reigning monarch, William IV. At His Excellency's departure, the entire population of the settlement—five hundred souls—assembled to give him a parting cheer. These five hundred settlers were possessed of 140,000 sheep, 2,500 head of cattle, and 150 horses—a very satisfactory state of progress. In this year (1837) the first government land sale in Melbourne took place, and the event is worthy of note as showing how enormously the value of land may increase by unforeseen circumstances. A small allotment in Collins Street (the aristocratic thoroughfare of Melbourne) purchased originally for £35 was afterwards bought for £24,000, and, at the present time, the average price of land in the same locality is £900 per foot. A gentleman was considered very foolish for having paid what was then regarded as the excessive sum of £80 for half-an-acre, but after the lapse of two years the same land realized £5,000, and twelve years later it was sold for £40,000. These are only two examples out of many that might be recorded.

Mr. William Kelly, a contemporary eye-witness, states the following facts: " Innumerable small lots, making in their aggregate immense breadths of property, were sold at nominal prices in the early part of 1851, which, ere its close, were 'pearls beyond price,' translated into the seventh heaven of appreciation by the fortuitous discovery of the Ballarat shepherd. I know the particulars of numerous cases of constrained fortune. One I will relate which occurred in the person of an humble man from my native country, who accumulated a very modest competence in Melbourne under the old *régime*—first by manual labour and then by carting at the moderate rates of the day. He purchased a town lot in Swanston Street, and erected a wooden house upon it, in which during the progress of his industrial prosperity he opened a little shop for the good woman. His decent thrift was as remarkable as his industry, so that in homely phrase he 'got the name of having a little dry money always by him;' and at the period in question he was beset by importunate neighbours and friends, imploring him, as he intended remaining, to purchase their town allotments at his own price. In some cases he yielded, not so much with the view of benefiting himself as of helping a few friends on the road to fortune, and much against his own will or conviction he secured, for some £450, property which in less than fifteen months he sold for £15,000, and which was resold within the subsequent year for nearly three times that amount. Had my humble countryman purchased to the full amount of his means and held over like other stay-at-home townsmen, he might now be side by side in the Legislative Council of Victoria with another Sligo man who came to Port Phillip without any capital but his brains and his hands, but who is reputed at present as possessed of property worth half-a-million sterling."

I have now before me the official list of purchasers of land at the first government sale in Melbourne, and, as might have been expected, Ireland is well represented. Amongst the principal buyers I find the names of Michael Pender, Michael Connolly, John Roach, James Connell, John McNamara, F. R. D'Arcy, Patrick Cussen, Patrick Murphy and E. D. O'Reilly.

In 1841 the revenue derived from the Port Phillip district had increased to £31,799, and, consequent on increasing prosperity, the colonists became dissatisfied with their political position. They had a nominal representation in the New South Wales Parliament, the Port Phillip district being allotted six members; but owing to the distance of the capital and the expense of living there during the session, no local candidates, no men having a personal interest in the prosperity of the new province, would come forward. As a necessary consequence, the choosing of parliamentary representatives soon became a merely formal matter in which not the slightest public interest was manifested. The choice of candidates being practically limited to Sydney residents, members were elected and re-elected for the Port Phillip district on the most approved old-world pocket-borough principle. As a matter of fact, many of the electors, probably the majority of them, were in complete ignorance of the names of their parliamentary representatives. To put an end to this stupid farce, a novel expedient was hit upon. In 1848, when the time again arrived to send representatives to Sydney, an ingenious elector suggested that they would be quite as well represented by residents of London as by residents of Sydney, and therefore he moved that Earl Grey was a fit and proper person to represent the electors of Port Phillip in the Sydney Parliament. This ludicrous proposal was immediately adopted and acted upon, and it must be admitted that no better means could be devised of showing the home authorities the absurdity of giving the form of parliamentary representation without the substance. When the news reached England that Earl Grey, Secretary of State for the Colonies, had been elected member for Melbourne in the Sydney Parliament, the irresistible drollery of the situation compelled attention to the remonstrances of the colonists. The agitation for separation was carried on with renewed vigour, and eventually, on August 5th, 1850, an " Act for the Better Government of the Australian Colonies " and providing for the separation of the Port

Phillip district from New South Wales, and its erection into a separate colony under the name of Victoria, passed the Imperial Parliament. The gratifying intelligence reached Melbourne in the following November, and it is needless to say there were considerable rejoicings, lasting several days. The Act came into operation on July 1st of the following year and the day has ever since been commemorated as a public holiday, under the title of Separation Day. Prominent amongst those who took an active part in directing the separation movement were Sir William Foster Stawell (afterwards Chief Justice, and now Lieutenant-Governor of Victoria), Sir Redmond Barry (subsequently Judge of the Supreme Court), Sir John O'Shanassy (three times Prime Minister of the colony), and Sir Francis Murphy (for many years Speaker of the Legislative Assembly)—four Irishmen to whom reference will again be made.

In the same year (1851) that witnessed the practical outcome of the separation movement—in fact almost coincidently with that historical episode, an event occurred that completely altered the destinies of the Australian colonies in general and Victoria in particular. It is unnecessary to state that the event alluded to was the DISCOVERY OF GOLD. Victoria up to that time was only known for the richness of its pastoral and agricultural resources, and the idea that mineral wealth of untold value lay concealed beneath the verdant soil never once entered the minds of the simple growers of wool and cultivators of corn. In 1849 the accounts of the golden treasures of California attracted adventurers from all parts of the world, and amongst those who left Australia for the American El Dorado were two intelligent colonists, named Edward Hammond Hargreaves and James William

Esmond. They were only ordinarily successful, but their visit to California gave them some valuable knowledge which they afterwards turned to good account. One thing they observed was the striking similarity in the geological formation of the two countries, and they rightly concluded that if the precious metal existed in the one place, it must also exist in the other. This conclusion they practically tested on their return, and were rewarded with immediate success. Hargreaves prospected the Bathurst district of New South Wales and found some nuggets and gold dust.

Esmond tried his luck in Victoria near the site of the present flourishing mining town of Clunes, then a squatter's run, and succeeded in finding some rich specimens, with which he hurried to the nearest town, Geelong, and made his discovery known. The news caused the most intense excitement amongst all classes, and the "gold fever" rapidly spread throughout the colonies. All ordinary pursuits were abandoned, and everywhere parties for the diggings were in process of formation. The first discoveries soon paled before the brilliant digging results that were daily brought to the surface. It was soon ascertained that the whole central portion of the colony was auriferous, and, as the various parties spread about in the hope of finding new and richer ground, the great goldfields of the colony became gradually opened up. Words cannot describe the delirium that ensued on reading the reports of the developments of the famous Ballarat, Bendigo and Mount Alexander mines. Not only were the other colonies literally drained of their population, but, on the wondrous intelligence being circulated at home, the old world sent thousands to swell the mining community at the antipodes. Ireland despatched a numerous contingent, whose members prospered in the main, invested their savings judiciously, and founded a patriotic and influential Irish-Victorian community. All the colonial towns were deserted, and people in the most reckless manner sold their houses and lands at an immense reduction on the cost price, and hastened away to the diggings. Hobson's Bay, the harbour of Melbourne, was a forest of masts; ships lay anchored in hundreds, unable to proceed on their voyages, the sailors having deserted in a body for the up-country goldfields. Every week a mounted escort brought down from Ballarat to Melbourne an average yield of 2,500 ounces of gold, and much larger quantities were sent away privately. But these astonishing yields were soon afterwards eclipsed by the discoveries at Mount Alexander, which proved to be literally and without exaggeration "a mountain of gold." The quantity sent from this mountain during the second week of December, 1851, was 23,650 ounces, more than one ton in weight. The influx of population consequent on the gold discoveries may be gathered from the fact that in the one month of September, 1851, 16,000 new arrivals appeared on the scene, whilst in the following month the number had increased to 19,000, and each succeeding month had to be credited with a similar rate of progress. At Bendigo, 25 miles north of Mount Alexander, 70,000 men were simultaneously seeking their fortune. The public revenue had jumped from £380,000 in 1851 to £1,577,000 in 1852. Melbourne, as the commercial centre on which the goldfields depended for supplies, and the principal point of departure for the up-country districts, had developed into an important city. Its streets were thronged with lucky diggers, some of whom were dissipating their easily-acquired riches in the wildest profusion, lighting their pipes with fifty-pound notes, purchasing gorgeous dresses for their female companions of the moment, chartering all the private carriages available, treating the floating population to unlimited champagne, and generally conducting themselves as if suddenly-acquired wealth had bereft them of their sober senses. But this high-pressure era in the colony's history was only of a temporary character. In a few years the rich alluvial deposits became exhausted, and a new and more scientific mode of mining had to be adopted. Companies were organised to crush the auriferous quartz that lay many hundred feet below the surface, and necessarily a considerable amount of capital had to be expended before the quartz rock was reached, before the crushing commenced, and before the shareholders received a dividend. But once the gold-bearing quartz was struck, the reef was worked systematically, and usually the promoters of the company received an immense profit on the capital they had originally invested. It is in this manner that mining as an industry is now carried on, and though the days of rich "nuggets" (solid masses of gold generally found near the surface) have apparently passed away, yet the auriferous resources of the colony are being successfully developed at enormous depths in the manner just described. The total amount of gold produced in Victoria from the time of the first discovery in 1851 to the year 1886 is no less than fifty-five millions of ounces, equal in value to more than two hundred million pounds sterling. From 1851 to 1861 was the most exciting time on the goldfields, and during that remarkable decade, the precious metal was raised to the surface at an average rate of £10,000,000 per year.

The unparalleled productiveness of her gold mines, principally, and the extent of her pastoral and agricultural resources, secondarily, have combined to place Victoria at the head of the Australian colonies, and have given her a lead that none of the others have yet been able to overtake. She is in the full enjoyment of Home Rule, having two chambers modelled on the principle of the British Constitution, the Legislative Council, corresponding to the House of Lords, and the Legislative Assembly, possessing all the powers and privileges of the House of Commons. Her capital, Melbourne, is a city, whose public institutions, principal churches and commercial buildings, will bear favourable comparison with those of the historic cities on the other side of the equator.

# CHAPTER II.

### GREATER BRITAIN'S METROPOLIS.

THE IRISH ELEMENT IN VICTORIA—PROGRESS OF MELBOURNE—TRADE AND COMMERCE—ST. PATRICK'S CATHEDRAL—ST. PATRICK'S AND ST. FRANCIS XAVIER'S COLLEGES—ST. PATRICK'S HALL—THE CHURCH OF ST. FRANCIS —IRISH GIRLS, A CREDIT TO THEIR RACE—THE PUBLIC LIBRARY, MUSEUM, AND NATIONAL GALLERY—THEIR FOUNDER, SIR REDMOND BARRY—THE UNIVERSITY—SUCCESSES OF IRISH STUDENTS—THE TOWN HALL AND MUNICIPAL GOVERNMENT—MR. ANTHONY TROLLOPE'S ATTACK ON THE IRISHMEN OF MELBOURNE—HIS UNTRUTHFULNESS EXPOSED—A RING OF PROSPEROUS SUBURBS.

ACCORDING to the census of 1881 Victoria has a population of, in round numbers, 900,000, of whom one-fifth are either Irish born, or of Irish parentage. Melbourne, the capital, with its numerous suburbs of Carlton, Collingwood, Fitzroy, Richmond, Hotham, Emerald Hill, Port Melbourne, Williamstown, Footscray, Prahran, Hawthorn, St. Kilda and Brighton, forms a splendid city of 350,000 inhabitants, embracing 90,000 of the Irish race. The principal provincial centres are Ballarat, Sandhurst, Geelong, Castlemaine, Echuca, Beechworth, Stawell, Belfast, Warrnambool, Kilmore, and Kyneton, in all of which the Green Isle is well and ably represented. Melbourne is the metropolis of Australia, the largest city in the Southern Hemisphere, the great centre of antipodean life and activity. When it is remembered that fifty years ago a forest of gum-trees occupied the site on which this bustling city now stands, and that, within the

* The latest statistical returns give the population of the colony at upwards of a million.

recollection of many living persons, black fellows have encamped where colossal banks and stately public buildings now rear their lofty heads against the blue Australian sky, it is not surprising that visitors should be amazed at what they see before them. The progress of Melbourne from the primeval wildness of less than half a century ago of its brilliant position to-day in the world of culture, civilisation, and commerce, fully justifies the epithet of " marvellous " applied to it by the much-travelled George Augustus Sala. The rapid growth of San Francisco is the only contemporaneous incident that suggests itself by way of comparison, but it remains to be seen whether the great American city of the West will eventually distance the great Australian city of the South in the race of material and permanent prosperity. Melbourne is situated at the head of a large inlet or land-locked sea called Port Phillip. It is bisected by the River Yarra, the native name for " ever-flowing water." This river is navigable for several miles, and thus the large intercolonial steamers are enabled to come up almost to the doors of the massive warehouses, and discharge their multifarious cargoes. But most of the ocean vessels and mercantile marine remain in the bay, Port Melbourne and Williamstown, the two ports of the capital, presenting all the facilities and conveniences that could be desired. Melbourne proper is built on two hills, gradually sloping to the river, the intervening valley, covered with shops and warehouses, being about a mile in width.

Sailing up the bay from the Heads, one of the first objects that arrest the stranger's eye is the magnificent Cathedral of St. Patrick, crowning the summit of the Eastern Hill—a monument of the undying faith and active piety of the

2—2

exiled children of the Isle of Saints. It has been in course of erection for more than a quarter of a century, the noble sum of £200,000 having been subscribed in voluntary contributions during that period to its building fund by the Irishmen and Irishwomen of Victoria. Though still unfinished, the elaborate and expressive design of its architect, Mr. Wardell, is rapidly being fulfilled. A portion of the main building has for years been used for public worship, accommodation being provided for a congregation of 3,000. When finished, the cathedral will accommodate more than double that number. It occupies the site of a smaller church which was hastily erected when Melbourne was not much larger than a village, but the prophetic eye of faith saw in that village not only the great southern metropolis of to-day, but the far greater city of a coming time. Short-sighted people of that early period were amused and astonished at the idea of the Roman Catholics building a grand cathedral in the " bush," but most of them lived to see what they then called the " bush " become the very heart and centre of the greatest city of Australasia. Addressing a large public meeting of his co-religionists on June 20th, 1880, the Hon. John Gavan Duffy, M.P. reminded his audience of " the wonderful and magnificent basilicas and cathedrals which Catholics in the ages of faith had erected in Europe, which were an honour to their builders, a glory to the earth, and would last as long as the world held together." " We have here," he remarked, " a noble site which should be crowned by a nobler edifice. It has often struck me, when sailing up the bay, what a thrilling spectacle it will be to a Catholic immigrant to see, as he approaches our shores, our noble tower crowned by the Catholic cross, telling him that even in this remote corner of the globe he will not be an outcast or a stranger, but will find himself amongst brethren of the faith." As a companion picture to this may be added the testimony of one of the ablest and most accomplished of Australian journalists, Mr. Howard Willoughby, who, in his collected series of sketches entitled " The Critic in Church," writes in this graceful and appreciative strain: " St. Patrick's Cathedral is a pile which looms above Melbourne, the first object starting into sight as we approach the city from any quarter ; a structure massive, isolated and grand, like the communion it represents. It is in its infancy just now, but the infancy is that of a giant. Already it is the wonder of the Eastern Hill, whose summit it crowns, and some time it must be its architectural pride. We may anticipate the day when the stranger, drawing rein on the Nunawading heights, or the Keilor Hill, or, as off Gellibrand's Point the liner's royals and to'gallants are reefed aloft, and the bellying canvas let fly below, will obtain his first glimpse of the double spires and of the lantern tower, near 350ft. in height, and will feel something of the glow of Chaucer's pilgrims when they caught sight of the 'Angel Tower' rising far away at the head of Canterbury's forest vista. In every way does the cathedral shed a glory on its founders, and probably they will not live to claim more than that title. They will begin, but others must finish. It shows how they can rise above the prevalent meanness and littleness of the present day, the selfishness which cares not about the future, which forgets that our buildings are the tombstones of the generation, and that by them our children will stand and judge us. England received cathedrals from her struggling forefathers ; Melbourne is likely, but for the builders of St. Patrick's, to send down nothing in ecclesiastical architecture but specimens of hard bargain-driving and cheap contracting—the greatest number housed at the least possible cost; the most souls accommodated at the least expense. We build for our present wants and forget the past and ignore the future, like the degenerate savages Goldsmith pictured, occupying turf huts in sight of palaces, and, like them, wonder that 'man should need the larger pile.' The Roman Catholics, true to nobler instincts, are not content to chant 'Day by day we magnify Thee and we worship Thy name ever, world without end,' in a barn. The painfulness of the incongruity strikes them. And they, free from schism and strife, can unite for a common purpose in the cause of the Cross as other men only appear able to do in the cause of the Dollar—a thing declared by some to be the devil, it being as easy for the author of evil to take the form of a coin as to assume the disguise of a reptile. Were this land blighted at its present stage, as Greece has been, or Spain, there would remain many magnificent temples erected in the service of Mammon. Thanks to the Roman Catholics, and them alone, there would be one temple dedicated to God."

At the rear of the cathedral are the Archbishop's Palace and St. Patrick's College, the latter being one of the leading public schools of the colony. It is conducted most efficiently by the Jesuit Fathers, and many of its pupils have won high honours, both in colonial and home universities. The Very Rev. J. Ryan, S. J., has been the accomplished rector of the college for some time past. It is an institution that has given to the Victorian priesthood much-needed recruits, and to the learned professions some of their most distinguished members. More recently the Jesuits have found it necessary to establish a second collegiate institution to meet the growing requirements of the rising Catholic population. This is situated on a commanding site in the suburb of

Kew, about five miles distant from the metropolis. St. Francis Xavier's College, as it has been titled, is built on a spacious estate of seventy acres in extent, and the view from its windows is superb, embracing the shining expanse of Port Phillip Bay, the picturesque panorama of the city and suburbs, and the mountain ranges in the background. Young Irish-Australians from all quarters are being carefully trained for a future honourable career in this delightful spot, under the careful supervision of its highly-successful rector, the Very Rev. C. Nulty, S. J.

Near the western end of the city proper, fronting Bourke Street, the main thoroughfare of the metropolis, stands St. Patrick's Hall, an unpretentious but historically interesting structure. Here the infant legislature of the colony assembled, and formed the machinery by which the measure of Home Rule granted by the Imperial authorities was brought into practical operation. Here, in 1854, the Victorian Convention, consisting of delegates from public meetings throughout the country, and guided by one of the purest patriots in colonial political life, the late Wilson Gray,* met and agitated for a reform of the land laws, and paved the way for future liberal land legislation. Here for forty years the Irish national sentiment has been kept alive and perpetuated by historical lectures, inspiring speeches, and frequent gatherings of the clans. Here every movement initiated in the old land has met with a generous, ready, and sympathetic response, whether its object was to raise immediate funds for the relief of our famine-stricken countrymen, or to help them to conquer the tyranny of bad and brutal landlordism, or to join with them in the

* Brother of the late Sir John Gray and uncle of the present Mr. E. Dwyer Gray, M.P.

righteous demand for the restitution of a native parliament, or to cheer the declining days of the men who have suffered for their love of country. Here is the head-quarters of the leading Irish organisation, the St. Patrick's Society, numbering 1,000 members, and having an accumulated fund of £15,000. Here were celebrated with the utmost enthusiasm the centenaries of Daniel O'Connell, Thomas Moore, and Henry Grattan. Here, on each recurring national anniversary, Irishmen of all shades of opinion and diversities of creed, unite to do honour to the common toast, "Our Native Land." And here, many a time and oft, has a political orator addressed the surging and excited crowd of free and independent electors, for St. Patrick's Hall is the polling-place for the West Melbourne constituency, which returns two members to parliament.

In the hollow between the two hills stands the popular Church of St. Francis of Assisium, occupying the position on which the early Irish Catholics first assembled in a little body to worship their Creator. A large cross, erected in the grounds attached to the present church, indicates the precise spot where the first Mass was offered up on Victorian soil by the late Father Patrick Bonaventure Geoghegan, the earliest Irish missionary to the infant settlement, and afterwards the energetic Bishop of Adelaide, South Australia. Its historical character as the cradle of Irish Catholicism in Victoria has made St. Francis' the most popular church of the city, and nowhere in the colonies, or even in Ireland itself, could a more genuinely Irish congregation be found. It can accommodate about 2,000 persons; but as a rule, the seating accommodation is wholly inadequate to the numbers in attendance. Not only are the passages filled, but many are to be seen kneeling outside the doors, unable to obtain admission. The national character of the congregation becomes manifest, when in the course of a sermon, the preacher makes an incidental allusion to the old land, her sufferings for the faith, the achievements of her sons, her fortitude and fidelity in the past, and her bright destiny in the future as "a nation once again." The panegyric of St. Patrick is here an annual institution. It is preached on the Sunday nearest the national anniversary, and then the throng becomes something astonishing. Several reasons have been given why St. Francis' Church should have taken such a hold on the popular liking, but the one advanced by a witty Irish priest, when asked his opinion, is rather ingenious: "You see," he said, "it is a nice walk down hill to St. Francis' from every quarter, and the people never think of the up-hill journey afterwards." And this is literally true, for, no matter in what direction you start for St. Francis', you walk down a decline, it being built, as already mentioned, in the hollow between the Eastern and the Western hills. This latter circumstance renders the locality at times both disagreeable and dangerous during heavy rains, for the running streams converge from all points in this hollow and flow past St. Francis' Church in a foaming torrent to the Yarra. According to tradition, after one of these temporary floods, a heavily-laden waggon and a team of horses once sank completely out of sight in the soft soil immediately in front of St. Francis'. But this occurred in the early days, when there were no smooth, substantial pavements, and strong macadamized roads as at present. It is in St. Francis' Church on Sunday evenings, at Vespers, that the Irish servant girls from all parts of the city and suburbs are to be seen in force. As a class they are a credit to their country and their creed. By the majority of Protestant masters and mistresses, an Irish girl is preferred before all others for her virtue, honesty, and integrity. "No Irish need apply" is reversed at the antipodes, for Irish girls are sought, asked, and invited, even by those who hold their country and creed in detestation.

The reason is obvious. Experience has taught them that an Irish girl, who is attentive to her religious duties, can be trusted under all circumstances, and in every position of responsibility in household affairs. It rarely happens that a bigoted master absolutely refuses to allow a servant girl to go to Mass or Vespers. Still such cases have occurred, but the girl was usually too high-spirited and too loyal to her faith to submit to such an unwarrantable deprivation of her liberty and her religious rights. She has informed her confessor of the circumstances—he has advised her to quit the place at once; she immediately takes the course recommended, and very soon she obtains another and a better situation, one in which no obstacle will be thrown in the way of the performance of her religious duties. Taken as a body, the thousands of Irish girls who emigrated to the Australian colonies during the past thirty years have worthily upheld the honour of their race.* The great majority of them married well and became the mothers of the fine body of Irish-Australians that are now growing to maturity. But in their material prosperity they did not forget the old land or those they left behind them. There is no means of ascertaining the total amount sent home by Irish girls from Victoria, but all contemporary evidence goes to show that it must have been a very large sum in the aggregate—many thousands of pounds. Every girl seemed to regard it as a

* "The best servants I found during my travels in the colonies were Irish girls educated at the Roman Catholic orphanages."—Mr. G. A. Sala.

duty incumbent upon her to send something regularly home to her aged parents, or to bring out a sister or a brother to the golden land. Not only that, but these hard-toiling girls were always amongst the first to subscribe to every national movement from the purest of patriotic impulses. They love to dress well in public, and this has given rise to a good deal of cheap wit at their expense, but what if they do indulge in a little harmless finery? It is but an innocent feminine weakness after all, and only deserving of censure when it passes into extravagance, which it certainly does not do in the case of the Irish girls of Melbourne.

"During my short colonial experience," remarks Mr. William Kelly, in his interesting "Life in Victoria," "I was much surprised at finding so large a proportion of the Irish leaven in the population, which, previous to the gold digging, I always understood was three-fourths Scotch with a good dash of English besides, in its lower and even secondary ranks. And the surprise was no more than natural, knowing as I did the alluring attractions held out by America to Irish emigrants—firstly in the extraordinary cheapness of the rate and the shortness of the passage; secondly, in the low price and easy acquirement of land, and thirdly, in the witching lures of consanguinity so inherent in Celtic bosoms. But notwithstanding these advantages and the discouragements of a voyage over five times as long and five times as costly, thousands of Irish poured in, independently of those who came out as free emigrants, all of whom were absorbed or found profitable occupations immediately after arrival; few, if any, contributing to swell the ranks of those discontented grumblers who were most eloquent when cursing the colony because they could not find gold on the surface, and who were always sure to be found sunning themselves lazily in the vicinity of the labour market, or propping up the portals of the lowest class of public-houses. Perhaps the explanation is to be found in the fact that any change from the impoverished and degraded condition of the Irish peasant on his native soil must necessarily have been one for the better, and that therefore, on arrival, he was only too glad to embrace the first opportunity that presented itself. However, whatever the reason, all impartial observers will agree, and statistics will bear me out in the assertion, that Irishmen constituted a very small proportion of the loafing population, or of the criminal crowd that filled the gaols and asylums; while I may affirm, without fear of contradiction, that the proverbial chastity of the Irish female was nobly sustained by those poor girls who found themselves standing alone, without parents or protectors, in the midst of the staring contaminations of the Victorian metropolis."

A few hundred yards to the east of St. Francis' is a magnificent block of buildings comprising the Public Library, the Museum, and the National Gallery, all founded by a distinguished, philanthropic, and scholarly Irish-Australian, Sir Redmond Barry, a native of Cork, and a fellow-graduate of Isaac Butt, with whom he was called to the Irish bar in 1838. According to one of his biographers, "Barry had scarcely been called to the bar when he formed the determination of emigrating to some less overcrowded field; for the Irish bar then presented no immediate prospects, but a very long and dreary expectation of the demise of a sufficient number of judges and leading barristers to raise the juniors to an amount of business sufficient for their support." In 1839 he arrived in Sydney, but only remained there for a few weeks, preferring to make the southern city his home. Even as early as 1841 he was the recognised leader of the bar in Melbourne. He took a prominent part in the agitation for separation from the parent colony, and very soon after the successful issue of that contest, when the settlement became an independent colony, he was elevated to the bench of the Supreme Court, and creditably filled that high position for the long period of twenty-nine years. One of Sir Redmond's ardent admirers has recorded that one of his first actions on arriving in Melbourne was the "founding of a reading club for working men. There were few books in the settlement, and no place where a poor man could have easy access to books or magazines. Barry set aside a room in his house as a little lending library, on the shelves of which stood *Frazer's Magazine, Blackwood, Cornhill,* &c., and a small selection of standard works. Here the working man of the neighbourhood could look in and select his book, no doubt having at times to listen patiently to one of those elaborate little addresses, in which Mr. Barry was fond of pouring out floods of inconceivably out-of-the-way erudition; but those who came in contact with him, all had the same impression of him, as a man who took a pleasure in seeing folks around him happy, even though it should be at the expense of some little discomfort to himself. This little institution is interesting as having been the means of suggesting the great library which he afterwards proposed and helped to found." The Melbourne Public Library now ranks among the great libraries of the world. It has a collection of 150,000 volumes and 20,000 pamphlets. All the year round it is open from ten in the morning until ten at night, and the average attendance of visitors is 1,000 per day. The present librarian is Thomas Francis Bride, LL.D., a distinguished young Irish-Australian, who passed from St. Patrick's College through the Melbourne University to the highest academic honours that were obtainable. Since his appointment, Dr. Bride has introduced an improved system of classification that has proved highly serviceable to students, who form a large proportion of the habitual readers. The department bearing the distinctive name " Ireland " is a fairly representative collection of some 2,500 volumes, comprising all the standard histories, the best-known biographies, complete sets of Swift, Burke, Goldsmith, Moore, Carleton, Griffin, Banim, Lady Morgan, and Miss Cusack, the publications of the Celtic and Archæological Societies, and complete files of the *Dublin Review* and the *Dublin University Magazine*. The latter was always a great favourite with Sir Redmond Barry, for he was associated with Isaac Butt in its establishment, and contributed regularly to the early numbers. In 1858 Sir Redmond commenced the formation of a Technological Museum at the rear of the Public Library, and here the industrial resources of the colony are now displayed in the most complete and interesting manner. A National Gallery of Painting and Sculpture was subsequently added, and this institution has given to the colony a number of promising young artists. There are at the present time 200 students in regular attendance. A statue of Sir Redmond Barry, raised by public subscription, now stands in front of the principal entrance to the Melbourne Public Library.

But there is one other Melbourne institution of noble proportions and beneficent scope, that owes its existence to the wise philanthropy of Sir Redmond Barry, viz., the University. It is modelled on the Oxford and Cambridge system, and governed by a council of twenty members, originally nominated by the Crown, but now elected by the Senate, or general body of the graduates. The University has power to confer degrees in arts, laws, medicine, and music. And here it may be appropriately remarked that the first student on whom the honour of LL.D. was conferred, was John Madden, a native of Cork, and son of John Madden, solicitor, of that city. He was until recently the representative of Port Melbourne in the Legislative Assembly of Victoria, and has twice held office as Minister of Justice. Another young Irishman, Patrick Moloney, was the first to receive a medical degree. Dr. Moloney is now not only one of the best-known and most highly-respected medical practitioners in Melbourne, but also a graceful speaker and accomplished writer. In the Melbourne University, it is gratifying to record that no religious test has ever been applied to students. Mr. Childers, now a member of the Imperial Parliament and a holder of high office under Mr. Gladstone for several years, was, when a young man, a member of the Victorian Legislature, and he succeeded in passing the Act of Incorporation, by which the University was brought into being. But all the hard work of organising the University fell on the shoulders of Sir Redmond Barry. He was appointed Chancellor at the first meeting of the council in April, 1853, and he held that distinguished office uninterruptedly to the day of his death, a period of more than a quarter of a century. He always presided in person at the annual conferring of degrees, and nothing could have been more appropriate than his handsome and dignified presence on such occasions. Both these eminently useful institutions —the Public Library and the University—that will perpetuate the fame of their founder to future generations of Australians, were ushered into existence on precisely the same day—July 3rd, 1854. "This," remarks Mr. Alexander Sutherland in his excellent biographical sketch of Sir

Redmond Barry,\* "was a memorable day in the history of the colony, for on it were laid the foundations of these two institutions of which we have reason to be most truly proud—the Public Library and the University. At twelve o'clock on that morning, the newly-appointed Governor, Sir Charles Hotham, who was then in the full tide of popularity, formed his procession and led the way to the forty acres which had been reserved at Carlton for the University. Here he was met by Redmond Barry in all the splendour of the Chancellor's robes. We can imagine the effect as the judge, then forty-one years old and considered the handsomest man in Melbourne, read his long and classically garnished address, and bowed with his stately gallantry to Lady Hotham, who occupied a chair at her husband's side. Sir Charles replied, and the stone was well and truly laid. Then the *cortège* wound its way to the corner of Swanston and Latrobe Streets, where two acres had been set apart for the magnificent pile which will eventually cover its site. There Dr. Palmer, afterwards Sir James Palmer, read the address, and Sir Charles laid another stone; after which he and the notabilities accepted Judge Barry's invitation to a magnificent repast, which had been prepared at his private residence. In 1859 Barry was able to inform the then Governor, Sir Henry Barkly, that there were thirteen thousand volumes on the shelves. Year after year, under his careful guidance, the institution prospered; additions were steadily made to the building, and by degrees the collection of books was converted from a merely respectable set of standard works into a most valuable and complete library, ranking amongst the finest that the world contains."

\**Melbourne Review*, July, 1882.

One of the most imposing of the public buildings of Melbourne is the Town Hall, situated at the corner of Collins and Swanston Streets, a little below the Public Library. It was erected about sixteen years ago at a cost of £100,000, and more recently a grand organ has been procured at an expenditure of £5,000. That Melbourne is a music-loving city is evidenced by the large audiences that are drawn together in the Town Hall by attractive concert programmes. It is the largest hall in Melbourne, and can give seating accommodation to four thousand. Its holding capacity is taxed to the utmost on each recurring St. Patrick's Night, when a programme of Irish national music is presented for popular acceptance. Lectures on Irish and Catholic subjects are occasionally delivered here with success, but for obvious reasons smaller halls are usually chosen for that purpose. The ruling spirit of the Town Hall is Mr. Edmond Gerald Fitzgibbon, for thirty years Town Clerk of Melbourne, and one of the most familiar figures within its corporate bounds. Mr. Fitzgibbon is a native of Cork, and, like many other ardent young Irishmen, was attracted to Victoria by the exciting accounts of the gold discoveries. After seeing a little of the rough digger's life at Mount Alexander, he returned to Melbourne, and very soon obtained more congenial employment. He is in point of fact, and has been for years, the municipal governor of Melbourne. The members of the City Corporation are invariably swayed by his recommendations. He is universally recognised as the best and most reliable authority in all matters relating to local government. The generally well-ordered condition of Melbourne, and its comparative freedom from most of the glaring evils of old-world crowded cities, are traceable in the main to Mr.

Fitzgibbon's salutary regulations and precautions. He has earned the lasting gratitude of future generations of Melbourne citizens by his watchful care and zealous guardianship of the public parks and gardens.

Melbourne is fortunately well supplied with these essential breathing-places. Within easy accessible distance from all parts of the city are the Royal Park, the Carlton Gardens, the Fitzroy Gardens, the Flagstaff Gardens, the Treasury Gardens, and the Botanical Gardens. But interested parties, selfishly inclined and forgetful of the needs of the future, are continually bringing pressure to bear on the government of the day with a view to having portions of the popular reserves submitted to sale in allotments. Against this numerous class of hungry land sharks, Mr. Fitzgibbon has waged an unceasing war, not always with success, but still he can point to more than one beautiful reserve that would have been either spoiled, disfigured or alienated, perhaps lost to the people for all time, but for his opportune interference, vigorous protests and strenuous exertions. In that capacity, as protector of the public parks, Mr. Fitzgibbon deserves to be long and gratefully remembered.

Melbourne has not escaped the gross misrepresentations and unfounded assertions of professional book makers, men who rush across the seas from the old world, put up at some leading hotel, remain for a few weeks in luxurious ease, accept everything they are told as gospel truth, and, having thus collected a miscellaneous budget of cheap and worthless information, rush back to London and publish what they are pleased to call, with sublime audacity, their "impressions of the colonies," save the mark! The mischief done by these parasitic excrescences of a book-loving age is deplorable. They listen with ready ear to the false or exaggerated tales of interested parties, jot down everything indiscriminately in their note-books, never go to the trouble of verifying in person the correctness of what they hear, or of seeing things as they are with their own eyes: and thus are circulated broadcast over the English-speaking world many infamous libels and disgraceful falsehoods. All that literary carpet-baggers of this description have in view is the obtaining of materials sufficient to fill a stipulated number of pages, and they are never particular as to the nature or quality of the material, so long as they get enough of it to suit their immediate purpose. This will account for more than one unfavourable reference to the Irish in Australia in latter-day books of travel, but the foregoing remarks will serve to show how densely stupid and utterly unreliable are all such gratuitous opinions, founded on chance remarks in casual conversation with bigoted or prejudiced individuals, speaking with no standing or authority. There is one prominent sinner in this respect, from whose recognised position in the literary world much better conduct might reasonably have been expected. Some years ago the late Mr. Anthony Trollope, the well-known popular novelist, paid a flying visit to the antipodes, and, on his return to Europe, published a bulky volume entitled "Australia and New Zealand," in which the following passage occurs:

"One cannot walk about Melbourne without being struck by all that has been done for the welfare of the people generally. There is no squalor to be seen, though there are quarters of the town in which the people no doubt are squalid. In every great congregation of men there will be a residuum of poverty and filth, let humanity do what she will to prevent it. In Melbourne there is an Irish quarter and there is a Chinese quarter, as to both of which I was told that the visitor who visited them might see much of the worse side of life. But he who would see such misery in Melbourne must search for it especially. It will not meet his eye by chance, as it does in London, in Paris, and also in New York."*

Here we have an eminent English writer demeaning himself to the level of the professional globe-trotter, and, on mere hearsay evidence, fathering a most offensive statement that, he might easily have ascertained from any respectable local authority, had no foundation whatever in fact. "In Melbourne there was an Irish quarter, and *he was told* (the old story) that the visitor who visited it might see much of the worse side of life." It will be observed that Mr. Trollope was *told* all this, not that he had ascertained the truth of it for himself. His reflections must have been the reverse of agreeable when he found out how cruelly he had been hoaxed into a belief in the existence of an "Irish quarter" in the city of Melbourne. Why, the oldest inhabitant of the city would have given Mr. Trollope a look of blank amazement if asked to point out the direction in which the "Irish quarter" lay. There is no such thing as a distinctive Irish quarter in Melbourne, known and recognised by that contemptuous term. Irishmen and their families are to be found in all parts of the city and suburbs, and everywhere they form a peaceable,

* "Australia and New Zealand." By Anthony Trollope. Page 250.

orderly, and industrious element in the general population, not a "residuum of poverty and filth," as Mr. Anthony Trollope insinuates, with lying and unblushing effrontery. There are nearly a dozen local governing bodies within a circle drawn five miles around the Melbourne general post-office, and there is not one of these municipal councils that has not two, three, or more Irish members, elected by their fellow-citizens in that particular neighbourhood. What does this prove? Beyond all question it proves that the Irish in Melbourne are not to be found herding together, like the Chinese, within a limited space or quarter. It proves that in each of the municipal districts there is a strong contingent of independent Irish ratepayers, men with a stake in the country, freeholders qualified to vote, and good citizens in every respect. Of course, some suburbs will be more representatively Irish than others. For instance, North and West Melbourne, from their proximity to the central terminus of the Victorian railway system, where many hundreds of Irishmen are regularly employed as porters, guards, pointsmen, engine-drivers, &c., have necessarily a larger Celtic population than South or East Melbourne. Naturally they settle down where they have obtained permanent employment, and here it may be observed that no finer or more patriotic body of Irishmen can be met with than those of North and West Melbourne. Their pastor, the Very Rev. Dean England, is a nephew of the illustrious Bishop England, who occupies so large a space in John Francis Maguire's account of the Irish in America. For many years they regularly returned, as one of their representatives in parliament, Sir Charles MacMahon, the son of the late Right Hon. Sir William MacMahon, at one time Master of the Rolls in Ireland. More recently they twice elected the late Prime

Minister of Victoria, the Hon. Sir Bryan O'Loghlen, Baronet, of Drumcondra, Ennis, Clare. In February, 1880, at a time of great political excitement, he was defeated by a narrow majority, but was subsequently returned by the agricultural constituency of West Bourke, which contains a strong body of well-to-do Irish farmers. Mr. John Curtain, a Limerick man, represented the North Melbourne electorate in parliament for a series of years. Mr. Thomas Fogarty has several times occupied the mayoral chair, and Dr. Lloyd, another Limerick representative, is one of the best-known and popular men in Melbourne. For a lengthy period, since 1865, he has been the chairman of the North Melbourne bench of magistrates. In law and medicine he is equally recognised as an authority of repute. South of the city proper, between the river and the bay, are the two flourishing suburbs of Emerald Hill and Sandridge, each of which has a considerable Irish element. The former was so named by one of its earliest Hibernian inhabitants, who was charmed with its beautiful verdant aspect, bringing up fond recollections of a "green isle" far away. Once it was temporarily known by the prosaic name of Canvas Town, which had at least the one merit of appropriateness, for, at the first great rush to the goldfields, the whole surface of the green hill was covered with tents, the temporary homes of thousands of intending diggers, who could find no accommodation or sleeping space whatever in the crowded city on the other side of the river. But all vestiges of that exciting time have long since vanished. Emerald Hill, or South Melbourne, as it is now officially called, forms a compact, substantial, well-built city of 25,000 inhabitants, of whom one-fourth may be set down as Irish-Australians. They are under the spiritual jurisdiction of the Very Rev. Dean O'Driscoll, who has had charge of the district for more than twenty years. Its splendid position, midway between the river and the sea, easily accessible from the city, and standing on an elevated and health-giving site, must needs ensure the permanence and prosperity of Emerald Hill. The river banks which form its northern boundary are literally hives of industry, presenting as they do an uninterrupted vista of foundries, factories, and stores of all descriptions. In them hundreds of able-bodied Celts may be seen constantly at work, and as many more are engaged in loading and discharging the fleets of intercolonial steamers at the contiguous wharves. This river trade is rapidly developing to an enormous extent, and the steamers now regularly trading between Melbourne and Sydney, Newcastle, Brisbane, Maryborough, Adelaide, Hobart, Launceston, Auckland, Christchurch and Dunedin may be counted by the score. A considerable number of Irishmen are also in the employ of the Harbour Trust, a body of commissioners elected to supervise the harbour generally, carry out all necessary improvements that will facilitate trade and commerce, and expend the large revenue they derive from the collection of appointed fees in the best interests of the port. Emerald Hill possesses a noble charitable institution in St. Vincent de Paul's Orphanage, which is under the management of the Christian Brothers and the Sisters of Mercy. Here some hundreds of Catholic boys and girls, bereft of parental care and supervision, are fed, clothed, educated and trained in some industrial pursuit. It is in receipt of an annual Government grant, which is largely supplemented by voluntary contributions from all quarters.

Sandridge, or Port Melbourne, occupies the flat on the western side of Emerald Hill, and owes its name to the immense quantities of sand, the accumulations of ages, that

are piled up in its vicinity. It is the chief port of the
metropolis, with which it is connected by railway. There
are two very fine piers running out some distance into the
bay, and capable of accommodating the largest vessels.
This is a favourite Sunday afternoon resort for the inhabitants of the city, and in summer the trains convey
thousands of excursionists to the neighbourhood. It has a
population of 15,000, who are mostly employed in those
multifarious pursuits incidental to a large and prosperous
seaport. Advantage has been taken of its proximity to the
sea, and the facilities thus afforded for safe and speedy
transit, to establish some large manufactories that give
constant and abundant employment to numbers. The Irishmen here are not so proportionately numerous as at Emerald
Hill, still, they form an influential and appreciable element.
One member of parliament is allotted to the district, and
Dr. Madden, the old St. Patrick's collegian and leading
barrister already referred to, sat for the place until he voluntarily retired in order to devote the whole of his time to the
practice of his profession.

Quite recently a Carmelite house has been established in
Sandridge by the Very Rev. Prior Butler, whose name enjoys
an Irish as well as a colonial reputation. As a pulpit orator
he stands in the front rank, as a controversialist he has
proved his power, and as a lecturer he has presented to the
popular mind some of the most instructive pictures of the
past.

St. Kilda forms one of the aristocratic southern suburbs
of Melbourne, and contains the residences of many well-
known, influential, and successful Irish-Australian colonists.
Here is a Presentation Convent, established in 1873 as an
affiliation from the parent house in Limerick. Nowhere are

religion and charity better or more systematically supported than in St. Kilda, Prahran, Windsor, and South Yarra, all of which contiguous districts are comprised within the parish that has been governed for many years by Dr. Corbett* and Father Quirk, two zealous and energetic Irish priests. Their efforts in the propagation of religion and the foundation of charitable institutions have been warmly seconded by the generosity of the good-hearted and sympathetic Irish girls, large numbers of whom are engaged in domestic service around St. Kilda. Indeed, Dr. Corbett has more than once publicly acknowledged his obligations to these humble but enthusiastic members of his flock. "From an experience of twenty years," he says, "I find it unnecessary to use much persuasion to induce the ever-generous Irish girl to lend a helping hand to anything that tends to the glory of God and the relief of the destitute. Out of her scanty income she is always willing to contribute to her parish church, school, and clergy, in many instances more generously than do her employers, without forgetting the sacred duty of assisting the poor aged parents and friends in the dear old land. From the Irish girl who neglects to assist her parents in their need, a priest will never get a pound in aid of the building fund of a church or a school." The number of Irish girls of the latter class in Australia is very limited indeed.

Richmond joins the city on the south-east, and is a flourishing town of more than 30,000 inhabitants. It is under the spiritual supervision of the Jesuit Fathers, and the fine bluestone church of St. Ignatius is a worthy tribute to the glorious founder of their order. For years the Very

* Within the last few months Dr. Corbett has been appointed Bishop of Sale, a newly-constituted diocese in Eastern Victoria.

Rev. Thomas Cahill (nephew of the illustrious Dr. Cahill, of Irish and American renown) was the local superior, and amongst the members is the Rev. Michael Watson, whose contributions on Australian subjects to the *Irish Monthly*, under the signature of " Melburnian," have been read with general and appreciative interest. Fathers William Kelly and Joseph O'Malley have also worthily upheld the reputation of their order in the colonies—the former by his varied scholarship and his remarkable eloquence in the pulpit, and the latter by the vigour and incisiveness of his controversial pen.

Collingwood, in a political sense the most democratic suburb of Melbourne, occupies an extensive and densely-peopled flat to the north-east of the city proper. Within its confines is the Convent of the Good Shepherd, at Abbotsford, a noble institution that has been conducted for many years by a self-sacrificing band of cloistered Irish and Irish-Australian ladies. It has the widespread sympathy and support of all denominations in its ceaseless and successful efforts to raise up and reform the Magdalens of Melbourne. Fitzroy, a suburb on the western side of Collingwood, also possesses a noteworthy convent, the parent-house of the Sisters of Mercy in Victoria, a massive pile of bluestone buildings in which a large array of sisters and several educational institutions are established. Mrs. Mary Ursula Frayne, a Dublin lady, who was the foundress of this extensive religious colony, enjoys the singular distinction of having been the pioneer of her order in two continents. As far back as 1842, she was sent from Dublin to establish a branch of the Sisters of Mercy in America, and she successfully accomplished the work. She was then sent on a similar mission to Australia, and, after spending some years on the western side of the continent, she migrated southwards at the invitation of the late Archbishop Goold, and laid the foundation of that striking centre of religious and educational activity to which reference has just been made. Under her energetic rule it grew from year to year; and, at the time of her recent death, after an active religious life extending over half a century, it had attained the distinction of being perhaps the largest, and certainly one of the largest, convents in the Southern Hemisphere.

Carlton, the suburb abutting on Fitzroy from the west, contains the Exhibition building, a vast structure with a lofty dome, erected at enormous expense for the purposes of the first Melbourne International Exhibition towards the close of 1880. During next year (1888) it will again be utilised in its original capacity, as another International Exhibition is to be held by way of fitly celebrating the close of Australia's first century of civilisation. To the north of the Exhibition building is a prominent and beneficent institution that is entitled to honourable recognition in this place, the Maternity Hospital, a national charity that owes its existence mainly to the zeal and practical philanthropy of an eminent Irish-Australian surgeon, the late Dr. Richard Tracy.

Beyond this immediate ring of suburban towns and cities, by which Melbourne proper is enclosed, several outlying suburban rings have been called into existence of late years by the imperative demands of a constantly-increasing population. But, as tramways and railways now give easy access to all parts of the metropolitan area, the numerous residents of these remoter suburbs experience no difficulty in getting to and from the heart of the city. Melbourne and its suburbs, near and remote, constitute, in point of fact, one great and homogeneous metropolis, whose inhabitants have at their command all the facilities for transit and convenience which the spirit of modern ingenuity and enterprise has supplied.

Though but an infant in comparison with the Old-World cities that can trace their growth and development through centuries, it would be difficult to find on the face of the globe a populated centre more amply endowed with the requirements and luxuries of contemporary civilisation than Melbourne, the Queen City of the South.

# CHAPTER III.

### THE STORY OF BURKE AND WILLS.

AMBROSE KYTE—HOW AN IRISH LAD ATTAINED TO OPULENCE—HIS MUNIFICENT BENEFACTIONS—STARTS AN EXPLORING EXPEDITION TO CROSS THE AUSTRALIAN CONTINENT—ROBERT O'HARA BURKE APPOINTED LEADER OF THE EXPEDITION—SETTING OUT AMIDST POPULAR ENTHUSIASM—THE FEAT SUCCESSFULLY ACCOMPLISHED—BACKWARD MARCH OF THE VICTORS—A RACE FOR LIFE—SERIES OF FATAL MISTAKES—TRAGIC CLOSE OF A BRILLIANT ENTERPRISE—DEATH OF BURKE AND WILLS—KING SAVED BY THE BLACKS—IMPORTANT RESULTS OF THE EXPEDITION.

"WE must regard him as one of the most striking instances of success which even Victoria affords. Of humble origin, and with but little education and few natural advantages, he, by a dexterous use of favourable circumstances, accumulated a large fortune and won his way to a leading place in the community. It is gratifying to be able to reflect that, when he had reached a position of affluence, besides performing many acts of charity known only within a limited circle, he distinguished himself by making several munificent donations to stimulate useful enterprise and advance the interests of the country in which his wealth had been won."*

It was in these words that the leading journal of Victoria concluded its account of the career of a remarkable Irish-Australian, whose life reads like a page from the "Arabian Nights' Entertainments." Leaving his home in Nenagh, County Tipperary, in his eighteenth year, Ambrose Kyte was

* The *Melbourne Argus*, Nov. 17, 1868.

one of a number of young Irishmen of spirit and determination who had resolved on building homes for themselves in the distant south. On landing in Melbourne in 1840, he hired himself at ten shillings a week, but it was not long before his salary was doubled. In five years' time he was able to start business on his own account, and he succeeded so well that he gradually acquired by purchase a considerable amount of property in the principal street of the city. Then came the gold discoveries, with their consequent rapid rise in the value of houses and lands. Thus it came about that the young Irish lad, who in 1840, was glad to accept ten shillings a week for the hard labour of his hands, was enabled in 1857 to retire from business with an annual rent-roll of £19,000, and to enter Parliament as the representative of East Melbourne. Unlike others who were enriched in a similar manner, he never overlooked the obligations he owed both to his native and his adopted land.

A moralist of the era has placed on record the reflections suggested to his mind by the contemplation of the noble philanthropy of Ambrose Kyte, as contrasted with the miserly selfishness of many others who had been equally favoured by fortune: "One act of splendid generosity is worthily followed by another, and the careful maintenance of the donor's *incognito* enhances the merit of the action by placing the motive beyond the reach of imputation. In proportion as such instances are rare, so should they be selected for special eulogy and pointed out as admirable examples. Of the hundreds and thousands who amass wealth or achieve an independence in these colonies, how few there are, who, by so much as a solitary act of beneficence, acknowledge their gratitude to the country which gave them fortune, identify themselves with its advancement, or leave any honourable trace of their

success upon its history." As was truly said by one of his contemporaries, " It would be well for Victoria if she had a few more such benefactors as this industrious, shrewd, yet withal free-handed son of Tipperary." From time to time prizes of £1,000 for the encouragement of agriculture and the development of the various resources of the colony, were offered through the medium of the principal metropolitan journal by " A Merchant of Melbourne." It was some time before people in general came to know that the anonymous merchant of Melbourne was Mr. Ambrose Kyte. His most memorable contribution of this kind, and the most far-reaching in its consequences, was the offer of £1,000 as the nucleus of an exploration fund for the fitting out of a Victorian band of explorers to cross the continent, and report as to what actually existed in the great unseen interior of Australia. In the words of an eminent Australian *littérateur*,*
" It was the munificent, but modest act of an Irishman—Mr. Ambrose Kyte—that gave the first impulse to the movement which resulted in the crossing of this continent from end to end ; and it was also an Irishman, Robert O'Hara Burke—who commanded that gallant band of explorers, and who, having commenced his heroic work, confronted death as calmly as he had conquered difficulties and disregarded dangers."

On the occasion of a complimentary address being presented to him, in the presence of more than 2,000 of his fellow-citizens, by way of recognising the philanthropy and public spirit by which he had been actuated in originating the first expedition across the Australian continent, Ambrose Kyte ably vindicated the rights and duties of Australian citizenship. He emphatically declared that every citizen

* Mr. James Smith.

owed a heavy debt of gratitude to the country which had
enriched him, and that he was called upon, instead of spending his fortune in distant lands, and purchasing with it the
means of indolent self-indulgence, to apply some portion of
it to promote the welfare and accelerate the progress of the
community, among whom he had risen to opulence. As to
the gift of £1,000 for exploration purposes, he looked upon
that sum as nought in itself, but it derived its value from
the fact that it was the donation of a working man, who out of
the proceeds of his hard earnings and years of toil, had made
a sacrifice as soon as he was able to do so. Out of that sacrifice had arisen a monument which would never be obliterated.

Mr. Kyte's patriotic offer elicited a response of £3,210
from the Victorian public, and the exploration fund was
further supplemented by a parliamentary grant of several
thousands. The work of organising the most ambitious
effort of exploration that had, up to that time, been attempted
by any of the colonies, was intrusted to a committee of
the Royal Society. General satisfaction was felt at the
appointment of Robert O'Hara Burke to the leadership
of the expedition, for he was a man who had given
signal proofs of courage, commanding ability, and the
possession of many qualities that peculiarly fitted him to
head the daring enterprise of crossing an unknown continent
from sea to sea. A member of an old Galway family, he
served in the Austrian army for some years, and retired
with the rank of captain. After a brief stay in his
native land, he decided on emigrating to the colonies.
His reputation had preceded him, and the Government
of Victoria secured his services in the capacity of inspector
of police, the position he occupied when his ardent temperament and love of adventure prompted him to volunteer

to take the leadership of the contemplated exploring expedition. No expense was spared in the equipment of the expedition, and on August 20th, 1860, the brave little band, with the soldierly figure of Burke riding in the van, left Melbourne, amidst the acclamations of the populace, to penetrate the mysteries of the interior. On arriving at Cooper's Creek, the farthest point in a due northerly direction that previous explorers were able to attain, Burke determined to establish a depôt to act as a sort of base of operations, on which he could fall back in the event of insurmountable obstacles opposing his progress through the thousand miles of country to which his face was turned, and on which no white man's foot had yet been placed. Leaving this depôt in charge of Mr. Brahe and a small party, Burke chose three companions, Wills, King and Gray (the latter two compatriots of his own) and, with the characteristic impetuosity of the Irish soldier, made a bold dash into the unexplored regions ahead. Had he been less enthusiastic in his enterprise, and less eager to earn the distinction of being the first man to cross the continent, the terrible series of disasters that enshrouded the close of an otherwise signally successful expedition would, in all human probability, have been averted. But Burke's ardent impulsiveness was not solely responsible for the calamitous close of this great event in Australian history. The exploration committee sitting in Melbourne, who should have sent a vessel round to the north of the continent to meet the explorers after they had finished their hazardous enterprise, did not do so until it was too late to be of any practical service. The result was that when Burke, Wills, King and Gray stood as victors on the shores of the Gulf of Carpentaria, on February 4th, 1861, none of their countrymen were present

to witness their triumph, no friendly steam
to bear them back to the popular ovatio
them in Melbourne; and so they had no o
than to retrace their steps, retraverse the
with their faces now turned to the south,
all possible speed for the depôt at Cooper's
literally a race for life, and poor Gray p
way. The surviving three, by a singularly
reached Cooper's Creek on the afternoon o
on which the depôt had been abandoned
whom Burke had left in charge. Brahe
command of the depôt, finding his stock
growing smaller, and feeling convinced tha
must have either perished, or else returned
districts by some other route, had broken
and started southwards in complete igr
immediate proximity of the returning b
leaving, he took the precaution of burying
at the foot of a tree which he had ma
word "Dig." When Burke and his compa
a few hours afterwards, weak, weary, and well-
and found the camp on which their salva
silent and deserted, their anguish, asto
cruel disappointment may well be imag
some time before the unfortunate little
the full extent of this wholly unexpected
having achieved the great work which all th
in the field of Australian exploration ha
complish, this was indeed a sad anti-clin
hopes and anticipations that had cheere
march across the wide Australian plains
a brief interval of dazed astonishment,

from the effects of this terrible disappointment, they raised their weak voices in unison in the hope that possibly some of their old comrades, who ought to have been there to meet and welcome them, might still be within hearing. But no answering cry brought relief to their strained ears. Then, looking around, they descried the marked tree, and, eagerly turning up the soil beneath, found the food of which they were so much in need, together with a brief note from Brahe, bearing that morning's date and recording how he had broken up the camp and started homewards with all his men "in good condition." This latter statement was not correct, for it was afterwards proved conclusively that several members of Brahe's party were weak and sickly. Brahe may be acquitted of entertaining any deliberate intention to deceive, but to his thoughtlessness in not setting down the plain unvarnished truth, the disasters that immediately ensued were in a great measure attributable. For the triumphant explorers held a consultation, and the opinion of Burke unfortunately prevailed, viz., that they could not hope to overtake a party "all in good condition" when they themselves were in the worst condition imaginable. If they had only pushed on for a few hours more they would actually have come up with Brahe and his party, who did not travel very far the first day. As the Rev. Father Woods remarks in his exhaustive "History of Australian Exploration," "they were camped within a few miles of each other, and either party would have sacrificed everything to know that the others were so near." In deciding to remain for awhile at Cooper's Creek to recruit their wasted strength, instead of at once advancing on the track of their comrades, Burke, Wills

4—2

and King committed the unfortunate error that cost two
of them their lives. And, when they did resolve to start
afresh, they made still another fatal mistake in branching off
towards South Australia as being, in the opinion of Burke,
the nearest goal of relief, instead of continuing on the
main homeward route. Had they adopted the latter course
they would most assuredly have encountered Brahe, who
was evidently not at peace with his conscience. His
desertion of the depôt, without knowing the fate of Burke
and his companions, was troubling his mind, and he determined to make a final effort to ascertain if the explorers
had returned. He accordingly retraced his steps to Cooper's
Creek and, to all appearance, the site of the depôt was
in just the same condition as he had left it a few days
before. All would yet have been well, if he had only
thought it advisable to verify appearances by seeing if
the cavity at the foot of his marked tree still contained
what he had deposited in it on leaving. Had he taken
that simple step, he would have found to his great surprise
that the provisions and his letter were gone, and that the
journals of the expedition occupied their place, thus affording conclusive testimony that Burke and his companions
had returned and were somewhere in the vicinity. But
Brahe, with characteristic thoughtlessness, forgot to do
what ninety-nine men out of an average hundred would
have done under similar circumstances. After a hurried
inspection of the scene, he went away, fully convinced from
very insufficient premises that no white man had visited the
place since the breaking-up of the camp. By an extraordinary piece of ill-luck, Brahe was not long gone when
poor Wills laboriously wended his way back to Cooper's
Creek from the new direction that the ill-fated explorers had

taken. He, in his turn, anxiously looked around but could see no signs of the presence of friends, Brahe, by another grievous oversight, having left no indication whatever to show that he had been there a second time. Then came the tragic close of this brilliant and successful enterprise. Burke and his two companions, enfeebled and emaciated by fatigue and privation, struggled on in the vain hope of reaching one of the outlying squatters' stations of South Australia. Wills was the first to succumb to exhaustion; Burke yielded up his brave spirit a day or two afterwards; and King would assuredly have shared the sad fate of his companions in misfortune, had he not luckily fallen in with a party of blacks who treated him very kindly and allowed him to live with them for several months. He was the hardiest of the three, and by his indefatigable exertions throughout the appalling difficulties and disappointments that met them at every step, he succeeded in prolonging the lives of Burke and Wills for days. The last words committed to paper by the dying leader of the expedition were: "King has behaved nobly and deserves to be well rewarded." King was in truth a remarkable example of the devoted Irishman of humble birth, who conceives an ardent affection for the brave leader under whose banner he is serving, and who is ready to follow whithersoever he goeth. As one of the historians of the expedition rightly remarks: "Having tended Burke and Wills to their death, this brave young soldier preserved their papers with a faithful devotion and constant heroism worthy of the Victoria Cross."

When Brahe arrived in Melbourne with the startling news that none of the explorers had returned to the depôt at Cooper's Creek, and when no tidings of them could be obtained from any source, the whole colony was thrown into a state of excitement; and the exploration committee, suddenly awakened out of its slumbers, began to exhibit an activity that would have prevented all the fatalities of the expedition, if it had only been exercised at the proper time. No less than five well-equipped relief parties were fitted out and despatched with all possible speed, each converging on the track of the missing explorers from different points, so as to make the search systematic and complete. The party headed by Mr. Alfred Howitt was the only one that achieved the immediate object in view, but it is worthy of note that the others, in searching for Burke and Wills, still further explored and opened up the great interior of the Australian continent. Thus, even in death, these vanished heroes advanced the cause for which in life they had worked with so much energy, enthusiasm, and self-sacrifice. Well and truly has Father Woods called this "the most glorious era in the history of Australian discovery." Howitt's party, after a diligent search of all the country around Cooper's Creek, at length discovered poor King sitting in a native hut. Howitt states in his diary that when they found this solitary survivor of Burke's party, he presented a melancholy appearance, being wasted to a shadow and hardly distinguishable as a civilised being but for the remnants of clothes upon him. The kindness and presence of friends, however, soon effected a considerable change for the better in his personal appearance, and enabled him to accompany Howitt's party back to Melbourne, where he received the warm and generous welcome that was due to the sole survivor of an expedition at once so successful and unfortunate. Parliament voted him a substantial pension, and also awarded liberal grants to the immediate relatives of Burke and Wills. A public funeral was decreed as a national expression of the pervading grief at the irreparable loss of "two as gallant spirits as ever sacrificed life for the extension of science and the cause of mankind." Accordingly, a second expedition was sent to bring back the remains of Burke and Wills from their lonely resting-place at Cooper's Creek, for interment in the same city, whose whole population had turned out not many months before to gaze on the dashing leader and cheer his cavalcade, as they started full of life and sanguine anticipations on their path of discovery through the untouched heart of Australia. Now, what a striking dramatic contrast! The city again sent forth its thousands, and deputations attended from every place of importance; but they all slowly followed in silence the hearse that contained the bones of the Irish-Australian hero who was the observed of all observers on that former day of pride and exultation. A huge monolith of granite marks the spot in the Melbourne Cemetery where Burke and his faithful coadjutor, Wills, sleep side by side, and on one of the city eminences their statues rest on the same pedestal, telling to each successive generation of young Australians a story of dauntless courage, chivalric heroism, rare fortitude, noble self-sacrifice, and ultimate triumph, only to be followed by the most painful and harrowing of deaths, with friends so near and yet so far.

Burke's dashing exploit, while it unhappily killed himself, also killed the theory that the centre of Australia was an arid impassable desert—a theory persistently promulgated by previous explorers, and which had met with almost universal acceptance until he practically demonstrated its utter fallacy. The journals of the expedition, when published, conveyed the gratifying intelligence that Burke and Wills had, for the most part, travelled through a rich pastoral country capable of feeding countless flocks and herds.

Settlers by the score followed in their track, and, in less than a year, the whole of the country along their line of march was occupied by the advanced guard of civilised progress. "So rapid has been the occupation of this hitherto unknown country," says an official report of the era, " that, on the east coast alone, the sheep stations now taken up and stocked extend from the settled districts in an unbroken line to within one hundred miles of the Gulf of Carpentaria." Burke's expedition in fact completely revolutionised the accepted notions of Australian geography, and filled the map of the great southern continent with the host of names that are now seen abounding where a huge blank space had previously existed. It is no small honour to the Irish in Australia that one of their number was the leading spirit in effecting so wondrous and beneficent a transformation in the face of the country which they had made their adopted home.

## CHAPTER IV.

### A BIRTHPLACE OF FREEDOM.

AN EARLY IRISH EXPLORER—PRIMITIVE SQUATTERS—ESMOND'S DISCOVERY OF GOLD—FEVERISH EXCITEMENT—RUSH OF GOLD-SEEKERS FROM THE OLD WORLD—LARGE PERCENTAGE OF IRISHMEN—THE GOVERNMENT ISSUES LICENCES TO DIG—ARBITRARY AND BRUTAL MODE OF COLLECTING THE LICENCE-FEES—TWO ZEALOUS IRISH PRIESTS—THEIR TREATMENT BY INSOLENT TROOPERS—GROWING AGITATION FOR REDRESS OF GRIEVANCES—MASS MEETING ON BAKERY HILL—12,000 DIGGERS BURN THEIR LICENCES—PETER LALOR CHOSEN COMMANDER-IN-CHIEF—THE DIGGERS OCCUPY THE EUREKA STOCKADE—ATTACKED BY THE MILITARY—THE STOCKADE CAPTURED—DIGGERS CHARGED WITH HIGH TREASON AND ACQUITTED—ABOLITION OF THE HATEFUL LICENCE-FEE—DEMOCRATIC FREEDOM WON BY THE DIGGERS—DEVELOPMENT OF MINING—DEEP SINKING—REMARKABLE CAREER OF THE BAND OF HOPE—FATHER DUNNE, THE PIONEER PRIEST—THE BALLARAT OF TO-DAY.

SITUATED at a height of 1,437 feet above the level of the sea, and at a distance of 70 miles from Melbourne, is Ballarat, the centre of the richest gold-field in the world. Ballarat is a compound native word, meaning in our language a camping or resting-place, "balla" being the aboriginal equivalent for elbow, or, in a figurative sense, reclining at one's ease with the hand supporting the head. No name could have been more suitable or appropriate during the decade that the locality remained a pastoral solitude, but it completely lost its significance when the mineral wealth of Ballarat became known to the world, and thousands of gold-seekers from every civilised country came rushing southwards like a mighty human avalanche. In every infant settlement it is only natural that adventurous spirits should be found form-

ing themselves into exploring parties, with the object of
ascertaining the capabilities of the back country. Such a
party was organised by Mr. D'Arcy, an Irish surveyor, very
soon after the settlement of Melbourne. With five kindred
spirits he started to explore the country to the west. On the
verge of the horizon they saw a solitary peak, Mount Buninyong, towards which they directed their steps. Ascending
it, they gazed with delight on the splendid expanse of
pastoral country all around them, little dreaming that they
were looking on what was destined to be the greatest gold-
field of the age, and the site of the future prosperous city
of Ballarat. It would appear that the members of this
expedition became separated in some manner, and only
succeeded in reaching the coast after much danger and privation. But the intelligence they brought was too valuable to
be overlooked. Several parties set out with the object of
making a permanent settlement, and the rich natural
pastures of the district were soon taken up by these early
squatters, most of whom became immensely wealthy in later
years through the discovery of gold on their lands. But, on
their first occupation of the country, they dwelt in primeval
simplicity, in the midst of their flocks and herds, without a
thought of the golden treasures beneath their feet. A little
township sprang into existence at the base of Mount Buninyong, and became the recognised centre of the district. Six
miles to the west was the site of the present city of
Ballarat, town of Ballarat East, and borough of Sebastopol,
described by those who viewed the scene at the time as a
"pleasantly-picturesque pastoral country. Mount and range,
and table-land, gullies and creeks and grassy slopes, here
black and dense forest, there only sprinkled with trees, and
yonder showing clear reaches of grass, made up the general

landscape. A pastoral quiet reigned everywhere. Over the whole expanse there was nothing of civilisation but a few pastoral settlers and their retinue—the occasional flock of nibbling sheep, or groups of cattle browsing in the broad herbage."*

An early settler has given a graphic description of the quietness that reigned supreme: "I often passed," he says, "the spot on which Ballarat is built, and there could not be a prettier spot imagined. It was the very picture of repose. There was in general plenty of grass and water, and often have I seen the cattle in considerable numbers lying in quiet enjoyment after being satisfied with the pasture. One day I met the keeper of a shepherd's hut, and he told me the solitude was so painful that he could not endure it. He saw no one from the time the shepherds went out in the morning till they returned at night. I was the only person he had ever seen there who was not connected with the station." Mr. F. P. Labillière, barrister of the Middle Temple, says he "well remembers the neighbourhood of Ballarat for two or three years before gold was thought of. Some months before the discovery he passed near the field, if not over it, on the occasion of a day's excursion, which as a boy he made to Lake Burrumbeet with some friends from Buninyong. The whole country then was devoted to sheep pasture. There were no farms, and not a fence was to be seen along the bush road, or rather track between the lake and Mount Buninyong."†

But a time was at hand when all this Arcadian stillness and simplicity would have to make way for the busy hum and strange ways of camping crowds of all nations, when the

* "History of Ballarat," by William Bramwell Withers.
† "Early History of Victoria," by F. P. Labillière.

nibbling sheep and grazing cattle would have to retire before red-shirted and loud-spoken miners, and when the clear pellucid waters of the Yarrowee would be ruthlessly diverted and discoloured in the eager and all-absorbing search for gold. The scene was indeed to be changed. After ten years of silence and slumber, Ballarat was to become a name famous throughout the world. It is now a well-established fact that the existence of gold was known to several of the early squatters, but such was their horror of change, and their fear of seeing their properties overrun by hordes of lawless adventurers, that they succeeded in keeping the important secret to themselves for some time, and staving off the evil day as long as possible. Some of them certainly did communicate privately with various colonial governors on the subject, but these latter dignitaries were still more alarmed at the possible consequences and the increased responsibility of their position, if the exciting news became generally known and a rush of gold-seekers set in from the Old World. Sir Charles Fitzroy, in an official despatch to Earl Grey, informed the Secretary of State for the Colonies that he had been shown a large mass of golden quartz, but he feared " that any open investigation by the government would only tend to agitate the public mind and divert persons from their proper and more certain avocations." But when Hargreaves and Esmond returned from California, fully impressed with the conviction that Australia also was auriferous, it became a matter of impossibility to conceal the golden secret any longer. Hargreaves immediately commenced prospecting for the precious metal at Summerhill Creek, in the Bathurst district of New South Wales, and succeeded in finding several nuggets and a considerable quantity of gold dust. His success naturally produced the greatest excitement throughout New South Wales and Victoria, and a general movement of the population set in towards the "diggings" discovered by Hargreaves. Victoria was in danger of losing all her able-bodied men, when, at the critical moment, Esmond published his still more astonishing discoveries at Clunes, about 20 miles to the N.N.W. of Ballarat. This timely intimation had the effect of not only stopping the exodus to New South Wales, but of inducing a general rush to Victoria from the other colonies. The result was the gradual development of the famous Ballarat gold-field, "the riches unearthed there," according to the historian of the era, "not only quickly attracting all the other prospectors, but setting the colony on fire with excitement from end to end." Patrick Connor and Thomas Dunn—unmistakable Milesian names—were the leaders of the first two parties that commenced actual work on this, the most celebrated gold-field of our century. Mr. Withers, in his " History of Ballarat," expresses the opinion that "the honour of discovery seems to be tolerably evenly balanced between the two parties, though it may perhaps be held that the balance of priority inclines to the side of Connor's party, and it is said in support of Connor's claim that he was always regarded as leader of the diggers at the meetings held in those first days when the authorities made their first demand for license fees." Connor is dead, but Dunn still survives at a ripe old age, and steadfastly maintains his claim to the title of " Father of Ballarat." " I shall give you," he says, " a full and true account of our gold prospecting and the first discovery of Golden Point, Ballarat. Our party consisted of Richard Turner, James Merrick, George Wilson, Charles Gerrard, James Batty, and myself, Thomas Dunn. We started from town (Geelong) on Tuesday, August 5th, 1851, met with an accident on Batesford Hill, the loaded dray passing over the driver's stomach, proceeded on our journey to the Clunes, but stopped at Buninyong nearly a fortnight. The party getting dissatisfied, Wilson and I agreed to go in search of better diggings, so we started from Buninyong on Sunday morning, August 24th, 1851, between ten and eleven o'clock, with a tin dish and shovel, reached the Black Hill\* at about two o'clock, and left at about half-past three. In coming over Winter's Flat I said to George, 'There is a likely little quartz hill; let us try it before we go home.' It was pouring rain at the time. So with that I cut a square turf, then partly filled the dish, and went to the creek to wash it. Oh, what joy! there were about ten or twelve grains of fine gold. So we left off, covered up the turf, and made for home as fast as possible through the rain; reached home like two drowned rats; started next morning early for our discovery; reached there in the afternoon, and had the cradle at work next morning. I firmly believe that I, Thomas Dunn, and George Wilson were the first men, and got the first gold, on the little quartz hill now known as Golden Point."

Such is Dunn's homely narrative of the circumstances surrounding the birth of Ballarat. The probability is that Dunn and Connor's parties were on the field almost simultaneously, but, at this distance of time, it is impossible to ascertain with any degree of certainty which of them actually raised the first gold. First discoverers, as a rule, are singularly unlucky and unfortunate, and the story of Columbus is continually repeating itself. Having sown the seed amidst danger and difficulty, they find themselves unscrupulously elbowed aside, whilst others gather in the golden harvest.

---

\* An eminence overlooking Ballarat. It was subsequently discovered to be literally a mountain of gold.

Such was the hard fate of Dunn and Connor, and the members of their parties. Their immediate followers were raised to rank and opulence by the riches of Ballarat, but they themselves were left in silence and neglect to earn a small and uncertain daily wage. Even in later years when the Victorian Legislature scattered thousands of pounds in rewards for the discovery of particular gold-fields, the undeniable claims of Dunn and Connor were completely overlooked, the prizes to which they were honestly entitled having been showered for the most part on obtrusive applicants, whose assertiveness, pertinacity and political influence constituted their chief claims to recognition. It was owing to the shrewdness of one Irish digger that the underground treasures of Ballarat came to be revealed in all their native richness. Speaking of this important discovery in his " History of Australia," Mr. Sutherland says : " The first comers began to work at a bend in the creek, which they called Golden Point. Here for a time each man could easily earn from twenty to forty pounds a day, and crowds of people hurried to the scene. Every one selected a piece of ground, which he called his claim, and set to work to dig a hole in it, but when the bottom of the sandy layer was reached, and there seemed to be nothing but pipe-clay below, the claim was supposed to be worked out and was straightway abandoned. However, a miner named Cavenagh determined to try an experiment, and having entered one of these deserted claims, he dug through the layer of pipe-clay, when he had the good fortune to come suddenly upon several large deposits of grain gold. He had reached what had been in long-past ages the bed of the creek, where in every little hollow, for century after century, the flowing waters had gently deposited the gold which had been carried

with them from the mountains. In many cases these
'pockets,' as they were called, were found to contain gold
to the value of thousands of pounds, so that very soon all
the claims were carried down a few feet further, and with
such success that, before a month had passed, Ballarat took
rank as the richest gold-field in the world. In October
there were 10,000 men at work on the Yarrowee; acre
after acre was covered with circular heaps of red and yellow
sand, each with its shaft in the middle, in which men were
toiling beneath the ground to excavate the soil and pass it
to their companions above, who quickly hurried with it
to the banks of the creek, where twelve hundred cradles,
rocked by brawny arms, were washing the sand from the
gold." The extraordinary excitement produced by the
Ballarat discoveries is thus described in a despatch of the
governor of the period, Mr. Latrobe, to Earl Grey: "It is
quite impossible for me to describe to your lordship the
effect which these discoveries have had upon the whole
community. Within the last three weeks the towns of
Melbourne and Geelong and their large suburbs have been
in appearance almost emptied of many classes of their male
inhabitants. Not only have the idlers to be found in every
community, and day labourers in town and the adjacent
country, shopmen, artisans and mechanics of every description thrown up their employments—in most cases leaving
their employers and their wives and families to take care of
themselves—and run off to the workings, but responsible
tradesmen, farmers, clerks of every grade and not a few of
the superior classes have followed; some unable to with-
stand the mania and force of the stream, but others
because they were, as employers of labour, left in the
lurch and had no other alternative. Cottages are deserted,

houses to let, business is at a standstill, and even schools are closed. In some of the suburbs not a man is left, and the women are known, for self-protection, to forget neighbours' jars and to group together to keep house. The ships in the harbour are in a great measure deserted, and masters of vessels, like farmers, have made up parties with their men to go shares at the diggings. Both here (Melbourne) and at Geelong all buildings and contract works, public and private, are at a standstill."

When the exciting news was published in the Old World, the natural result was an exodus on a very large scale to the Golden Land of the south. All the nationalities of Europe were represented in this huge rush of gold-seekers. Every county in Ireland sent its thousands. Indeed, the large percentage of Irishmen on the gold-fields soon became a very noticeable feature. Mr. J. D'Ewes, who was the stipendiary magistrate in charge of Ballarat during the early period of its history, relates that on one occasion he witnessed a purchase, made by one of the banks, of five thousand four hundred ounces of gold, the produce of one claim at Eureka, discovered by a party of twelve Irishmen. The price paid by the bank to the lucky Hibernians was £4 2s. per ounce, so that each man received £1,845 as his share of the profits of this one golden hole.

For a time the Victorian Government, taken by surprise, was utterly powerless in the presence of this unexpected influx of population, but it eventually recovered its self-possession, proclaimed the right of the Crown to the gold, despatched officials to preserve order, and issued licenses to dig for the precious metal. At first the license fee was fixed at £1 10s. per month, but it was soon doubled in the hope of thinning the crowds that continued to travel to the gold-fields from all the points of the compass. In course of time this poll-tax, as it really was, assumed a most arbitrary and unjust character. It was levied alike on every digger, whether successful or unsuccessful, and the brutal and insulting manner in which it was enforced became an insupportable grievance, and led to a bloody conflict between the outraged diggers and the tyrannical authorities. The ridiculous idea seemed rooted in the minds of the governor and his advisers, that the gold-fields' population could only be ruled and regulated on military principles. Hence the diggers were allowed no representation whatever in the Victorian Parliament, although the great majority of them were respectable men of good family and education. They were tyrannised over by ignorant and insolent officials, many of whom were originally expatriated for their crimes, and were afterwards promoted into the ranks of the colonial constabulary. These ex-convicts took a demoniac delight in annoying and insulting the free-born diggers, and straining their petty authority to the utmost. No sooner had an intending digger arrived on the field than he was compelled to appear before one of these insolent officials, hand over his first monthly payment of £3, and receive in return a license to the following effect:

### Gold License.

No——                    Date—— 185—

The bearer ——, having paid to me the sum of £3 sterling on account of the territorial revenue, I hereby license him to dig, search for, and remove gold on and from any such Crown lands as I shall assign to him for that purpose during the month of ——, 185—. This license is not transferable, and must be produced whenever demanded by me or any other person acting under the authority of the government.    Signed ———,

*Commissioner.*

It was the custom of the gold-fields' officials, supported by bodies of armed mounted troopers, to sally out unexpectedly, surround the diggers whilst at work, call upon them, with many oaths and insults, to produce their licenses, and arrest all who could not exhibit the necessary document. The prisoners would then be marched off to the " Government Camp," and kept chained to large logs within its fortified lines until such time as their friends came forward with monetary assistance to their relief. One incident out of hundreds that might be narrated will serve to show the coarse, reckless and unjustifiable manner in which these ignorant officials carried out the duties intrusted to them, and which eventually drove the gold-fields' population into open rebellion. Father Patrick Smyth was one of the first of the Irish priests to arrive on the Ballarat gold-fields. He had a devoted personal attendant named John Gregory, who was one day paying a visit of charity to some Catholic friends. A license-hunting party of troopers came up, surrounded the tent in which they were, and the officer in charge " commanded the ——— wretches to come out of the tent and show him their licenses." Gregory quietly told him that he was the servant of Father Smyth, and had no such document. The troopers thereupon profusely damned both him and Father Smyth, and took him into custody. As Gregory was not a very able-bodied man, he asked his captors to take him to the Government Camp at once, and not drag him after them all over the diggings in their search for unlicensed miners. This reasonable request was refused with many curses and blows, and the poor fellow was compelled to follow the brutal troopers through the whole of the day's campaign. Next morning, although it was evident at a glance that Gregory was physically unable to dig for gold, he was fined £5 for having no license, and an additional £5 for having committed an imaginary assault on one of the troopers! "In the whole affair," says a contemporary account, "the Rev. Father Smyth was certainly treated with but little courtesy, and the trumpery story of a cripple assaulting an able-bodied mounted trooper is too ridiculous to warrant serious attention." Treatment of this description naturally engendered a bitter feeling of resentment against the law and its local administrators. The late Venerable Archdeacon Downing, who came up to Ballarat almost simultaneously with Father Smyth, was frequently the victim of the harsh tyranny of the insolent officials of those early days. On one occasion Father Downing had pitched his tent at the Brown Creek diggings, and, with his coat off, was hard at work digging a trench round it to carry off the water, when a brutal trooper, coming up, insisted that the priest was a digger, bailed him up, demanded his license, and subjected him to the grossest indignities. Mr. William Kelly, author of "Life in Victoria," thus describes what happened to himself and his friends on the very day of their arrival in Ballarat: "While still sitting round the hole, musing and chatting on the strange vicissitudes of life and the infinite mutability of fortune, we were favoured with no very pleasing exemplification in our own persons by the unexpected appearance of a 'brace of traps' (police), who demanded our licenses; and, so far from being satisfied with our explanations, they were rude and insolent, and, pretending to discredit our statements, ordered us to march as prisoners to the camp, first to pay fines of £5, and then to take out our licenses. Expostulation was vain; promises were sneered at; nothing short of £20, that is £5 each, could procure our liberation; so off we marched in the worst of humour. The first mandarin before whom we were brought, took the cue from the captors, pretending to laugh at 'our ruse,' assuming at the same time an air of menace, in which he hinted at locking up in default; but on my asking 'if one of his brother-commissioners, to whom I had a letter of introduction from a certain person in authority at head-quarters, was in the camp,' the matter assumed another complexion. The other commissioner soon arrived, and, glancing at the signature, he grasped my hand and shook it almost to dislocation; but, had I not had the letter, the consequences would have been both expensive and disagreeable. Reflecting on this, I began for the first time to think that the diggers' outcry against official tyranny and exaction was not altogether a baseless grievance. I could well imagine the state of feeling likely to be generated by a persistence in such a system of arbitrary persecution, and I was not surprised when it reached its climax soon afterwards."

These are only samples of the intolerable wrongs the mining population was compelled to endure at the hands of an irresponsible *régime*, and when it is added that the diggers were not permitted to cultivate the smallest portion of land for the maintenance of themselves and their families, it may be supposed that they would have been more than human if they had remained quiet under such grievous oppression. They organised a peaceful and constitutional agitation, to which all the gold-fields of the colony unanimously gave their assent and support. Its object was twofold—the abolition of the oppressive monthly license-fee and the representation of the gold-fields in parliament—two very reasonable and the reverse of revolutionary requests. Nevertheless, they were contemptuously rejected by the new governor, Sir Charles Hotham, and his responsible advisers. Sir Charles succeeded Mr. Latrobe on June 21st, 1854, and soon showed himself to be eminently unfit for his position. A retired navy captain, he tried to rule the colony like a martinet, and, by his headstrong and senseless policy towards the exasperated diggers, he precipitated a collision with the authorities. He professed to regard the agitation on the gold-fields as the result of the machinations of foreigners and, in the true spirit of the quarter-deck, defiantly declared his intention to put down all seditious manifestations with a stern hand. The underlings bettered the instructions of their chief, and the raids by the troopers upon the diggers became more numerous and irritating than ever. At last the utmost limits of patience having been reached, the probability of a successful insurrection was openly discussed on the gold-fields, and the agitation came to a crisis on November 29th, 1854, when 12,000 diggers held a meeting on Bakery Hill, Ballarat, under the presidency of Mr. Timothy Hayes, one of the most genial and popular Irishmen on the diggings. After carrying a series of resolutions setting forth the grievances of the gold-fields' population, and the unavailing efforts to induce the authorities to redress them, the meeting unanimously determined then and there to burn all their licenses, and thus bid open defiance to the government. Amidst enthusiastic cheering a huge bonfire was made, and every digger consigned his Crown permit to the flames. The two Irish priests already mentioned,

Father Patrick Smyth and Father Matthew Downing, were present at this historical meeting, and naturally exerted all their influence to induce the excited diggers not to take the irretrievable step of burning their licenses. But however willing the Irishmen, who constituted no small percentage of that crowd of 12,000 diggers, would be under ordinary circumstances to heed and obey the voice of their pastors, their blood was now boiling with indignation at the wrongs they had so long endured from their tyrannical oppressors, and whilst they listened to their priests with patience and respect, they could not be diverted from their fixed determination to summarily and decisively end such intolerable persecution. Messrs. Lalor, Quinn, Murnane and Brady were four of the principal speakers, and the most important resolution agreed to was couched in the following terms: " That this meeting being convinced that the obnoxious license-fee is an imposition and an unjustifiable tax on free labour, pledges itself to take immediate steps to abolish the same by at once burning all their licenses, and that, in the event of any party being arrested for having no licenses, the united people under all circumstances will defend and protect them."

Affairs on the gold-fields had now reached a crisis, but the governor and his advisers were resolved to pursue their tyrannical policy towards the diggers to the bitter end. According to them, what had just transpired in Ballarat was but a cloak to cover a democratic revolution, which must be stamped out at all hazards. The day following the burning of the licenses witnessed the last " digger hunt " on the Australian gold-fields. It was carried out with a great display of military force, in the hope of overawing the rebellious diggers and striking terror into their hearts. A large body of police, supported by the 12th and 40th regiments of the line, skirmishers in advance and cavalry on the flanks, advanced from the Government Camp on the diggers to demand the production of their licenses, knowing full well that those precious pieces of paper had been committed to the flames on the previous day. Not expecting this sudden attack, the diggers were unprepared for effective resistance. They retired as the troops advanced, rallying occasionally and receiving the enemy with a mingled fire of stones and bullets. The result of that day's work was open war between the gold-fields' population and the Crown. No sooner had the police and the military returned with a number of prisoners to the Government Camp, than the diggers assembled *en masse* on their old meeting-ground, Bakery Hill, appointed a council of war, and elected Peter Lalor (son of the late member for the Queen's County, and brother of the present member) as their commander-in-chief.

Up to this point, the diggers would seem to have had no designs of a revolutionary character. Their sole object was to secure a redress of their grievances and the abolition of an intolerable system of vulgar official tyranny. Now, however, when they found themselves treated as outlaws, the movement assumed a wider significance; a declaration of independence based on the American model was drawn up and signed, and a new silken flag—the Southern Cross—five silver stars forming a cross on a blue ground—was unfurled to the breeze. Beneath this diggers' standard, Lalor, as commander-in-chief, took his stand and administered the following oath to his men: "We swear by the Southern Cross to stand truly by each other and fight to defend our rights and liberties." It was in that portion of the gold-

## A BIRTHPLACE OF FREEDOM.

fields known as the Eureka * and principally inhabited by Irish diggers, that the fortified camp of the "rebels," as they were now officially described, was erected. It consisted of an entrenched stockade, that was capable of being made a place of great strength if the diggers had had time to utilise its natural advantages, and place it in a proper state of defence. It occupied an area of about an acre, rudely enclosed with strong slabs. Within the stockade drilling now became the main business of the hour; the diggers' council of war sat almost continuously; blacksmiths were kept at work night and day forging pikes. "Let those who cannot provide themselves with firearms procure a piece of steel five or six inches long, attached to a pole, and that will pierce the tyrants' hearts," were the words of the commander-in-chief to his men. Patrick Curtain was the chosen captain of the pikemen, and Michael Hanrahan was their lieutenant. Meanwhile the authorities were grievously alarmed at the spectre their stupidity, barbarity, and truculent insolence had created. They had never reckoned on the persecuted diggers turning at bay and presenting an unbroken military front to their oppressors. Sir Charles Hotham and his ministers were in an agitated state of perplexity; Melbourne, the capital, was in a panic, and the mayor was swearing in citizens by the hundred as special constables to resist the victorious diggers, whom the wild rumours of the hour described as marching in a body from

---

* Why it was so designated has been thus explained: Dr. Doyle was one day walking over the ranges when he came across a gully about two miles from Ballarat, in which he picked up a few stray nuggets of gold. The classical exclamation, "Eureka!" at once rose to his lips, and he resolved to give the place that name. A rush of diggers was the natural result of the doctor's discovery, and "The Eureka" soon became famous as one of the richest spots on the Ballarat field.

Ballarat to pillage the city. Hearing that the rebellion was spreading and that the men of the other gold-fields were hastening to the relief and assistance of their Ballarat comrades, the authorities of the Government Camp decided to attack the diggers' stronghold before any of these reinforcements could arrive. Early on the morning of Sunday, December 3rd, 1854, the assault was made by the combined forces of the military and the police under the command of Colonel Thomas, of the 40th regiment. The insurgent diggers, commanded by Mr. Peter Lalor, made a brave and desperate resistance; the pikemen (an almost exclusively Irish detachment) stood their ground in double file around the enclosure and repelled several charges of cavalry; volley after volley was poured into the stockade and answered by the diggers, until their want of ammunition and comparative unpreparedness became apparent. After half-an-hour's desperate hand-to-hand fighting, the Eureka stockade was surrounded and carried by storm.

The scene that followed was of a brutal and barbarous character. The ruffianly soldiers and troopers behaved towards their discomfited opponents in the most cowardly fashion. Not content with making a large number of them prisoners, they did not scruple in their savage glee even to shoot non-combatants down in cold blood. The official list of casualties on the diggers' side reports 22 killed, 12 wounded, and 125 taken prisoners; but these figures must not be accepted as literally accurate, as many lives were sacrificed and many persons wounded in the encounter, whose names were not officially recorded. Subjoined are some of the names of the Irishmen who fell or were wounded in this first struggle for freedom on Victorian soil:

## KILLED.

| | |
|---|---|
| John Hynes | County Clare. |
| Patrick Gittings | ,, Kilkenny. |
| Patrick Mullens | ,, Kilkenny. |
| John Diamond | ,, Clare. |
| Thomas O'Neil | ,, Kilkenny. |
| George Donaghy | ,, Donegal. |
| Edward Quinn | ,, Cavan. |
| William Quinlan | ,, Cavan. |

## MORTALLY WOUNDED.

| | |
|---|---|
| Thaddeus Moore | County Clare. |
| James Brown | ,, Wexford. |
| Edward M'Glynn | ,, Wexford. |

## WOUNDED AND SUBSEQUENTLY RECOVERED.

| | |
|---|---|
| Peter Lalor | Queen's County. |
| Patrick Hanofin | County Kerry. |
| Michael Hanly | ,, Tipperary. |
| Michael O'Neil | ,, Clare. |
| Thomas Callanan | ,, Clare. |
| Patrick Callanan | ,, Clare. |
| James Warner | ,, Cork. |
| Luke Sheehan | ,, Galway. |
| Michael Morrison | ,, Galway. |
| Denis Dynon | ,, Clare. |

Lalor, commander-in-chief of the diggers, was in his place when the attack was made on the stockade, and fought with conspicuous bravery until he received a ball near the shoulder of the left arm. Some of his men placed him under some protecting slabs within the stockade, and there he was discovered after the engagement was over, lying in a pool of blood. Fortunately his friends, and not his foes, found out his place of concealment, and they carried him to a safe retreat in the neighbourhood, where the wounded arm was successfully amputated by a friendly surgeon. Then, under the protection of the good priest, Father Patrick Smyth, arrangements were made to have the rebel commander removed as speedily as possible from the hot and vengeful pursuit of the authorities. A few days after the storming of the stockade, Patrick Carroll, an Irish carrier, arrived in Ballarat with a load of goods from Geelong, and on the return trip he had a solitary passenger, the man for whose body, dead or alive, the government emissaries were scouring the country in all directions. Carroll did his best to conceal the fugitive leader under a tarpaulin and the boughs of trees, and, by keeping as far as possible from the frequented roads and driving through lonely bush tracks, he succeeded in reaching Geelong without having attracted any hostile notice. Camping outside the town until night came on, the faithful Irishman drove his distressed compatriot to the appointed place of refuge. Notwithstanding that a large money reward was offered by the government for Lalor's apprehension, and although his place of concealment was well-known to many, not a solitary scrap of information did the government receive, so loyal and hearty was the sympathy of the people at large with the oppressed diggers and the cause for which they had suffered. "It is a curious commentary on the events of those times," remarks one of the historians of the colony, "that whereas the Government of Victoria then offered so large a sum for Mr. Lalor's dead body, they are now glad to pay him £1,500 a year to live." This is an allusion to the fact that the erstwhile rebel of 1854, with a price on his head, is now the first commoner of Victoria and admittedly one of the ablest

Speakers in the Australian colonies. The diggers captured in the stockade were brought to Melbourne to await their trial for high treason against Her Majesty. So determined were the authorities to convict at any cost, that they did not hesitate to resort to the hideous system of packed juries. Every Irishman, and every citizen suspected of sympathy with the miners, were promptly told to stand aside. Nevertheless the current of popular opinion was so powerful, and the sympathy with the persecuted diggers so widespread, that prisoner after prisoner was acquitted, amid the ringing cheers of a crowded court and the more boisterous demonstrations of satisfaction from the thousands outside. Eventually the State trials were wisely abandoned by the Crown; the proclamations of outlawry against Mr. Lalor and his fellow-leaders were unconditionally withdrawn; the concealed chiefs came forth into the light of day once more; a Royal Commission, with the late Sir John O'Shanassy as one of its principal members, was appointed to inquire into the grievances of the miners; the oppressive license-fee was soon abolished on their recommendation; parliamentary representation was given to the gold-fields, and before the first anniversary of the storming of the Eureka stockade came round, Mr. Lalor was one of the members for Ballarat, and the mining population was as quiet, law-abiding, and industrious as any other section of the community.

That the armed resistance of the diggers on the Eureka paved the way for democratic freedom in the Australian colonies, and abolished for ever a semi-military despotism over free-born men, is an historical fact that cannot be called into question. Irishmen played the most important part in that exciting episode, and to this day Irishmen continue to be the backbone and sinew of the flourishing city of Ballarat, that has developed from the thousands of diggers' tents that occupied its site in 1854. Nowhere could be found a more hospitable and patriotic people, a more enlightened community, a more intelligent body of electors. The Irishmen of Ballarat have not only been foremost in building up the Golden City and gathering its auriferous treasures, but they have always been found in the van of liberal progress and useful legislation. Their respected leader, Daniel Brophy, a sterling Celt from Castlecomer, Kilkenny, has been several times mayor of the city, and was for years one of their representatives in the Legislative Assembly.

In the early years of Ballarat, the operations of the diggers were confined to the surface workings, or the sinking of shallow shafts into the rich alluvial. Fabulous wealth was thus raised by thousands of men in a comparatively easy manner. Scientific mining for gold was not attempted at this early stage, the men merely digging and delving into the golden soil to the depth of a hundred or one hundred and fifty feet, when they were stopped by a huge layer of solid rock. Beneath this they did not attempt to penetrate, though their shrewd observation convinced them that if they could only succeed in piercing that rocky barrier, they would strike still richer leads of gold in the underground river-beds. Still, so long as the gold was to be procured within easy reach of the surface, there was no inducement to expend a large amount of capital and labour in the risky experiment of cutting several hundred feet through the underlying rock in the hope of striking another payable gold-field. It was only when the surface workings gave unmistakable signs of exhaustion, that the sanguine and speculative spirits of Ballarat turned their attention to the new and still untouched sources of wealth that lay deep down in the earth. The glorious result of this new development of antipodean enterprise soon became manifest. Individual mining gradually gave place to co-operative mining; companies were formed in which the shareholders provided the capital necessary for so much expensive deep-sinking; after many dangers and difficulties the rocky barrier was pierced at last, an extensive and permanent gold-field was opened up, and the prosperity of Ballarat was assured.

Perhaps the most remarkable of the companies that, by their energy, perseverance and pluck, contributed to this magnificent result, was the "Band of Hope," in which Irish enterprise and industry were very largely represented. Its history is of the most chequered character. Originally inaugurated by 120 working miners, it took no less than twelve months' continuous labour to get to the bottom of the hard basaltic rock. In the effort to sink their first shaft, an underground stream broke in upon them, and a powerful steam engine had to be employed to pump up an immense quantity of accumulated water. To keep out this enemy they built a wall of clay around the shaft, but the work was hardly finished before the water broke through and flooded them out again. A second time they rebuilt the wall, and once again it gave way to the pressure of the underground streams. Undaunted by their continued ill-luck, they erected it a third time and at last succeeded in keeping out the water. Continuing their descent through the rock, after being flooded out from time to time, they eventually reached a depth of 340 feet. Then they commenced to drive a tunnel to the south-east, and once again their old enemy, the water, came down upon them, accompanied this time by an immense quantity of sand. "It was now over six years since the starting of the company," remarks Mr. George Sutherland in one of his graphic descriptive sketches of the Victorian gold-fields. "Fortunes had been spent upon it; many shareholders had dropped out. But still the faithful few persevered under every disadvantage, determined to deserve their first adopted name of 'Band of Hope.' The miners retreated higher up the shaft, and opened up a new drive at a point beyond the level of the water. Profiting by their former experience, they carried their drive in the proper direction this time; and thus they arrived once more at the gold-drift. Again the water and sand poured in, and there was no chance of proceeding with the work until these enemies were subdued. Thick walls of clay were constructed, backed by immense barriers of beams and logs. And still the water burst through these obstacles and swept them away. So much sand and water had obtained access to the shaft, that it took two years' labour to clear it out again. It was now the middle of 1866, or over eight years from the date of the commencement; the sinking of the shaft had cost £30,000, and still the company was in a 'progressive' state—that is to say, the shareholders were continually putting money into it, instead of receiving any profit from it." Two years more of rebuff and disaster had to be experienced before this brave body of men secured the just reward of their persevering toil. As if to recompense them for their indefatigable industry in conquering obstacles that would have overwhelmed any less determined band, the treasures for which they had been so long in search exceeded their most sanguine anticipations. "The amount of gold," says Mr. Sutherland, "collected in this famous mine astonished the world. In one day over £6,000 worth was obtained, and for a long time the weekly reckoning of the profits showed that the company was making over £1,000 per day." The total quantity of gold raised from this mine—a mine possessing the strange history thus summarily reviewed —has exceeded in value £4,000,000 sterling. It is no small compliment to the Irishmen of Ballarat that they formed the backbone of this great pioneer deep-sinking company, that they manfully continued the work when the faint-hearted fell away, that disaster following disaster only excited them to renewed exertion, and that after ten years' unflagging toil they reaped the reward of their extraordinary activity, and established fortunes for themselves and their families.

The Ballarat of to-day is one of the finest inland cities of Australia. Its main artery, Sturt Street, is admittedly one of the noblest thoroughfares in the Southern Hemisphere, being unusually wide and beautified by trees for nearly the whole of its length. Prominent amongst the many striking buildings that line this lengthy and lovely street, are the City Hall with its lofty tower, and St. Patrick's Cathedral, a splendid and capacious edifice that does credit to the Irish Catholics of the Golden City. Ballarat, formerly a deanery in the diocese of Melbourne, was, in 1874, erected into a separate bishopric. Its first prelate was the Right Rev. Dr. O'Connor, who at the time of his appointment was parish priest of Rathfarnham, Dublin. Bishop O'Connor was enthusiastically welcomed on his arrival, and very soon the enthusiasm of his people was manifested in a more practical form by the erection, at a cost of £10,000, of the handsome Bishop's Palace that now ornaments the margin of Lake Wendouree, in Ballarat West. Dr. O'Connor travelled through every part of his extensive diocese, and made himself personally conversant with the needs and requirements of every mission that was under his jurisdiction. For some years the Legislature of Victoria has given no aid whatever to Catholic schools, whilst lavishing thousands on thousands of pounds on godless secular schools, the teachers of which are sternly prohibited by legislative enactment against imparting religious instruction in any shape or form. By voice and pen Dr. O'Connor unceasingly denounced this iniquitous law, and, from the first day of his landing, he laboured energetically and successfully in the work of building up a sound Catholic system of education for the benefit of the little ones of his flock. During the eight years that he ruled the diocese of Ballarat, he raised no less a sum than £70,000 for educational purposes alone. He introduced a community of the Loretto Nuns from the parent house of Rathfarnham, and, with the willing assistance of his devoted people, built a commodious convent and schools for them, in close proximity to his own residence, at a cost of £15,000. The Loretto Nuns have proved themselves to be highly-successful teachers, a number of their pupils having passed the Civil Service Examination; and not a few have taken high honours at the Melbourne University. In Ballarat East there is a convent of Sisters of Mercy, who are doing noble service by undertaking the management of the girls' primary school in that populous portion of the city. Near the cathedral in Sturt Street the Christian Brothers have established themselves, and are conducting boys' schools in accordance with the excellent and well-known system of their order. Unfortunately, Dr. O'Connor did not live long to supervise the efficient educational machinery he had set in operation. The health of the good bishop failed, and to the great regret of his flock, he died in 1883. His Vicar-General, Dr. James Moore, succeeded him and continues to carry on the good work that the first Bishop of Ballarat so devotedly and energetically initiated. Under the vigorous administration of Bishop Moore, the diocese of Ballarat has become wonderfully well-equipped with all that is requisite for the active promotion of religion, morality, and Christian education.

At the consecration of Bishop Moore in St. Patrick's Cathedral, Ballarat, on April 27th, 1884, there was one amongst the number of clergy and dignitaries within the sanctuary, for whom the ceremony had a deep and pathetic interest, recalling to his memory, as it must needs have done, the marvellous days of thirty-three years before, when Ballarat was at its beginning, and when he was the first and only priest amongst its tent-living population of thousands of adventurous diggers. He had travelled a long distance to be present at the first consecration of a Bishop in Ballarat, for a generation had passed away and his eyes had not once beheld the place since he saw it in the first stage of its golden existence. This was the Very Rev. Patrick Dunne, D.D., Vicar-General of the Diocese of Goulburn, which embraces the great southern district of New South Wales. Father Dunne was the first priest who came direct from Ireland to the infant see of Melbourne. He was educated in the College of Maynooth, which has not only supplied Ireland for a century with a zealous and patriotic priesthood, but has nobly upheld the traditions of the island of saints by sending fearless missioners to preach the gospel and plant the Cross in almost every quarter of the habitable globe. Ordained a priest and appointed to a curacy in his native diocese, Kildare, during the terrible famine year of 1846, Father Dunne, in common with his brother-priests, did his duty manfully during that most trying time in the history of the country. When, in 1850, the Rev. Dr. Geoghegan, Vicar-General of the newly-founded diocese of Melbourne, came to Ireland as a delegate from the infant Australian Church, and feelingly represented the spiritual destitution of many of the Irish Catholic immigrants, for whom he had no means of providing the consolations of religion, Father Dunne was the first to volunteer to fill the breach, leave his native land, and follow his fellow-countrymen to the far-distant south. At Liverpool there embarked with him for Australia another priest who had been stationed near that city for some time—Father Gerald Ward. This clergyman was not destined to labour long in his new sphere, but he left after him an enduring monument of his active zeal in the splendid orphanage of St. Vincent De Paul, in the populous city of South Melbourne. When these two good priests arrived in Hobson's Bay, the harbour of Melbourne, after a voyage of five months' duration, they were landed in one of the ship's boats on the sandy beach, which is now occupied by the busy town of Port Melbourne, but which then displayed only one outward sign of civilisation in the shape of a solitary public-house. After making their way over sandy hills and through silent wastes, they came to a punt on the river Yarra, by which they crossed over to the then little village of Melbourne. Away to the north in what was at that time considered the "bush," but which is now in the centre of the city, they found the humble four-roomed cottage in which the young Bishop of Melbourne had established himself. Dr. Goold was naturally delighted at the unexpected advent of two much-needed clergymen, and gave them a very cordial welcome. To Father Dunne was allotted the pastoral charge of the extensive Geelong district, and soon afterwards he was appointed to supervise the country stretching to the north of Melbourne. At Coburg he was engaged in building a church, when the exciting news of the gold discoveries at Ballarat was proclaimed. All the men employed on the building left at once for the gold-fields. As a priest was very much wanted amongst the digging population, Father Dunne lost no time in responding to the request of his ecclesiastical superiors. Mounting his horse and taking nothing with him save the clothes he wore and his sacred vestments, he started for the golden centre. In such a dreadful condition was the road, that some days elapsed before he reached the spot where ten thousand people were living in tents and digging for gold. He found shelter in the tent of Mr. John O'Sullivan, a timber merchant of Melbourne, who had come up with the rest in the hope of achieving a fortune more expeditiously than in the ordinary ways of trade.

On the Sunday after his arrival, Father Dunne celebrated the first mass that was offered up in what is now the episcopal city of Ballarat, and afterwards it became a familiar and a very edifying spectacle to see, every Sunday morning, hundreds of rough, red-shirted, long-bearded diggers devoutly kneeling outside in the open air, whilst the Holy Sacrifice was being offered up in the tent. The pioneer priest of the gold-fields made himself in all respects as one of the people around him. He slept on a sheet of bark with a blanket rolled about him; he often prepared and cooked his own meals, and every morning at six o'clock, he could be seen making his way to the nearest water-hole with two large bottles in order to secure a supply for the day. An hour later not a drop of clean water was to be had, every available hole and creek being surrounded by diggers, washing out the clay in search of the precious metal.

Dr. Dunne has kindly supplied the subjoined interesting recollections of his visit to early Ballarat: "The scenes on the first gold-field at Ballarat were something to be remembered. The camp fires at night, the echo of the songs and choruses in the tents after the evening black tea and damper, the barking of dogs, for every tent had its dog, the discharge of firearms, all resounding through the primeval forest, made up such a chaos of sounds as no words could describe. In the morning all were up and stirring at early dawn, the fires were lighted to prepare for the morning meal, the sound of the axe was heard, and the crashing of falling trees made those who were not early risers feel rather uncomfortable whilst sleeping under a frail canvas tent. After breakfast all were off to their different occupations, some sinking with pick and shovel, others carrying the auriferous clay to the nearest water-hole or creek to have it washed in some of the most primitive constructions imaginable. Tin dishes were most generally used, but cradles with perforated zinc were adopted by the most experienced. In the absence of anything better, old hats were sometimes called into requisition. The ten thousand people at Ballarat during the first two or three months after the discovery of gold were almost without an exception as intelligent, orderly and respectable a body of men as you would meet in any part of the world. Mr. Blair, the police magistrate from Portland, was there more as a spectator than in his official capacity. There were members of parliament, lawyers, doctors, and men of every class and grade in society, and during the two or three months that I remained at Ballarat I never saw a man the worse for drink. There were no rows or robberies, but everything went on in the very best order and good feeling. The Irish element at Ballarat was in the early days very considerable, and Irishmen fell in for their fair share of the gold. Melbourne and Geelong were nearly drained of their male population, agriculture was completely neglected, and flour, and hay and oats went up to fabulous prices. It was soon found that it was more profitable to keep to the ordinary occupations than to go gold seeking; so society soon began to find its level, and trade and commerce were again in a most flourishing condition."

## CHAPTER V.

### A GOLDEN CITY.

SANDHURST, THE GREAT CENTRE OF QUARTZ MINING—AN INVADING HOST OF DIGGERS—INDIGNANT REMONSTRANCES AGAINST OFFICIAL TYRANNY—THE BANNER OF THE IRISH DIGGERS—" BENDIGO MAC "—HOW HE AVERTED A REBELLION — AN IRISHMAN WHO LITERALLY ROLLED IN WEALTH — AN IRISH DIGGER'S TENT—HIBERNIAN PERSEVERANCE REWARDED—TIPPERARY GULLY—THE "SHAMROCK"—AN ENTERPRISING IRISHMAN—SOME PROMINENT SANDHURST IRISHMEN, AND WHAT THEY HAVE ACHIEVED.

MUCH that has been said about Ballarat is equally true of the city of Sandhurst, the second great gold-fields' centre of Victoria. Distant 100 miles from the metropolis, in a north-westerly direction, it is surrounded on all sides by an abundance of mining wealth that will ensure the prosperity of the place for many a year to come. Indeed, some scientific experts have given it as their opinion that the quartz reefs of Sandhurst are practically inexhaustible. Without acquiescing in that professional prediction, there is no denying the fact that the production of gold from the Sandhurst mines during the past thirty-five years has been something marvellous, and the immense depths at which the golden stone continues to be procured at this day strengthen the belief that it will take at least half a century to extract all the gold from the available quartz. The first great " rush " to Sandhurst or Bendigo, the name by which it was known for many years, happened soon after the discovery of Ballarat, and in a few weeks' time the gold-seekers were tramping from Melbourne in their thousands. They occupied the field in force, and lost no time in turning up the soil in all directions, and washing out the golden grains. To quote the words of the genial Hibernian historian of Sandhurst, Mr. John Neill Macartney, who was the government mining registrar of the district for many years, " all around resembled ant-hills with their teeming numbers, and the diggers' tents reminded one of a serried and invading army." The license-fee, or rather its mode of collection by the insolent Crown officials, soon became in Bendigo, as in Ballarat, an insupportable grievance, and it was only by a lucky chance that hostilities were at one stage averted. As Mr. Macartney very truly says, many a scholarly and polished gentleman's heart was beating under the blue shirt of many a digger, and it is not difficult to understand how men of that stamp were wrought into a dangerous state of exasperation by the wanton insults of brutal and ignorant troopers. Bendigo, at that time, numbered a considerable proportion of honest Hibernians amongst its tent-living population, so it is not surprising to read in the contemporary records of a great diggers' demonstration held towards the close of 1853, that " flags of all nations were present, but a splendid Irish banner was most conspicuous in the van."\* Deputies from mass meetings of the diggers were sent down to Melbourne to remonstrate with the governor in person, and to point out the inevitable consequences of denying the gold-fields' population the rights of freemen, and of leaving them at the mercy of a ruffianly police. But His Excellency turned a deaf ear to all remonstrances, and insisted on ruling in quarter-deck fashion. If the peace was preserved

---

\* "First marched the Irish—always first in every agitation"—is the comment of Mr. William Howitt on this demoustration, in his "Two Years in Victoria."

in Bendigo at the time that the diggers of Ballarat were in armed rebellion, it was not the Governor of Victoria, Sir Charles Hotham, who was to be thanked, but the newly-appointed resident magistrate, Captain M'Lachlan, who arrived just in the nick of time, and, with the shrewdness of the Scotchman, took in the situation at a glance. He saw the imperative necessity of conciliating the exasperated diggers, and, by his first administrative act, he won their confidence and appeased their indignation. That act was the instant dismissal of a number of the black sheep amongst the police force—scoundrels who had been transported from the mother country for their crimes, and, by a strange irony of destiny, were afterwards placed in a position of authority which enabled them to tyrannise at will over men of birth, breeding, education, and honesty, to whom their touch was contamination and their very presence an insult. This in itself was one great stride in the direction of reform, and Captain M'Lachlan followed it up with a distinct and deliberate refusal to carry out the governor's instructions to collect the diggers' license-fees at the point of the bayonet. By this disobedience he jeopardised his position and rendered himself amenable to a court-martial, but he had the satisfaction of knowing that he had saved Bendigo from the bloodshed and loss of life that resulted from obeying the governor's instructions at Ballarat. When affairs cooled down a little, and the diggers were granted those rights that should never have been denied them, every one admitted that the captain was in the right and the governor stupidly in the wrong. So far from suffering any official degradation for declining to enforce an order by the representative of the Queen, which he knew meant precipitating a civil war, he was continued in his office and applauded on all sides for the sound common sense, tact, and discrimination he had displayed under most trying and exceptional circumstances. "Bendigo Mac," as he was ever afterwards familiarly and affectionately called, presided as stipendiary magistrate over the Sandhurst court for the succeeding seventeen years, and when he retired into private life, all classes of citizens combined to present him with a large monetary testimonial.

People who have plenty of money are often said, by a figure of speech, to be "rolling in wealth," but the expression was literally true in the case of a certain eccentric Irishman in the early days of Sandhurst. His name was Flanagan, and, finding that he had dug £3,000 worth of gold out of the earth, some demon prompted him to run down to the metropolis and enjoy himself for a season. On arriving in Melbourne he engaged a room in a hotel, and then proceeded to the bank, where he presented his draft. Instead of taking his £3,000 in notes, he insisted on having 3,000 sovereigns, with which he filled a sack that he had brought with him for the purpose. Returning to his hotel, he went straight to his room, locked the door, and emptied the sack of sovereigns on the floor. He then stripped himself stark naked, and spent the remainder of the day in rolling himself over and over upon his golden heap. Next day he commenced to get rid of his golden store as fast as he could by senseless drinking, dissipation, and extravagance of all sorts; and, before the end of the month, the foolish fellow was trudging back to the diggings without a solitary shilling to bless himself with.

Though the tragic element necessarily predominated in those digger-hunting days, the comic was by no means wanting at times. Mr. Macartney relates one amusing incident that came under his personal observation. "Early in

1854 two well-known diggers, John Murphy and Garrett Brennan, were rounded up by the police on a part of the diggings called Jackass Flat, and taken before Mr. Dowling, the police magistrate, their offence being not having their licenses upon them. Although they had paid for their licenses, Murphy, who was a droll dog, a rough Irish diamond, requested to see 'his honour's riverince.' Mr. Dowling replied, 'Well, my man, I am the man you want.' Murphy then asked, 'Would your honour's riverince order that fellow (pointing to the policeman on guard) to fire on a man who had paid for his license and had left it in his tent, if he ran away after being rounded up by the police?' Mr. Dowling replied, 'Certainly not.' Murphy exclaimed, 'Thin, be jabers, I'm off,' saying which, he knocked over the police guard, jumped the picket fence, and ran like a greyhound into the bush. His companion, Brennan, having proved that he had paid for a license, was dismissed with a reprimand."

Neither was conviviality of the old-land type unknown at the close of the day's gathering-in of the golden harvest. A contemporary eye-witness has given a graphic description of an Irish tent, in which an old fiddler is reviving fond recollections of a dear isle far away by playing the beautiful melody of "Erin-go-Bragh." "Hold a moment! He is resining his bow. Now he begins, and as the charming strain falls upon the ears of his sensitive countrymen, they here and there chime in with a part of the song and dissolve in tears from the warmth of their emotions. Of what a complication of joys and sorrows is the human heart made up! Listen. He now plays 'Paddy Carey,' and see—every face that was this moment suffused with tears is radiant with joy, and the tent, as a matter of course, being now no longer capable of holding its inmates, throws them forth to the open air to have a trip on the gravel, which here serves as a substitute for the bright green sod of their own native 'isle of the ocean.'"

In a community composed of so many inflammable elements, and gathered from all the nations under the sun, with every man desperately eager to build up a golden pile, and return home with the utmost speed to astonish his family and friends with the richness of his rapidly-acquired wealth, it was to be expected that there should be not unfrequently personal disputes as to the right of possessing particular pieces of coveted ground. As a rule the contending parties were allowed to fight the matter out for themselves; but occasionally their sympathising countrymen would appear on the scene of strife, hot words would be interchanged, and very soon, what was originally a purely personal quarrel would develop into a *mêlée* between opposing nationalities.

Mr. C. R. Read, an official on the gold-fields, in a work describing his experiences in that capacity, narrates how, on one occasion, there was a dispute between a Tipperary boy and an Englishman about a piece of ground, and in the inevitable scuffle that ensued the Irishman fell headlong into a hole full of muddy water, and the Englishman partly so. This trifling incident a few hours afterwards led to a desperate fight between the Irishmen and Englishmen on the field. One Irishman was shot through the lungs and another in the head, whilst the leader of the Englishmen had his head split open with an axe.

The same official states that the Irishmen were generally the most fortunate on the diggings. The most unfortunate class of gold-seekers were those that came under the denomination of "swell" or gentleman diggers—members of the learned professions and younger sons of good families, who had never before handled a pick in their lives. But, whilst this was the rule, there were some exceptions. Mr. Read says he was personally aware of several instances of great success attending gentlemen who were digging. One with whom he was intimately acquainted cleared upwards of £3,000 in six weeks.

Perseverance was richly and deservedly rewarded in the case of a party of four Irishmen who sank eighteen holes in succession, and only got one ounce of gold each for their trouble. They did not lose heart, but sank nine more, with little better result, realising just one pound per man. They were naturally somewhat discouraged at such poor returns after months of labour, and believed themselves to be very unlucky indeed. Still, they were determined to make one effort more, and, on sinking their twenty-eighth hole, they struck a splendid patch of gold which yielded them £1,000 per man.

Mr. James Bonwick, the most industrious and voluminous of Australian authors, visited Bendigo in 1852, and, in his "Notes of a Gold Digger," he speaks of the Irish who occupied Tipperary Gully, near his tent, as consisting entirely of families conspicuous for their order, cleanliness, kind-heartedness and happiness.

Sandhurst is not to be compared with Ballarat for beauty of site or surroundings, but by means of various artificial embellishments and the almost universal planting of umbrageous trees along its thoroughfares, its civic rulers have in great measure succeeded in overcoming its natural defects of position, and introducing some of the elements of the picturesque. No doubt, on entering the city the observing eye is at first liable to be offended by the repulsive heaps of upturned earth that lie ruthlessly scattered in all directions—perpetual reminders of the early days when the gold was readily found near the surface, and diggers acquired enormous fortunes without much bodily labour or risk of life. But this is a prevailing characteristic of nearly all gold-fields, though Sandhurst, by reason of its low, flat situation, suffers in appearance more severely from this cause than its sister cities. But when the visitor leaves the outskirts of Sandhurst behind him and enters the city itself, the disagreeable impression produced by the sight of dreary wastes of torn and disembowelled earth will speedily be dissipated. For he will be ushered into a bustling and animated scene; he will see himself in the centre of a well-planned and well-appointed town; a long succession of handsome shops will spread out before his gaze, and all around he will discern indubitable evidences of material prosperity and intellectual life in a host of fine public buildings, imposing banks, numerous churches, and a variety of literary and educational institutions. That once popular Hibernian governor of New South Wales, Sir Hercules Robinson, was perfectly right when he declared that "Sandhurst surpassed all other districts in the marvellous wealth of its mineral resources." It has been of recent years the richest and most productive of Victorian gold-fields, and the auriferous quartz continues to be found so abundantly at enormous depths as to lead to the widespread belief that Sandhurst is in reality a series of gold-fields, one underneath the other.

One of the great institutions of Sandhurst is the "Shamrock," a capacious and comfortable hostelry that, notwithstanding its aggressively Hibernian title, has been the head-quarters of visitors from every nation under the sun, and a favourite resort of successive generations of gold-diggers. Its founder, Mr. William Heffernan, was an Irishman of extraordinary enterprise, who made fortunes and lost them again with equal rapidity. To him Sandhurst is also indebted for a beautiful theatre and a commodious public hall. In the palmy days of gold-digging, he spared no expense in bringing up to Sandhurst all the musical and theatrical celebrities who crossed the equator into the Southern Hemisphere.

Sandhurst was constituted a bishopric by Pope Pius IX. simultaneously with Ballarat, and its first resident prelate, the Right Rev. Dr. Martin Crane, continues to rule the extensive diocese that was then committed to his charge. Prior to his arrival in Australia, Dr. Crane was long and intimately associated with the Irish Church, and was twice elected by his Augustinian brethren to the high office of Provincial of the order. The handsome church of SS. Augustine and John that adorns the Irish metropolis, is a monument of his zeal and untiring energy. Bishop Crane laboured with great earnestness and success in his new Australian sphere until he was unfortunately prostrated by a painful affection of the eyes. His Lordship is now assisted in the administration of the diocese by a coadjutor-bishop, Dr. Stephen Reville, formerly president of the seminary of St. Laurence O'Toole, Usher's Quay, Dublin. There is a prosperous community of the Sisters of Mercy in the city of Sandhurst; and, in the town of Echuca, at the northern end of the diocese, the Brigidine nuns have recently established a convent. The members of both those orders devote themselves to the education of Catholic girls.

Amongst the public men that Sandhurst has produced, the

Hon. James Forrester Sullivan and the Hon. J. J. Casey (now Judge Casey) occupy a prominent place. Mr. Sullivan, a Waterford man, came to the front as a trusted leader of the diggers in the days of oppression, and was chosen as the president of the league they established for the defence of their liberties and the assertion of their rights against official insolence and tyranny. When the battle was over, and brutal officialdom was humbled in the dust, and the diggers received the rank and the privileges of freemen, they showed their gratitude to their champion by sending him first to the newly-created municipal council, and soon afterwards to the greater parliamentary council of the colony. Mr. William Kelly, the author of "Life in Victoria," visited Sandhurst in its early days, and he describes its town council at that time as being "generally composed of most intelligent and energetic men, but containing one master-mind in the chairman, Mr. Sullivan, whom I yet look forward to see occupying the highest positions in the infant state of Victoria." This prophecy received its full realisation in after years. In parliament Mr. Sullivan sat for many years and took office as Minister of Mines—a position he held for a lengthened period, and for which he was admirably fitted by the practical experience of gold-fields work which he acquired when a young man, his intimate knowledge of the wants and the wishes of the mining population, and the strong admixture of common sense in his composition. His administration of the Mining Department was most successful and satisfactory. As a leading member of the Victorian Board of Commissioners to the Dublin International Exhibition of 1865, he deserves a word of recognition for the devoted zeal and earnestness with which he laboured to secure a creditable display of the productions of his adopted home in the metropolitan city of his native land.

Judge Casey was also closely connected with the public affairs of early Sandhurst. His daily journal, the *Bendigo Advertiser*, rendered good service to the cause of the diggers, and it continues to be the leading newspaper of the district. After serving his apprenticeship in the local municipal council, Mr. Casey entered parliament in 1863, and held his seat almost continuously until his elevation to the bench a few years ago. As a Minister of the Crown, he is best known and remembered for his able and popular administration of the Lands Department. He succeeded, where most of his predecessors signally failed, in effectually checking the land-grabbing propensities of unscrupulous squatters. Taking advantage of the liberal land legislation of the colony, these wealthy pastoral princes were in the habit of getting their hirelings to personate *bonâ fide* selectors and take up land from the Government, ostensibly for the purpose of settling on the soil, but in reality to transfer the land to the squatters as soon as the Government regulations would permit them to do so. In this fraudulent manner several of the valuable large estates of Victoria were put together piece by piece, and their owners, so far from being ashamed of having acquired their possessions by such dishonourable and underhand practices, very often glory in their successful evasion of the law, and take much credit to themselves for their smartness. This baneful and illegal system of land-grabbing is known thoughout the colonies by the expressive name of "dummyism," the persons professing to be genuine selectors, desirous of establishing themselves on the soil, being actually the agents or the "dummies" of the adjoining squatters. So craftily was the system pursued, and so difficult was it to legally prove collusion between the parties, notwithstanding that the facts pointed unmistakably in that direction, that for years this baneful practice flourished like a noxious weed, and all the precautions of Government officers were powerless to check it. But when Mr. Casey came into power, he firmly grasped the nettle and saved the public estate from further spoliation. He instituted boards of inquiry at most of the principal pastoral centres, and so energetically were these investigations conducted that several lords of the soil were at last convicted of dummyism, and punished by the forfeiture of the selections they had unjustly acquired as well as the lands they had originally leased from the government. In thus making an example of some of the aristocratic dummy-mongers, Mr. Casey administered a salutary check to the pernicious practices that had previously prevailed, and rendered good and lasting service to the colony of Victoria. Another prominent Irishman long connected with Sandhurst was Judge Macoboy, who, in his early years, was an active promoter of the Tenant League of Ireland. The names of Edward O'Keefe, founder of the first society of Irishmen on the gold-field and chairman of the mining board of the district, and Patrick Hayes, the present popular mayor of the city, during whose reign many civic improvements have been effected, are also entitled to honourable mention amongst the civic worthies of Sandhurst.

# CHAPTER VI.

### A FEW IRISH CENTRES.

GEELONG—ITS EARLY PROSPERITY—MANUFACTURING ENTERPRISE—THREE DISTINGUISHED IRISH PRIESTS—ADDRESS TO SMITH O'BRIEN—IRISHTOWN—HIBERNIAN TITLES FOR AUSTRALIAN ESTATES—ENORMOUS PRICE OF LAND—VISIT OF SIR RICHARD BOURKE—HIS DESIRE TO MAKE GEELONG THE CAPITAL—ITS CATHOLIC INSTITUTIONS—KILMORE—A TYPICAL IRISH CENTRE—LOVE OF KINDRED—LARGE REMITTANCES TO RELATIVES AT HOME—KYNETON—A FLOURISHING COMMUNITY—BELFAST—A CHILD OF THE ULSTER CAPITAL—AN ABSENTEE LANDLORD—AN IMPORTATION OF IRISH FARMERS—A CELEBRATED POTATO COUNTRY—SOBRIETY OF IRISH SETTLERS—GIPPS LAND—ITS WILD LUXURIANCE—A MEMORABLE TOUR OF EXPLORATION—SIR CHARLES GAVAN DUFFY'S LAND ACT—HOW IT PROMOTED THE SETTLEMENT OF GIPPS LAND—"THE GARDEN OF AUSTRALIA"—A MILLION OF MONEY IN DIVIDENDS—THE STRANGE CASE OF PATRICK COADY BUCKLEY.

GEELONG, once the only rival of Melbourne in the race for metropolitan pride of place, may be described as a city of arrested development. Beautifully situated on the shores of Corio Bay, the western arm of Port Phillip, it was the natural port for the extensive pastoral and agricultural district that stretched away for hundreds of miles in the direction of the setting sun. Its progress as a commercial centre was exceedingly rapid, and for a time it really seemed as if Geelong was destined to wrest from Melbourne the honour of being the capital city of Victoria. This anticipation was materially strengthened by the opening up of the Ballarat gold-fields fifty miles to the north. It was in Geelong that the first glad tidings of gold were announced, and it was from Geelong that the largest contingent of the diggers' army started to try their luck. When they reached their destination and settled down to the work of gold-finding, they drew their supplies from Geelong, as being the nearest and most accessible sea-port. Thus the lovely harbour of Geelong became crowded with shipping, and at the western end of the town there sprang into existence the bustling suburb of Kildare, which was peopled almost exclusively by Irish carriers and their families. These carriers made hay while the sun shone. They were the only means of regular communication between the diggings and the coast, and the storekeepers often paid them £100 per trip for the carriage of a ton of goods. In this way many of the carriers made fortunes in a few years' time, and, whilst some of them exemplified in their own persons the truth of the old saying, "Easily got, easily gone," others judiciously invested their money and established their families in opulence. For years past nearly the whole of the lucrative carrying trade of the Geelong district has been in the hands of one self-made Irishman, who from small beginnings has risen to a position of wealth and influence. Councillor Joseph Kerley, the gentleman referred to, is an enterprising Celt, a popular president of the Geelong and Western District St. Patrick's Society, and a generous benefactor to the Irish and Catholic institutions of the community in which he lives.

To ensure the continuance of the prosperity enjoyed by Geelong during the years that immediately followed the discovery of gold, two steps were necessary—railway communication with Ballarat, the leading gold-fields' centre, and the removal of a shoal or bar that formed a dangerous impediment to navigation at the entrance to the harbour. But, with a want of foresight they have ever since regretted, the people of Geelong took no thought of the future. To all appearance they believed that the days of lucky diggers, and the consequent plentiful circulation of money in their midst, would last for many a year. They foolishly adopted no means of removing the only drawback to the permanent utilisation of their capacious harbour, and the result was the gradual centralisation of the shipping trade in the metropolis. When they did take action in the other direction, their procedure was equally disastrous to the interests of their town, for, instead of connecting themselves by railway with Ballarat and thus securing the gold-fields' traffic, they constructed a line to Melbourne, and only succeeded in killing the goose with the golden eggs, that is, in diverting a most lucrative trade from their own doors and into the coffers of the rival, Melbourne.

It took some years before Geelong recovered from this double blow inflicted by its own unthinking inhabitants, but after a period of depression, the place gradually regained to some degree its old position of importance, and it is now the leading manufacturing centre of provincial Victoria. Woollen mills, tanneries, foundries, a paper mill and a rope factory, give constant employment to a large section of its population. The last-named is a most extensive establishment, occupying three acres of ground, with a rope-walk of 1,650 feet in length. It was originally founded in 1853 on a very humble scale by an honest, hard-working Irishman, Michael Donaghy, under whose industrious hands it grew year by year, and finally developed into the largest establishment of its kind in Victoria. It is now directed by the founder's son, Mr. John Donaghy, a good citizen, and one of the three Parliamentary representatives of the town. Geelong is also noted for the number and the excellence of its educational institutions, its healthy and salubrious situation inducing many inland colonists to send their children there for scholastic training. It possesses the oldest provincial newspaper in the colony—the *Geelong Advertiser*, and in it the first Victorian literary periodical was started in 1849, under the title of the *Australia Felix Monthly Magazine*. Most of the public buildings of Geelong were designed in the heyday of its brief period of golden splendour, when it aspired to be the metropolis of Victoria, and it is therefore not surprising to find that they were projected on a great scale of magnificence. But long ere they were completed, Geelong's dream of future prosperity and pre-eminence had vanished, and its suddenly-awakened people had the good sense to swallow their pride, accept the situation, and suspend the building of the gorgeous edifices they had in hand. The suspension has lasted ever since, and the result is that every visitor to the town is immediately struck with the quantity of ambitious architectural work left in an unfinished condition. The two most striking examples of these unaccomplished aspirations are to be found in the Town Hall and St. Mary's Roman Catholic Church. The former, a massive and highly ornate structure as originally designed, has only its southern front completed, and this presents a curious contrast to the baldness and incompleteness that are so conspicuous on the other faces of the building. But, more than anything else, a glance at the accepted design for St. Mary's Church will supply convincing evidence of the strong faith in the future of Geelong as the coming capital, that was entertained by its early inhabitants. It exhibits an edifice of colossal cathedral proportions, such as one might expect to find in the episcopal city of some ancient Catholic continental nation, but which excites astonishment when associated with an antipodean town of yesterday. Still, it speaks well for the faith and enthusiasm of the first Catholics of Geelong, that they planned and set about building so noble a fane, at a time when most of their fellow-citizens were thinking of little else but the making of rapid fortunes for themselves, when the place was in a state of continual feverish excitement through the presence and extravagance of thousands of returned lucky diggers, when, to quote a contemporary narrative, "men clad in blue shirts and fustian trousers were hourly bringing into Geelong gold dust and nuggets wrapped up in rags, old stockings, pieces of handkerchiefs, and such like, to the amount of thousands." In after years the original design of the church was considerably modified to suit the altered circumstances, and a portion of the nave was completed, sufficiently large to answer the requirements of the reduced population. Even in this incomplete condition, the building is the most conspicuous, commodious and elegant ecclesiastical edifice in the town. Its *façade* contains a beautiful circular stained glass window in memory of a popular pastor of the place for many years, the Very Rev. Dean Hayes, who was on a visit to his native Ireland when he died, after having just been designated as the first Bishop of Armidale in New South Wales. His successor in Geelong was the Venerable Archdeacon Downing, who has already been mentioned as one of the pioneer priests of the goldfields, and who endeared himself to all classes of the community by his abounding liberality and his practical philanthropy. With him was associated a highly-accomplished Irish priest—the Rev. B. H. Power—one of the most accomplished preachers the Victorian church has possessed, a musician and composer of acknowledged attainments, and in his younger days a skilful editor of the Sydney *Freeman's Journal*. A sterling patriot, he established the Geelong and Western District St. Patrick's Society, as a bond of union amongst the Irishmen of the district, and the organisation continues to flourish, and to maintain the principles of loyalty to faith and fatherland which he eloquently enunciated in his opening address.

From its earliest days Geelong has been largely peopled by the Irish. No better evidence of this could be furnished than the significant fact that the address of welcome to Victoria, presented to William Smith O'Brien on his liberation from captivity in Van Diemen's Land, was actually signed by every member of the Geelong Corporation. In the Corporation of Melbourne the address to the exiled patriot was far from meeting with so unanimous and so favourable a reception.* And further, when Smith O'Brien

* The address was in these terms and was presented by the late Sir John O'Shanassy on behalf of the Irishmen of the Colony:

" To William Smith O'Brien, Esq.

" Dear Sir,—We the undersigned citizens of Melbourne and Geelong avail ourselves of the opportunity afforded us by your visit to this country, to congratulate you and your companions in exile, Messrs. Martin and O'Doherty, upon your liberation from a painful and protracted bondage.

" We beg to express to you our most sincere gratification for having afforded us, by your visit to Victoria, the pleasure of offering to you, personally, an assurance of our sympathy and esteem ; and, transient as we know your stay necessarily is, we rejoice at the occasion which enables us to greet you with a hearty welcome.

" We deeply regret to learn that the fond hope so long and so ardently cherished by men of every shade of political sentiment, indeed by every generous mind acquainted with your character and history, has not been fully realised by the graceful concession, on the part of Her Majesty's Ministers, of the full measure of your freedom.

" We desire to acknowledge the immensity of the sacrifice which you made from the noblest feeling that can actuate the heart—a pure and disinterested love of country. We appreciate and honour the manly bearing and dignified fortitude which have characterised you under a terrible adversity, and anxiously trust that the impolitic restriction which debars you from a return to all you hold visited Geelong in person, he was received with a general cordiality, and with popular manifestations of respect and goodwill such as are ordinarily reserved for the representatives of royalty. For years there was direct emigration from the home country to Geelong, and on one occasion the local government agent thought it his duty to direct the attention of his superiors to the fact, that "during the year 1855 the number of Irish people brought to Geelong in the government immigrant ships exceeded that of the English and Scotch put together." It was on the outskirts of the town proper that the Irish immigrants mostly settled, because there they could purchase land on reasonable terms. The government, in the hope of raising a large revenue, had divided the town into two parts, calling the portion near the harbour North Geelong, and the part further back, South Geelong. The minimum price of land in the former they fixed at £300 per acre, and in the latter £150 per acre. These of course were practically prohibitory prices to the great majority of the immigrants. As suburban allotments were to be had at £5 per acre and even less, new and more populous towns sprang up outside the two proclaimed government towns, and thus were created the extensive suburbs of Geelong known as Ashby, Newtown and Irishtown. The latter filled a spacious valley to the west of the government town of South Geelong, and was apparently occupied principally by the Irish immigrants. It was there that Mr. Michael Donaghy first started the extensive industry which has already been referred to. When municipal privileges were conferred on

dear—to home and family—may be speedily removed, and that you, consoled for the reverses and trials of the past by a nation's gratitude, may enjoy many years to witness in your native land the prosperity and happiness of her sons. We remain, &c."

the district, in common with the adjacent but elevated suburb of Newtown, the government thought proper to change the name from Irishtown to Chilwell, the name it now bears. Kildare, the other Hibernian suburb, and Little Scotland, a Caledonian centre, became merged in the extensive borough of Ashby, or Geelong West, as it is now officially designated. Irish names figure very conspicuously in the first government land sales at Geelong, and the purchasers all seem to have been actuated by the patriotic desire to perpetuate in a new land the titles which had been familiar to their lips in childhood's days. On this account a large map of Geelong and its suburbs forms a very interesting study. There we see the " Avoca Estate " at the junction of the Moorabool and the Barwon, with Herne Hill rising up abruptly in the background—a pretty spot that suggested to its exiled owner a reminiscence of " the vale in whose bosom the bright waters meet." An Irish-Australian author, Samuel Hannaford, describing this portion of Geelong in his " Sea and River Side Rambles in Victoria," says : " Here the banks remind us of the dark glen-like scenery of some parts of Ireland; high hills whose declivities reach to the water's edge, and dark hollows intersecting, into which the daylight scarcely seems to glance." Other suburban estates, which have since been subdivided and built upon, originally bore such names as Kilkenny, Roscommon, Ballinasloe, Drumcondra, Cashel, Dunboyne, &c. As showing the exceedingly high value that was once set upon these lands, it may be mentioned that the late Frederick Griffin, a pioneer Victorian squatter, refused an offer of £50,000 for a small estate of five acres adjacent to the before-mentioned suburb of Irishtown. This was in the palmy days of Geelong, when its people revelled in glowing anticipations of a glorious future, and land speculation was the chief business of the hour. When the brief period of splendour had departed, and it became evident that Geelong was not destined to be the first of Victorian cities, the land became in consequence considerably depreciated in value, and the little estate, for which £50,000 had been refused, was afterwards sold for one-twentieth of that sum.

Sir Richard Bourke, the brave old Limerick soldier who was the Governor of New South Wales at the time, visited the infant settlement at Port Phillip in March, 1837, and was so delighted with the picturesque appearance and surroundings of Geelong, and so struck with its natural capacity for accommodating a large population, that he strongly favoured the proposal to make it the capital in preference to Melbourne. He advocated this view before a conference of government officials and leading colonists, which he had convened for the purpose of finally selecting the site of the capital. The balance of opinion, however, was against the Governor, and having gracefully acquiesced in the decision of the majority, he proclaimed Melbourne as the metropolis of the rising colony. Mr. Richard Howitt, who visited the place not long afterwards, remarks in his book of Australian impressions: " I reached Geelong in the evening, and was much pleased with the neighbourhood. With the locality of Geelong itself no one can be undelighted. The town is secondary only to Melbourne. It has progressed wonderfully, and, should this country become more prosperous, must at no distant date almost equal its more fortunate prototype, the metropolitan city of Australia Felix."

To the energy and public spirit of one of its mayors

of Irish birth, Mr. J. H. Connor, now a member of the Legislative Council of Victoria, Geelong is indebted for the existence of the massive Exhibition building, which is one of the chief ornaments of the town. Another conspicuous building is the Convent of Our Lady of Mercy, a direct affiliation from the parent house in Baggot Street, Dublin. Within the convent enclosure are an extensive orphanage and industrial school for Catholic girls, both of which institutions are partially subsidised by the State. St. Augustine's Orphanage, in the same neighbourhood, is a commodious establishment for boys, and is under the skilful management of a community of Christian Brothers.

The typical Irish centre of the colony of Victoria is Kilmore. Its name, its history, its people, and its general characteristics combine to make it the most distinctively Catholic and Celtic town at the antipodes.* Occupying an exceptionally fertile valley about forty miles to the north of Melbourne and on the main road to Sydney, it was discovered by some early Irish immigrants, who settled down upon the land, prospered amazingly, and, with that generous warm-hearted love of kindred which is one of the finest traits of the Irish character, they lost no time in sending for and bringing out their poor and oppressed relations at home, to share in their prosperity and freedom under southern skies. Thus Kilmore soon became a little Irish colony in itself. To quote the words of a book-making traveller: "It gave me the idea that Tubbercurry had been rafted over holus-bolus from the Emerald Isle, so

---

\* "In certain well-known districts, such as Kilmore in Victoria, where they (the Irish) form the majority of the farming community, they retain to a great extent the national characteristics of their parents."—*Edinburgh Review*, April, 1868.

completely and intensely Irish was the entire population in appearance, in accent, and in the peculiarly Milesian style in which the shops were set out." And this is still true, not only of the town of Kilmore, but of the whole of the surrounding country, which is mostly in the hands of as fine a body of Irish and Irish-Australian yeomanry as one could wish to see. When the gold discoveries so suddenly and marvellously changed the face and fortunes of the colony, Kilmore was lucky enough to be just in the position to profit exceedingly by the unexpected revolution that was brought about. It became a recognised halting-place for troops of intending and returning diggers, and its farm produce was bought up at fabulous prices to supply the wants of the huge mining population that was congregated at Bendigo and other northern goldfields. In after years the people of Kilmore found to their surprise and delight that there was plenty of gold at their very doors. The mines at Reedy Creek in particular have produced a very large quantity of the precious metal, and have contributed greatly to the progress and prosperity of the Kilmore district. Rich in a double sense is the soil on which this pleasant Hibernian settlement stands—rich in agricultural wealth and in mineral treasure. From what has been said of the history and peculiarities of the place, no one will be surprised at the information that the most prominent building in Kilmore is its Catholic Church—a splendid Gothic pile dedicated to Ireland's patron saint, and built at a cost of £19,000, the voluntary contributions of the Irish exiles around, whose faith and fidelity to the religion of their fathers and the land of their birth, so far from being diminished by time and distance, became intensified by thought and by absence from well-remembered scenes. Neither will it be any surprise to learn that Kilmore gave to the church in Victoria its first native nun and its first native priest. St. Patrick's Church in Kilmore contains the remains of Father O'Rourke, the devoted Irish priest who lovingly superintended its erection, and who, during life, was almost idolised by his faithful Celtic flock. An antipodean *Soggarth Aroon*, when priests were few and far between, he brought himself to a premature grave by the unsparing activity with which he strove to overtake the spiritual requirements of the extensive district which had been committed to his charge. The present pastor of the Kilmore mission, Father Farrelly, is the *beau idéal* of the genial, good-natured Irish priest, and he has achieved a widespread popularity.

Kilmore was necessarily a place of considerable political importance during the long period when it was represented in Parliament by the late Sir John O'Shanassy, the head of three Victorian Ministries. It was the platform to which the eyes of the whole colony were turned at more than one momentous crisis, and from which more than one statesmanlike policy was propounded. When Sir John retired from its representation in order to enter the Upper House, he was succeeded by his Attorney-General and the most brilliant advocate at the Victorian bar, Mr. R. D. Ireland, Q.C. The district is now well and capably represented by Mr. Thomas Hunt, the proprietor of its *Free Press*, and an energetic, patriotic Irish-Australian.

In his "Life in Victoria," Mr. Kelly gives an interesting account of his meeting in the early days with a countryman in Kilmore, who had been a great gainer in every respect by emigration. "During my first stroll through the town," he says, " I observed a man following me in all my movements. At last, on hearing my voice, he exclaimed, as he confronted me with a beaming countenance, 'Arrah, sure you're Master William.' 'That's my name, certainly,' I replied; 'have we ever met before?' 'Ah, thin, blud-an-ouns, how's every inch of you? Meet afore is it?—at Bomore, in ould Sligo, where you carried the day on Irishman.' 'So, you recollect me, I see,' said I, 'though that race came off some years ago.' 'Remimber you, indeed; why thin I'd be far gone wid sore eyes if I wouldn't know your skin on a bush. But there's no use in talkin',' he continued, 'come down wid me, sir, an' see the place an' family.'

"I went with him accordingly, and, in explanation, was enabled to bring to mind some home reminiscences of his family and neighbourhood, which delighted him beyond measure. His name was Carty; he lived in the town, but had a fine block of land of sixty acres in the suburbs, all under crop, and every inch his own. At home, a few years before, he was one of that poor spalpeen class who rented an acre of land and a mud cabin, and went over to reap the harvest in England in order to make up the rent; but on the occasion of our meeting, he owned a plot in the town, and built the house he inhabited by means of his earnings from the farm, which he purchased at the upset price of £1 per acre before the diggings commenced—rather a radical change in his condition in a very brief period. He explained to me the reason of the aggregation of Irish in the neighbourhood in a very simple and natural way—one that will be very easily understood by any person familiar with the invariable habits of the Irish emigrants on the American continent, where the first use an exile of Erin makes of his savings is to remit every penny beyond that required for his own immediate and pressing wants to his friends at home, to enable them to join him in the land of promise.

" In the early, or pastoral days of the colony, Scotchmen vastly predominated over all others in the aggregate, while the Irish counted a miserable minority; but now the tables are turned, and the Irish, as far as numbers go, are in the ascendant beyond any other distinct race, notwithstanding their original poverty and the expense of the voyage, and without seeking an explanation in any excess of partiality in the selections of free emigration. In fact and truth it was and is altogether owing to the national characteristic alluded to above; and in the instance of Kilmore, Carty informed me such was the case, in confirmation of which he ran over a list of late remittances within his own knowledge, the magnitude of which completely surprised me, and satisfactorily accounted for the great and growing increase of the Irish family in Victoria."

Kilmore occupies the south-eastern corner of the county of Dalhousie, but the south-western section of the same county, surrounding the substantial town of Kyneton, is also largely peopled by settlers of Irish birth or parentage. Kyneton is beautifully situated on the River Campaspie, is connected by railway with the metropolis, and is the centre of a farfamed flourishing community of cultivators. Its agricultural show-day is only exceeded in splendour and popularity by the bright moving spectacle seen at its annual racemeeting on each St. Patrick's Day. On both these festive occasions Kyneton becomes crowded with visitors from far and near—friendly gatherings of the Irish clans, well-fed, well-dressed, and well-behaved. Kyneton's prosperity, it has been well said, " rests upon the firm foundation of a rich soil and a good climate," and no inland town of Victoria is characterised by more of the elements of permanence and stability. Kyneton is a deanery under the jurisdiction of the Archbishop of Melbourne, and the mission possesses quite a host of churches, but not too many in view of the numbers and the extent of the Catholic population. Dean Geoghegan has been in ecclesiastical charge of Kyneton for more than a quarter of a century, and is held in the highest esteem throughout the district. Mr. Martin McKenna, a leading local Irishman, represented the Kyneton Boroughs in Parliament for a long series of years, and Mr. John Gavan Duffy—worthy successor to an honoured name in the records of colonial statesmanship—has been repeatedly returned for the county of Dalhousie.

The Victorian town of Belfast is a direct descendant of the Ulster capital; but, unlike the Irish parental city, it is a quiet, peaceable, and well-nigh unanimous community, undisturbed and undisgraced by riot or disorder of any description. Its history is unique in the annals of the Australian colonies. It presents the only example to be found in Australia of a large town belonging entirely to one man, and he an absentee landlord, living in Ireland and drawing a princely revenue from an estate where his corporeal presence was but a memory of a long-vanished past. The Irish people have suffered exceedingly from the curse of absenteeism, and the inhabitants of the antipodean Belfast were also, until quite recently, severely and unjustly handicapped by this incubus of a non-resident landlord. Within the last year or two, however, Belfast, to the great joy of its people, was rescued from its anomalous position amongst Victorian towns, its tenants being allowed the privilege of buying out their holdings or allotments—a privilege, it is needless to say, that was exercised with considerable pleasure and alacrity. Having obtained the freehold of the land which they were previously only permitted to occupy on annual leases, the people of Belfast are now carrying out extensive permanent improvements in every direction, and pushing their town into that prominence as a Victorian centre which it would have attained long ago but for the adverse circumstances of its birth.

Briefly these circumstances are the following: About the year 1840 the Colonial Office in London, with a full belief in its own infallibility and a self-satisfied ignorance of what it was really doing, initiated a system of "special surveys," by which capitalists were allowed to select blocks of 5,000 acres each, payment to be made at the rate of £1 per acre and no competition to be permitted. The mere statement of the scheme is sufficient of itself to show its utter stupidity and recklessness. To part for ever with splendid blocks of land in rising colonies, and on such ridiculously easy terms, was playing into the hands of the capitalists with a vengeance. The Australian people, who were on the spot and could see the injurious effects of this ill-conceived project, naturally protested with all their strength against its continuance. The governing authorities in London soon recognised the blunder they had made, but not before some mischief was done. One of the few capitalists who were in a position to seize the golden opportunity was a shrewd Irish attorney, named Atkinson, who was living in Sydney and who had previously made some unsuccessful attempts to acquire a large tract of land. He now lost no time in putting in his application for a special survey of 5,000 acres on the conditions laid down by the Colonial Office. The locality he chose was the land abutting on the beautiful harbour of Port Fairy, in what is now the western district of Victoria, and which had been described with perfect truth as "surprisingly fertile" by the rescued crew of a vessel that had been wrecked in the vicinity. But it so happened that the local government in Melbourne had also an eye to the probable future value of this spot, not only on account of the richness of the soil, but also by reason of the possibilities of the place as a leading seaport in the days to come; and before Mr. Atkinson's application received official approval, the land to the extent of five miles around Port Fairy was proclaimed a reservation by the State for the purposes of a future town and seaport. Most men would have withdrawn from the field after the issue of such a proclamation as this, but Mr. Atkinson was not to be daunted by obstacles of any shape, and he resolved to persevere in his determination. He summoned all the influence at his command into operation, with the result that on January 6th, 1843, Mr. Latrobe, the head of the government in Melbourne, was astonished to receive a communication from the Colonial Secretary, instructing him to "allow Mr. Atkinson to select his special survey." So indignant was Mr. Latrobe at this barefaced over-riding of the government proclamation, that he returned a reply absolutely refusing to order the survey until he received distinct and definite instructions. He further deemed it his duty to emphasise the injustice and the unwisdom of giving to one man a monopoly of one of the finest harbours in Australia, but all his remonstrances were without avail. After the lapse of a year he got the more precise instructions without which he had previously refused to act, and then of course he had no alternative but to order the survey and place Mr. Atkinson in possession of his coveted and most valuable estate.

As soon as he entered into possession, the first thing Mr.

Atkinson did was to lay out a township around the harbour and give it the name of his native Belfast in Ireland. He then sub-divided 4,000 acres into farms of convenient size ; and with the very laudable object of making the place Irish in reality as well as in name, he went to Sydney, and, when he returned, he brought back with him a shipload of his countrymen, their wives and their families. It is to be recorded to his credit that he did not insist on his future tenants being of Belfast or Northern origin. On the contrary, the great majority of them were Catholics from Munster and Connaught, and to this day the Belfast district continues to be one of the distinctively Catholic centres of Victoria. Having placed each family in possession of its future farm, Mr. Atkinson provided them all with seed, and with the means of maintaining themselves until the ripening of their crops. The first harvest fully realised all the anticipations that had been formed of the fertility of the soil, and at once lifted Belfast into the front rank of agricultural areas—a pride of place that it has continued to occupy ever since. " The farm lands on the Belfast estate," writes an authority on the subject, " are capable of growing excellent crops of potatoes or wheat, and other cereals. As an instance of its productiveness, it is related that one of the blocks has been under wheat continually during the past fifteen years without manuring, and the crops at the end of the period are as good as those obtained at the beginning. Yields of 16 tons to 21 tons per acre of marketable potatoes are stated to have been obtained from some paddocks in the district : and with regard to the grazing capabilities of the land, it is said that in a paddock of 86 acres, about seven miles from the town, 110 bullocks are being fattened, and 10 to 15 sheep to the acre are usually put to fatten in the neighbourhood."

As an agricultural settlement, Belfast thus became rapidly prosperous, but as a seaport town, in which respect it was also fully qualified to excel, its progress was far from being so satisfactory. The local government being naturally indignant at the manner in which their reservation of the place for public purposes had been ignored by the higher authorities, revenged themselves on the successful interloper by spending as little State money as possible on the development of the natural resources of Belfast and its harbour. But Mr. Atkinson had a firm faith in the future, and could afford to wait. Having founded his thriving farming colony, and appointed an agent to collect and remit his annual revenue of thousands of pounds from the estate, he retired to spend the rest of his days in his native Ireland, strong in the belief that the town he had marked out on the shores of Port Fairy would grow of itself, and be to him an additional abundant source of wealth. And the event proved that he was quite right in this anticipation. An infant town in such a commanding situation, and surrounded by the richest of agricultural areas, could not be kept back either by government neglect or by the ungrateful indifference of its absentee owner; and slowly but surely building sites in Belfast were sought after and became increasingly valuable. Thus the town grew apace through the operation of its own unaided resources, but, except to the very oldest of its inhabitants, the landlord of the place was only known through the reflected medium of his regularly-calling rent-collecting agent. It was apparently Mr. Atkinson's intention to make the town of Belfast, and the neighbouring agricultural settlement, a splendid hereditary estate, for, when he died, he bequeathed the whole of the lucrative property to his son. But this attempt to plant the evil seed of absentee landlordism on Australian soil was happily frustrated, and the second Mr. Atkinson was induced to part with the property for a good round sum to three gentlemen who possessed large interests in Belfast. These gentlemen, by selling the land in small allotments, which brought remarkably high prices, gave the leaseholders under Mr. Atkinson's sway the opportunity of converting themselves into independent freeholders, and this long-wished-for opportunity was embraced with general joy and eagerness. In this manner Belfast has been placed on an equal footing with other Victorian towns, and is no longer drained of several thousands of pounds annually to support an absentee owner in idleness. The money is retained where it has been raised, and circulates for the benefit of its producers. The good results of the abolition of the old insecure tenure, one of the greatest disabilities with which Belfast had to contend in its days of private ownership, are now seen in a vastly increased stability and self-confidence, and in the variety of improvements that would never have been undertaken but for the fortunate change from foreign to local proprietorship. The Victorian Government, too, is now making amends for past neglect by providing all necessary harbour facilities, and improving the navigation of the River Moyne, so that vessels may come up, discharge, and reload in the town itself.

Whether regarded as a maritime, a manufacturing, or an agricultural centre, Belfast has now a most promising future before it, but it may be hoped that in the era of its coming prosperity, it will not lose that Celtic atmosphere and those Hibernian attributes with which the eminent scientist, Dr. J. E. Taylor, was so particularly struck. In the record of his tour through "Our Island Continent," he says that the suburbs of Belfast reminded him wonderfully of a well-to-do

Irish town—"The same kind of houses and potato-patches, the same paddocks with the same kind of cows, the same kind of stone-walls." The town of Belfast, it only remains to add, has been represented for some years in the Victorian parliament by its present member, Mr. J. J. Madden, a stalwart young Irish-Australian Catholic. The county triumphantly returned Sir Charles Gavan Duffy soon after his arrival in the colony, and was subsequently represented for a lengthy period by a typical true-hearted Celt in the person of the late Hon. Michael O'Grady. Mr. James Toohey, its present member, has been continuously returned at all the recent elections.

Another estate known as Farnham adjoined Mr. Atkinson's in the early days, and like his, it was subsequently subdivided into small farms and largely occupied by industrious Irish immigrants. It extends to the eastward from Belfast towards the town of Warrnambool, and from its rich volcanic soil are produced the very best potatoes in Australia. As many as 40,000 tons of potatoes have been exported from Warrnambool in one year, and the quantity annually sent away from Belfast has, at times, been even greater than this. "As a potato-grower the Irishman has no equal, and as a pig-raiser he is hard to beat," was the conclusion arrived at by a candid critic after travelling through this district. "Leasing land for potato-growing," writes a gentleman intimately acquainted with the locality "is the great event of the year with the small proprietors in the district, and the prices paid per acre are a source of the greatest astonishment to the residents in less favoured districts of Australia. The leaseholders get possession of the land on the 1st July, and give it over on the 1st May ensuing, and for this they pay the high rent of from

£4 up to £8 per acre. The persons carrying on this industry are, as might be guessed, of Irish birth or descent, and their judgment and skill in the conduct of the business is remarkable. Before offering for a lease of any land, they have an intimate knowledge of the quality and depth of every yard of soil in the field, and what crop they may expect on an average season." An eye-witness has given an interesting description of one of these sales of annual leases for potato land. "The whole assemblage," he says, "with the exception of the auctioneers and one or two others who, like myself, are simply present from a feeling of curiosity, are dressed in their work-a-day clothes, but under these well-worn coats there are some deep pockets, as the subsequent proceedings testify. Meeting an acquaintance in the crowd, an old resident in the locality, I remarked that there was a poor prospect of a satisfactory sale, as the appearance of the crowd certainly indicated no plethora of cash. He shook his head, and in a whisper remarked, 'There will be high prices given to-day, they are all so quiet—that means business,' and, pointing to one individual in the crowd, who apparently was more likely to be an applicant for admission to the benevolent asylum than a purchaser of land at extreme rates, he remarked, 'that man, poor as he looks, is worth thousands, and, take them all round, I believe they are worth more man for man than the same number selected indiscriminately at one of your town sales :' and the result, as far as the prices realised were concerned, justified his prediction. A few minutes afterwards a well-appointed buggy and pair drove up, containing the burly and genial form of the senior partner in a leading Warrnambool firm, who, after exchanging cheery greetings with the assemblage, to whom he was evidently well known, at once commenced business. As soon as the conditions of sale were read a storm of dissent greeted them, and all sorts of suggestions were made for their amendment, but, finding it impossible to meet their various ideas, the auctioneer exclaimed, ' Well now, gentlemen, the conditions of sale just read hold good without any alteration, so take the land or leave it, or regulate your biddings by them.' This gave the opposition its quietus, and the bidding began at £7 an acre the first jump, which was rapidly increased to £8 7s. 6d., when the lot was knocked down. The purchaser stepped forward and marked his allotment on the map, after carefully comparing it with the one held in his hand. The next block was then offered, and so on continuously, till the whole area of 125 acres found purchasers at an average rental of £6 10s. per acre." After describing the conditions of payment—one-third of the purchase-money on the fall of the hammer, another third on the 1st of August, and the balance on the 1st of February—our observant friend concludes with a sort of left-handed compliment: "At the settling the purchasers put down the cash for their several instalments, amounting in some cases to upwards of £50, and eight o'clock saw the last of them. I was certainly surprised to find the whole assemblage disperse without a drunken man to be seen or a row. Surely Pat is degenerating from the traditions of his ancestors!"

If by "the traditions of his ancestors" are meant the many doubtful stories of the bacchanalian revels and the quarrelling propensities of Irishmen in a bygone age, then the sons of Hibernia to-day, all the world over, must be entitled to every commendation for refusing to recognise, as their national model, the reckless, rollicking, contentious, six-bottles-a-day Irishman of exaggerated tradition. The

Celts of the great potato-producing district of Victoria are far from being singular in their good behaviour as an assembled body; for, in every part of Australia, Irishmen meet together both for business and for pleasure, and afterwards return to their homes in the most sober and peaceable fashion that any honest well-wisher of the race could desire.

Gipps Land, the eastern province of Victoria, is now almost as Irish in the composition and the character of its inhabitants as that older western district which has just been described. This extensive and marvellously-productive province was named after the governor of the day —Sir George Gipps—by Count Strzelecki, an expatriated Polish exile and an enthusiastic scientist, who, in the beginning of 1840, explored what was then a wild and trackless region, with a young Irishman named James Riley for his companion, and a few personal attendants. They approached the district from the settled portions of New South Wales, and had no sooner crossed the dividing range than they entered on what they described as a new and splendid country, clothed with the richest pasture, and intersected with numerous rivers, forming an immense inland lake and its ramified lagoons. They saw opening up in every direction fresh fields for the operations of the settler, such as no other part of the colony with which they were acquainted presented to the gaze of the pioneer. As the party advanced the vegetation became so dense that it was with the utmost difficulty they could make any appreciable progress southwards. Finding that the horses retarded rather than accelerated the advance of the party, it was resolved to abandon them, and the adventurous explorers proceeded on foot through the *terra incognita*.

At a subsequent stage it was deemed advisable to bury all unnecessary baggage, so as to leave the party as free as possible to force their way onwards through the heavily-timbered country that surrounded them on every side. The count, not without a pang, had even to leave his mineralogical and botanical collections behind him. Day by day the party pushed their way through the tropical undergrowth, but with the exception of their wiry leader, they all gradually became so exhausted as to be physically unable to cope with the difficulties that beset their progress. According to a contemporary narrative,* the count, being more inured to the fatigues and privations attendant upon Australian exploration, alone retained possession of his strength; and, although burdened with a load of instruments and papers of forty-five pounds weight, continued to pioneer his exhausted companions day after day through an almost impervious forest, closely interwoven with climbing grasses, vines, willows, ferns and reeds. Here, the count was to be seen breaking a passage with his hands and knees through the centre of the forest; there, throwing himself at full length among the dense underwood, and thus opening, by the weight of his body, a pathway for his struggling companions. Thus the party inch by inch forced their way, and to add to their discomfort, the incessant rains prevented their getting rest either by night or day. During the last eighteen days of their journey their provisions consisted only of a very scanty supply of the flesh of the native bear. On the twenty-second day after they had abandoned their horses, the travellers, to their intense delight, came in sight of Western Port, and descried a vessel riding at anchor.

* *Port Phillip Herald*, June 2, 1840.

At this infant settlement they received every hospitality, and were soon restored to their former health and vigour.

The intrepid count immediately published a report of this perilous journey, and of the discoveries he had made. He described the new country he had found as "ready to reward the toil and the perseverance of the unwearied and thriving settlers of Australia. Scarcely any spot I know, either within or without the boundaries of New South Wales, can boast such advantages as Gipps Land." He then speaks in terms of rapture of its " 3,600 square miles of forest, and its valleys, which in richness of soil, pasturage, and situation could not be surpassed."

The publication of this report was speedily followed by the settlement of Gipps Land, but only to a comparatively limited extent, for the difficulty of conquering the country deterred all save the hardiest and most resolute of pioneers. Its fierce, wild, black men, its dense forests, its huge mountain ranges, and its swiftly-rushing, almost uncrossable rivers, frightened away many who would have dearly loved a slice of its splendid soil, if they could achieve it without undergoing such a fearful preliminary penance. But the liberal provisions of Sir Charles Gavan Duffy's Land Act induced hundreds to stifle their fears and to settle in Gipps Land, and though at first they had a very hard fight with the forces of nature, most of them have now completely subdued the forest and are well-to-do farmers and graziers. It was of one of these successful settlers that Sir Charles once related this pleasing little incident: " I was in the house of a yeoman proprietor at Briagolong, who brought me to see a cheese factory established by a joint-stock company of farmers in his neighbourhood, where the milk of twenty farms is taken daily at a fixed price and manufactured into excellent cheese. 'I do not employ one additional hand,' he said, 'on this account. That girl who is playing Moore's Melodies milked a dozen cows this morning, and nearly every one in the house did as much. The result is a profit of £10 a week, the greater part of which would otherwise be lost.'"

Now that the Victorian Government is systematically opening up the wide and fertile expanse of Gipps Land with railways and roads, it has become the favourite field for land selection and scientific agriculture. Everywhere the axe of the woodman is heard resounding through the forest; cleared and cultivated spaces are beginning to be numerous; rivers are being bridged and brought under subjection, and the whole face of the country is losing its primeval wildness and gradually assuming an aspect of civilisation and advancement. Gipps Land is becoming, in short, what Henry Kingsley, the novelist, looking down from an Alpine height upon its untamed luxuriance more than thirty years ago, predicted it would one day be—" the garden of Australia." It is also one of the most popular resorts for excursionists during the summer season, its lake and mountain scenery being unsurpassed on the southern continent. Another great attraction to strangers are those gigantic gum-trees still to be seen in different parts of the province, some of them towering aloft to a height of 450 feet, and more than 80 feet round at their base. There is no unmixed good, it is said, on this mundane sphere, and the evil that has accompanied the extensive settlement of Gipps Land during recent years is to be found in the widespread destruction of the forests, resulting in a disturbance of the atmospheric conditions and the banishment of an ever-active agent in the preservation of health, for these eucalypts, or gum-trees, as they are generally called, possess the peculiar property of arresting fever germs and poisonous exhalations. They have been transplanted for this especial purpose to some of the malaria-infected districts of Europe and America, and with pronounced success. Australia, to which they are indigenous, has mercilessly hewn them down in the past, but is now repenting of its folly in that respect, and is replanting them on every seasonable opportunity.

Apart from its rich grazing grounds and its teeming farms, Gipps Land has immense stores of mineral wealth only partially developed—coal, tin, iron, copper, and gold. One of its principal towns—Walhalla—contains a gold mine known as the Long Tunnel, which has recently achieved the unique distinction amongst the gold mines of the world, of paying one million pounds in dividends to its fortunate shareholders.

Gipps Land has been the scene of many romantic incidents, from that early period when several expeditions started from Melbourne in search of a white woman supposed to be held in captivity by its ferocious blacks, down to the recent time when the "Buckley will case" took its place amongst the most remarkable legal puzzles of the century. One of the few fearless pioneers, who followed in the footsteps of Count Strzelecki in the memorable tour of exploration already referred to, was a young penniless Irish-Australian named Patrick Coady Buckley. He chose the wildest part of Gipps Land for his home, leased a pastoral area from the government, and, by his bull-dog bravery and determination, soon struck such terror into the marauding blacks of the neighbourhood, that they wisely gave his homestead a wide berth in the future, though in other parts of the country they continued their favourite pastime of spearing shepherds, sheep, and cattle. Buckley prospered year by year, added station to station, accumulated wealth, never married, never mentioned whether or not he had any relatives, and never referred to his early life. In religion he was a Roman Catholic, and during his lifetime he was a generous contributor to charitable institutions in general. As a rule, he was reserved and unassuming in manner, and was little known beyond the contracted circle of his immediate neighbours. It was only after his death on June 16th, 1872, that his name became familiar to the outer world. He died worth £63,000, but he left no will, and not a solitary relative came forward to claim the property. Under these circumstances the Crown, as usual, through its officer, the curator of intestate estates, stepped in, and the litigation that ensued lasted for nearly ten years and swallowed up the greater part of Buckley's accumulated wealth. An elderly man from New South Wales, named Thomas Maher, appeared on the scene and produced a dilapidated will, purporting to have been signed by Buckley in his favour more than thirty years before. He accounted for the dampness of the document by stating that during his absence from home a flood inundated the house and moistened the will. There was only one surviving witness to this alleged will, and he corroborated the story of Maher. But the Equity Court of Victoria refused to recognise the will as a genuine document, and Maher was thereupon arrested for perjury, but he died before the day fixed for his trial. Everybody who rejoiced in the name of "Coady" or "Buckley," or who was married to a lady maidenly known by either of these titles, now claimed relationship with the deceased squatter, and sent in an application to share in his estate. These applications came from every quarter of the globe. One English gentleman is reported to have written to the Secretary of State for the Colonies to the effect that he had a servant named Buckley who was next-of-kin to the deceased, and airily requesting that the value of the estate should be transmitted to him by return of post. A similar appeal was made by Lord Henniker, of Eye, on behalf of a servant of his, who was also a Buckley. After a long delay, during which the responsible legal officers were busily engaged in examining the proofs and sifting the claims of hundreds of aspirants to the honour of relationship with the late lonely Gipps Land squatter, the Master-in-Equity finally reported to the Court that the following were first cousins and next-of-kin to the deceased Patrick Coady Buckley:—Mary Coady, wife of John Coady, of Kilkenny, Ireland; James Maher and Thomas Maher, of New York, America; Ellen Tobin, wife of John Tobin, of Newfoundland; Mary Grace and Edward Grace, of East Newark, United States; Patrick Coady, of Burrin, Newfoundland; Catherine Browne, wife of Hugh Browne, of Nova Scotia; and Bridget Murphy, of Benalla, Victoria. But, when the unlucky estate emerged from the ten years' conflict in the courts, only £20,500 out of the original £63,000, was left for distribution amongst the nine duly-certified first-cousins. That is to say, two-thirds of Buckley's wealth went into the capacious pockets of the lawyers, and one-third was divided amongst his poor relations. One cannot but feel a regret that the major part of the savings of a lifetime of courage and toil, energy and perseverance, should have been thus scattered to the four winds of heaven.

# CHAPTER VII.

### IRISH IMMIGRANTS IN THE COLONIES.

CAROLINE CHISHOLM, "THE EMIGRANT'S FRIEND" — HER PROTECTION OF HOMELESS GIRLS—A DIVINE MISSION—CONVERSION OF A GOVERNOR—THE SYDNEY FEMALE EMIGRANTS' HOME — CORRECTION OF A CRYING EVIL — THE "BUSH JOURNEYS" OF MRS. CHISHOLM — WANTED, A TIPPERARY GIRL—WHAT THE IRISH RACE OWES TO MRS. CHISHOLM—ANECDOTES OF HER PHILANTHROPIC CAREER — LORD SHERBROOKE'S EULOGIUM — A TRIUMPHANT VINDICATION OF IRISH FEMALE IMMIGRANTS—OFFICIAL TESTIMONY IN THEIR FAVOUR — LIFE ON AN EMIGRANT SHIP—GENEROSITY AND AFFECTION OF IRISH GIRLS—THE DANGER OF DRUNKENNESS—SOCIAL IMPROVEMENT DURING RECENT YEARS.

IF one were asked to name the most genuine, devoted, and unselfish philanthropist that has ever trod Australian soil, the name of Caroline Chisholm would at once rise to the lips.

Her affectionate title of "The Emigrant's Friend"—a title conferred with the unanimous consent of the young nation that profited so largely from her self-imposed mission of love—tells its own story, and will ever remain one of the most pleasing phrases in the history of the great southern continent. It was towards the end of the year 1838 that Mrs. Chisholm, with her infant family (one of her daughters is now Mrs. E. Dwyer Gray, of Dublin), first landed in Sydney, the place that was soon to be the base of her benevolent operations. Her womanly heart was sorely afflicted by the crying evils she saw all around her in that young disorganised community. What horrified her most was the hapless fate of so many of the helpless ones of her own sex—the poor emigrant girls who were turned adrift without friend or counsellor in that city of sin, and but too frequently were inveigled into houses of ill-fame in less than twenty-four hours after leaving their ships. Against this monstrous evil Mrs. Chisholm determined to wage a ceaseless combat. The brave-hearted woman commenced her campaign—more glorious in its results than any recorded in the military history of nations—by systematically meeting every emigrant ship on arrival, gathering the unprotected girls around her, giving them sound motherly advice, and, when necessary, sheltering and protecting them in her own house. She often had nine of these friendless girls at a time under her hospitable roof; but, as ship after ship arrived in the harbour, she saw the absolute necessity of establishing an institution large enough to afford protection to the many who stood so urgently in need of a temporary asylum. With a view to arousing the respectable public opinion of the place to the pressing urgency of what she proposed, Mrs. Chisholm contemplated publishing a large collection of letters in her possession, detailing the miseries of young women on their first landing in Sydney, but she was dissuaded from this step by representations of the injury that would be inflicted on the colony by such an exposure. Then she sought the co-operation of a few influential ladies—Lady O'Connell, Lady Dowling, Mrs. Roger Therry, Mrs. Richard Jones, Mrs. Mackenzie, Mrs. Wallen and Miss Chambers—all of whom promised to assist in founding a Female Emigrants' Home in Sydney.

Mrs. Chisholm has left on record a frank confession of her feelings at the inception of the unique philanthropic movement which was ever afterwards to be associated with her name. She says: "I felt convinced the evil which struck me so forcibly, would soon be made apparent to the good people of Sydney; and I felt assured that the God of all mercy would not allow so many poor creatures to be lost, without disposing the hearts of the people to unite and save them. I now considered the difficulties and prepared the plan: for three weeks I hesitated and suffered much. I was prepared to encounter the opposition of some, the lukewarmness or the actual hostility of others, to the plan I might suggest. I saw I must have the aid of the press; for I could only anticipate success by soliciting public sympathy for the cause I had undertaken, notwithstanding which, as a female, and almost a stranger in the colony, I naturally felt diffident. I was impressed with the idea that God had in a peculiar manner fitted me for the work, and yet I hesitated. About this time several young women, whom I had served, advised others to write to me. I did all I could to aid them in their prospects by advice, or recommending them to situations; but the number increased, and I saw that my plan, if carried into effect, would serve all. My delay pressed on my mind as a sin; and when I heard of a poor girl suffering distress, and losing her reputation in consequence, I felt that I was not clear of her sin, for I did not do all that I could to prevent it. During the season of Lent of that year, I suffered much; but on the Easter Sunday I was enabled, at the altar of Our Lord, to make an offering of my talents to the God who gave them. I promised to know neither country nor creed, but to try to serve all justly and impartially. I asked only to be enabled to keep these poor girls from being tempted by their need to mortal sin; and resolved that, to accomplish this, I would in every way sacrifice my feelings, surrender all comfort ; nor, in fact, consider my own wishes or feelings, but wholly devote myself to the work I had in hand. I felt that my offering was accepted, and that God's blessing was on my work ; but it was His will to permit many serious difficulties to be thrown in my way, and to conduct me through a rugged path of deep humiliation. With one exception every person I wrote or spoke to on the subject acknowledged the need of such an institution, promised to subscribe when one was established, though with few exceptions all declared they thought the thing impossible."

It will thus be seen that the great difficulty Mrs. Chisholm had to encounter, on the threshold of her noble undertaking, was to awaken the people to a sense of the evils that were rampant in their midst, and to communicate to them some of the reforming zeal and enthusiasm that animated herself. The Governor of the colony, Sir George Gipps, did not scruple to describe her as a wild enthusiast, and her letters beseeching his patronage to a movement that he should have been the first to encourage, were merely acknowledged with the severest official brevity. The newspapers contented themselves with mildly debating the project, and the clergy, whilst admitting that the idea was laudable in itself, shook their heads and gravely doubted whether it could be made a reality. But Mrs. Chisholm was not depressed in the least by these prophecies of failure. Their effect was rather to make her work more energetically than ever, and her perseverance was at length rewarded by the Governor granting a reluctant interview to the "lady labouring under amiable delusions," to quote his own condescending phrase.

"I expected," said Sir George Gipps many years afterwards, "to have seen an old lady in white cap and spectacles, who would have talked to me about my soul. I was amazed when my *aide-de-camp* introduced a handsome, stately young woman, who proceeded to reason the question as if she thought her reason, and experience too, worth as much as mine."

Mrs. Chisholm succeeded in converting the Governor so far to her way of thinking, that he consented to give her the conditional use of a government building. True, it was but a low wooden structure; still, it was not to be despised in a city which had a nightly average of 600 homeless emigrant girls. With characteristic energy, Mrs. Chisholm had soon transformed the old, abandoned storehouse—for such it had originally been—into an institution answering, in some degree at least, to the title she attached to it—that of "Female Emigrants' Home." Sacrificing every domestic comfort, she took up her abode in the institution that had been called into being by her untiring exertions, and, every night before retiring to rest, she made it a point to visit every one of the hundred homeless girls that the place was made to accommodate by economising space to the utmost. A number of these poor but virtuous girls—a large proportion of them Irish girls—had, before being admitted to the Home, slept out for many nights in the public parks or in the sheltered recesses of the rocks around the harbour, rather than expose themselves to the dangers of the streets. Nothing was more discreditable than the deplorable want of foresight exhibited by the New South Wales Government at this time, in encouraging female immigration to its shores, whilst making little or no provision for the safety or protection of the girls, either on the voyage or when they landed.

The abuse of power by ship captains, and the immorality of the inferior officers, were considerably checked by a prosecution, which Mrs. Chisholm compelled the Governor to institute against parties who had driven a girl mad by their violence. When Sir George Gipps, hesitating, said, "A Government prosecution is a very serious matter," she answered, "I am ready to prosecute; I have the necessary evidence, and if it be a risk whether I or these men shall go to prison, I am ready to stand the risk." That trial established a precedent, and corrected a crying evil.

Mrs. Chisholm, having now successfully established her Female Emigrants' Home in Sydney, threw all her energies into the supplementary work of obtaining honest employment for her *protégés*. She saw clearly that, for the most of them, the Home would be but a brief respite from destruction unless, in their unprotected state, they were speedily removed from the dangers and pitfalls of the city, and placed in the way of earning an honourable livelihood in the country. To this end, the indefatigable lady went boldly into the interior, visited every provincial centre, established local Homes as branches of the central institution in Sydney, and formed local committees for the purposes of management and supervision. At first she had some little difficulty in consequence of the natural dislike of the girls to venture into "the bush," as the whole of the back country was called, but her commanding personal influence always prevailed in the end.

Thus was commenced Mrs. Chisholm's memorable series of "bush journeys," during which she travelled through all the settled districts of the colony, accompanied by successive batches of emigrant girls, whom she placed, one by one, in domestic service, chiefly in the houses of respectable farmers. Just as in the city she was invariably under the roof of her Emigrants' Home, so in the country this devoted apostle of her sex never allowed her girls out of sight, many a time sleeping out with them in the wild bush, or occupying the dreary floor of a barn when no other shelter for the night was available. Her contingents of girls varied from 15 to 60 in number, but on one occasion she started from Sydney with the little army of 147 under her command, for all of whom she found suitable places. On one occasion she received a batch of 64 girls from a newly-arrived vessel, and their aggregate wealth was found to be exactly fourteen shillings and three half-pence. And yet, through the instrumentality of Mrs. Chisholm, for every one of the girls who thus landed in such a miserable plight, was found a good place in the country, and the great majority of them married well. "I have been able," she says, "to learn the subsequent progress in life of many hundreds of these emigrants. Girls that I have taken up country in such a destitute state, that I have been obliged to get a decent dress to put upon them, have come to me again, having every comfort about them, and wanting servants for themselves. They are constantly writing home to get out their friends and relatives."

It will hardly be believed that Mrs. Chisholm experienced most trouble in getting places for those of her girls who were blessed with personal attractions, but that such was the case is evident from her own words: "Pretty girls, no matter what their qualifications or characters, were difficult to dispose of; they are not, it appears, liked as servants, though they are preferred as wives. Mrs. —— wanted a servant. I sent one—a good servant girl and a very beautiful girl, I must acknowledge. I thought the place would suit her; no son in the house; no nephews; the cook married; the groom married; in short, quite a safety. In less than an hour the girl returned with the following note: 'My dear Madam,—What can you be thinking of, to send such a handsome girl to my house? Heavens, the place would be beset! Besides, I do not like such showy women in my house. Send me a plain, homely-looking girl, and oblige, yours, &c.'"

It is narrated that on one occasion, just as she came to a solitary point of the road, near a valley, she heard a man shouting to her "Stop, stop!" A stout, rough bushman, clearing a few bushes at a leap, placed his hand on the horse's head, and said "Are you Mrs. Chisholm?" "Yes; what do you want?" "Want—want—why, what every man like me wants when he sees Mrs. Chisholm. Come now, do look up that hill, and see that nice cottage and 40 acres under crop. The land is paid for, and the three cows—oh, it would do you good to see the cows." Then, pulling out a roll of papers, he continued: "See what a character I have got from the magistrates in charge of the district; and look here, ma'am, at this roll of notes. Come now, Mrs. Chisholm, do be a mother to me and give me a wife; the smile of a woman has never welcomed me home after a hard day's work—you'll have pity on me—you don't mean to say No; you'll never be so cruel as to say No. It makes a man's heart light to look at your camp. Now, you don't mean to say you have not got a nice girl from Tipperary. Never mind the breakfast; I could keep the whole party for a week; and what peace of mind it would be to you to know what a kind husband I shall make for one of your girls." The appeal was irresistible, and the lonely bushman, who was so anxious to be mated with " a nice girl from Tipperary," was gratified with his heart's desire.

At the expiration of the first year of its existence, the Female Emigrants' Home, under the guidance of Mrs.

Chisholm, had provided no less than 735 young women with temporary protection and permanent situations—a record of good to which no other woman of our century, fighting against similar adverse circumstances, can conscientiously lay claim. Of these 735 unprotected female emigrants, the great majority, 516, were of Irish birth, the minority being composed of 184 English and 35 Scotch. It was the same during the subsequent years of what may be truly called Mrs. Chisholm's missionary career. As a rule, two girls out of every three brought by the emigrant ships were of Irish nationality. By systematically taking these lonely exiles under her protecting roof, saving them from the perils of a demoralised city, piloting them to worthy households in the country, and thus fitting them to preside in the near future over happy homes of their own, Mrs. Chisholm conferred an amount of good on our race that is simply incalculable, and that should ensure for her memory the everlasting gratitude of the Irish people, not in Australia alone, but all the world over. It was she who preserved the purity of the stream at its fountain-head, and there are thousands of Irish homesteads on Australian soil to-day that, in all human probability, would never have been erected but for her loving and practical philanthropy. The government official records credit this wonderful woman with having settled altogether 11,000 souls upon the soil; but that number, large as it is, can only be accepted as a rough estimate, falling far short of the reality. In the later years of her mission, she added to her supervision of the female emigrants the serious responsibility of taking whole families into the interior, and planting them on the fertile areas that only needed to be tickled with a plough to laugh with a harvest. This work needed many of the qualities that go to make up a skilful general—tact, firmness, courage, foresight, and strong common-sense; but Mrs. Chisholm proved herself equal to every emergency. Here is a characteristic little anecdote, recorded by herself: "When we landed from the steamer and entered the bush, we found there was no water. I had thirty women and children in the party, all tired, hungry, and thirsty, and the children crying. Without saying a word, I sent one of my old bushmen off on horseback three miles to get enough of milk or water for the children. In the meantime some of the emigrants came up and said, in a discontented tone, 'Mrs. Chisholm, this is a pretty job. What must we do? there is no water.' I knew it would not do for them to be idle; anything was better than that in their frame of mind; so, partly judging from the locality, I said to them without hesitation, 'If you will dig here I think you will find water.' Directing the tools to be got out, they immediately set to work, and, providentially, they had not dug many feet when they came to water. This had such an exhilarating effect upon their spirits, that they instantly threw off their coats, began to dig two other fresh holes, and did not leave off till moonlight."

On another occasion, when in charge of a party of emigrants, she reached a river that had overflowed its banks during the night. There was but one means of crossing—a punt that had been moored to the bank on the previous night, but was now separated from the land by a hundred yards of rushing water. It was necessary that she should get her people to the other side without delay, and she was determined to do it. "Pick me up and carry me to the punt," she quietly but firmly said to the man in charge of the ferry. He was astounded at the request, but all his objections were of no avail, and, despite his declaration that it was tempting destruction to do what the lady asked, he had in the end to carry her bodily through the storm-waters to the punt. The whole of her party were soon on board along with her, and they all crossed the flooded river in safety. "Ah! sir, she's a bold woman," was the very natural comment of the puntman, when telling the story in after years.

On many of those journeys with emigrant families, Mrs. Chisholm has been known to travel 300 miles into the interior; but such was the general admiration for the sterling character of the woman and the exalted unselfishness of her colonial life, that, wherever she went, squatters, settlers, and store-keepers vied with each other in extending unbounded hospitality to herself and the pilgrims whom she was guiding to the promised land. As to her paying for provisions, they would not listen to the suggestion, and this helps to explain the otherwise incredible statement that during seven years' travelling on benevolent expeditions to all parts of New South Wales, her personal expenses for the whole of that time did not amount to more than £1 18s. 6d. Sleeping one night in a wealthy squatter's mansion, and on the next in an humble settler's hut, she was equally welcomed and beloved wherever she went.

In the early part of 1846 family reasons induced her, but evidently with great unwillingness, to leave the noble work in which she had so long and so advantageously been engaged, and to return to the home country. Her departure, as may easily be imagined, was regarded as a national loss, for, through the agency of her philanthropic schemes, she had visibly founded a new nation. The farewell addresses and testimonials that were showered upon her but imperfectly translated the gratitude of the whole colony to the high-minded, warm-hearted, sympathetic lady, who, unaided by any force outside her own lofty enthusiasm and unexampled energy, had effected an abiding moral and social revolution.

A general address was signed by members of the Legislative Assembly, magistrates, landholders, merchants and representative citizens. It tendered to Mrs. Chisholm a warm expression of thanks for her zealous and active exertions on behalf of the emigrant population during her seven years' residence in the colony. It was universally acknowledged that the extraordinary efforts which she had made in the cause of practical philanthropy had been dictated by a spirit of the most enlightened benevolence. The address concluded by stating that signal advantages had been conferred on the community by her establishing an Emigrants' Home in Sydney, and procuring the satisfactory settlement of great numbers of the emigrant population in the interior.

Out of the many eulogiums that were pronounced on Mrs. Chisholm's seven years' work in Australia, one is especially worthy of note, as coming from a remarkably close and critical observer. Mr. Robert Lowe, now Lord Sherbrooke, was a young barrister, a prominent politician and a contemporary of Mrs. Chisholm's in Sydney many years ago, and this is his testimony: "One person only in the colony has done anything effectual—anything on a a scale which may be called large—to mitigate this crying evil and national sin, and to fix families on our lands in lieu of bachelors. And, strange to say, that one is an humble, unpretending, quiet-working female missionary—an emigrant missionary, not a clerical one. The singularity of her mission, looking to the nature of her work, is one of the most original that was ever devised or undertaken by either man or woman; and the object, the labour, the design, are beyond all praise."

It goes without saying that Irish immigrants, as a class, and Irish immigrant girls in particular, had their detractors and calumniators in almost all of the Australian colonies. In every quarter of the globe there will surely be found some representatives of that prejudiced and insignificant faction, to whom the name of everything Irish is hateful, and whose chief delight it is to concoct vile charges against the faithful sons and daughters of St. Patrick. At the time when emigration to the colonies was in full swing, these ill-conditioned slanderers did their little best to poison the minds of their fellow-colonists against the Irish immigrants. They were never weary of reiterating sweeping charges of incapacity, dishonesty, and immorality against the Irish girls who were passengers in the immigrant ships. In Melbourne their perpetual mud-throwing prevailed so far as to cause the city council on one occasion, in a moment of weakness, to carry an address to the Queen praying for an immediate stoppage to the immigration of Irish girls. But this unworthy act on the part of the municipal rulers of Melbourne was promptly neutralised by the action of Archbishop Goold and the late Sir John O'Shanassy, who convened a public meeting, at which the reckless assertions of the bigots were shown to be a wilful contradiction of facts and experience. A counter-memorial to the Queen was adopted by that large assemblage of representative citizens, who further pledged themselves to the protection and encouragement of the Irish girls as a highly virtuous and deserving class of immigrants. The discomfiture of the cowardly slanderers was complete when Mr. Edmund Finn, the vice-president of St. Patrick's Society, diligently searched the records of the police-courts, and obtained the evidence of immigration agents, detectives, and constables, with the result that the good name and the fair fame of the daughters of Erin were triumphantly vindicated on appeal to these official sources of information. Mr. Finn laid the results of his investigations before a crowded meeting in St. Patrick's Hall, and the charges, born of malignity and prejudice, were unanimously branded as being without a particle of foundation to rest upon. The disgraceful part played by the city council in the matter was also strongly condemned by the meeting, as a most uncalled-for and unjustifiable abuse of representative power. It sometimes happened that the anti-Irish bigots were summarily silenced by the candid testimony of honest English immigration officers. For instance, Mr. Arthur Perry, secretary to the Tasmanian Female Immigration Association, on one occasion addressed this conscientious and in every way creditable report to Lieutenant-Governor Sir William Denison: "I have the honour to report, for the information of His Excellency, that the conduct of the immigrants by the ships 'Beulah' and 'Calcutta,' whilst in the depôt at the wharf, was very satisfactory. All the immigrants by those ships, with two exceptions, have obtained respectable situations and been discharged from the depôt. The very large majority of the immigrants were Irish Roman Catholics, and have for years past been brought up in different union workhouses and establishments in Ireland; consequently they knew little or nothing of domestic service; but experience has now proved that very many of these girls are likely to make most valuable servants, particularly in those instances where their mistresses have used kindness and forbearance towards them, and have taken the trouble to instruct them in their new duties. Their aptitude for and quickness at learning how to perform the services required of them is, in many instances that have come under my notice, surprising. The girls sent out are very well adapted for country servants, and, as many of them have gone into situations in the country, their conduct has been so good that many applications have been made to me by the settlers lately with which I could not comply, there being no girls at the depôt. I must not omit to mention that the moral character of these Irish girls has not, to my knowledge, in one single instance been brought into question. Some few of the English girls who came in the 'Beulah' from Portsea have, I am afraid, gone astray; but out of nearly 400 single females who arrived in the ships 'Beulah,' 'Australasia,' and 'Calcutta,' I have not heard of more than four instances where the girls have left their situations, and preferred obtaining a livelihood in an improper and immoral manner. If more instances had occurred, I think I should have heard something of them, as many persons here are over-anxious to mark anything amiss or improper in the character, conduct or management of the free immigrants. I consider the arrival of these girls here, and their distribution throughout the island, has been a great public good, and I only sincerely hope and trust that the further supply will not be stopped."

Colonel Mundy, who had special opportunities of obtaining accurate information, declares that in some cases the Irish girls were shamefully treated on board the emigrant ships, and there are certainly cases on record of young women being punished in the most brutal manner for alleged breaches of discipline, at the instance of inhuman surgeon-superintendents. Whilst many of those officials were commendably strict, but courteous, in their relations with the emigrants under their charge, there were others in whom the spirit of the petty tyrant was uppermost, and these, particularly if they had previous anti-Irish prejudices, took a savage delight in wounding the susceptibilities and even outraging the bodies of the Hibernians on board. As a result of official inquiries instituted on arrival in Australia, more than one of the privileged ruffians who thus abused their power and position, were heavily fined and dismissed for disgraceful conduct on the voyage. A perusal of the sickening evidence in these cases, as set forth at length in government blue-books, leaves no room to doubt that fine and degradation from office was too light a punishment altogether for such offences against manliness and decency, as were sheeted home to these "gentlemen" by Act of Parliament. However, it is gratifying to record that the number of such scoundrelly surgeon-superintendents was comparatively small. Colonel Mundy assures us that "the majority of the ships were admirably conducted,"* and he adds his weighty personal testimony, that many of the Irish girls brought out in them succeeded remarkably well in the colonies. He says he was particularly struck, on visiting the immigration depôt, with the cleanly, decent appearance of the Irish girls as a body, as well as by their marked superiority in good looks.

There are not very many accessible pictures of life on board an Australian emigrant ship, but a few graphic

* Reports to this effect repeatedly occur in the blue-books: "The immigrants, with a few exceptions, were Irish nominees and conducted themselves throughout the voyage to the entire satisfaction of the surgeon-superintendent."

examples of portrait and character painting may be met with in a charming little collection of "Waifs and Strays, by an Irish-Australian Emigrant." Glancing around for the first time on his fellow-passengers, he says: "It was not difficult to recognise the frank, intelligent face of the Irish Celt; the cold, self-important bearing of the Englishman was equally unmistakable; upon every side resounded the pleasant dialect of the Scot; and scattered here and there might be seen natives of Poland, Germany, Italy and France, still retaining a little of their picturesque national costumes. There was a large number of my countrymen on board, and one of the few real pleasures I enjoyed was to observe the good sense and the good nature by which they were habitually distinguished. Avoiding every unreasonable ground of quarrel, they associated in a kindly brotherhood with their fellow-voyagers of every country and creed; and it was equally novel and delightful to see Irish, English and Scotch doing justice to each other, and avoiding the dismal feuds which originate in the vices of their rulers. But still the exiled Celts seemed proud of their old historic island, and evidently regarded themselves as defenders of her fame. Some stupid insult having been offered to Ireland by a few ignorant malcontents one evening, it was resented in a manner which effectually prevented its repetition. 'Although we have been driven into exile,' observed one of the actors in this scene (a fine young fellow from Cork), 'don't think that we have forfeited our nationality.'"

The departing emigrant was denied the sorrowful favour of seeing his native shores fade away in the distance. "At about eight o'clock a.m. we knew that the dark outline which loomed on our left was Holyhead, but not even thus dimly could we discern to the right the ' green, holy hills of

Ireland.' At noon we saw Bardsey Island, bearing southeast, but not a glimpse of the pleasant homes of Dublin or the romantic glens of Wicklow. I had anticipated the sad, sweet pleasure of taking a last glimpse of the Irish coast, and yet, although I knew we were sailing past it the entire day, I strained my eyes in vain endeavouring to pierce the invidious curtain of clouds that intervened."

Of that very important personage on board a ship—the cook—an amusing anecdote is recorded: "All the passengers' food was cooked at the ship's galley—a small dingy-looking apparatus enough, but which executed its enormous task with admirable punctuality. The chief *artiste* was a negro, named Bill, whose salient characteristic was a decided weakness for rum, and it was often amusing to see him cajole some unsophisticated passenger out of his favourite beverage. 'Massa,' said he one evening to a group of good-natured young Celts, 'Lor' knows, I'm an Irishman myself—only I was born in Demerara!'"

Mr. James Smith relates a touching little incident that was communicated to him by the late Irish-Australian philanthropist, Ambrose Kyte. One afternoon in the leading street of Melbourne, Mr. Kyte's attention was attracted towards a group of his countrymen and countrywomen. They were evidently members of the same family, some of whom had only lately arrived, whilst others had been in the colony for some time. The new-comers had brought with them a little box upon which great store appeared to be set, for, when it was opened, the eyes of the older settlers glistened with tears, and the aged mother of the party devoutly made the sign of the Cross. The box contained a sod of shamrock, fresh and green as when it was first cut from the surrounding turf. "And who," exclaims the narrator of the story, "will refuse to sympathise with the emotion which that simple memento of a far-distant land excited in the breasts of those who were thus feelingly reminded of the emblem of their country and the verdure of its soil?"

Speaking of the strength and the perpetuity of the chain of affection that has always connected the Irish abroad and their kindred at home, the same gentleman once publicly stated from a Melbourne platform: "It is a fact—without a parallel I should suppose in the world's history—that in seven years the Irish in America sent £7,520,000 to their friends and relations at home. The aggregate remittances from the colony of Victoria to Ireland must be something considerable, and the eagerness with which our Irish fellow-colonists poured in their applications and their money for passage-warrants, under the Assisted Immigration regulations, is another and a most creditable proof of the strength of their family affections. I know of three sisters—unsophisticated but warm-hearted Irish girls, domestic servants in this city—who regularly remit one-third of their earnings every year to Ireland in order to support an aged and widowed mother in comfort and independence. Acts o:< filial piety like these—and they are very common among the class I speak of—say more for the character of the Irish people, and for the depth and durability of the ties which bind them to their kindred, than the most eloquent eulogy which could be pronounced upon them. These are not such actions as court notoriety [and obtain applause. They are secretly performed, and spring from a loving impulse, while they are consecrated by a solemn conviction of duty; and believe that no Australian mail is delivered in Ireland th does not carry succour to the destitute, comfort to the age health to the infirm, a gleam of pleasure to many a solitary cabin, and a sense of solace and companionship to many a lonely fireside." \*

The Irish emigrant to Australia, who systematically abstained from intemperance and cultivated habits of industry, always attained to success and frequently arrived at affluence. Thousands of such instances might be quoted. On the other hand, it is equally true that some of our emigrant countrymen fell victims to the ever-open public-house and the prevailing sociable conviviality of the colonies. Drinking there is quite a common practice, and what is familiarly known as "shouting" was at one time almost universal, though of late years this peculiarly dangerous evil has been considerably diminished in extent. To " shout" in a public-house means to insist on everybody present, friends and strangers alike, drinking at the shouter's expense, and, as no member of the party will allow himself to be outdone in this reckless sort of hospitality, each one "shouts" in succession, with the result that before long they are all overcome by intoxication. By reason of their characteristic temperament and their superabundant sociable qualities, Irishmen were peculiarly liable to tumble into this pitfall, and whenever they did fail in the colonies, in nine cases out of ten the failure was clearly attributable to this baneful source of temptation in their path. In the middle of 1852, when people were hurrying from all quarters of the globe to the newly-discovered Australian gold-fields, Patrick O'Donohoe, one of the transported men of '48, acted like a true disciple of Father Mathew, and, from his place of exile in Tasmania, addressed an earnest exhortation to his

\* Lecture on " The Irish Character," by Mr. James Smith.

emigrant countrymen to be on their guard against the foul
fiend of drunkenness. "Since the era when the standard of
temperance was first raised in the green old Western Isle—
the Isle of the Saints—at no period, and in no country, was
the rigid fulfilment of all the duties connected with
teetotalism of such importance as it has now become in the
great continent of Australia and the adjacent colonies." He
goes on to declare that "very many of the political, social
and moral evils of Ireland owe their origin or continuance to
the baneful vice of drunkenness," and he pathetically pleads
with his fellow-countrymen who were coming out to the new
southern land, to live in accordance with the principles of
Father Mathew. The only reason, he says, that induced him
to pen this well-timed address was the " hope of lending a
helping hand in the work of regeneration, and thereby laying
the foundation of great, free, and united states in the
Southern Hemisphere." Looking back at the past history
of the colonies, he sees them possessing the incalculable
advantages of a pure salubrious climate, a soil abounding in
fertility, producing all the necessaries and even the luxuries
of life, and covered with flocks and herds and gathered
harvests. Then, lifting up the curtain of the future for the
benefit of the emigrating Irish thousands, the man of '48
observes : "And in addition to all those blessings of heaven,
there are now thrown open mines of the richest metal.
Isolated though you stand, deeply embedded in the bosom
of the boundless Pacific, you offer to the world an emporium
of wealth. You have become a sort of magnet which will
attract tens of thousands from the Northern Hemisphere—
from the Old and New World to the Antipodes. The progress of the arts and sciences, civilisation, liberty, and independence ought to be the results of those unexampled sources

of prosperity, but to secure such desirable results, perseverance, fortitude, and wisdom must lead the way and govern your conduct. In this incipient stage on the highway to your future greatness and renown, all the religious and moral virtues should be encouraged and cultivated. Of the latter class, I hold temperance and the absence of all excesses to be of paramount importance."

Answering the question, what is the cause and source of crime in Australia?—an Irish-Australian judge,* in his address at the opening of the first circuit court at Brisbane, now the capital of the flourishing colony of Queensland, gave his personal testimony and experience in very startling language. "I think," he said, "I may claim some authoritative right to answer that question correctly, as a person having had an experience second to few in this or any other country in the administration of criminal law. The result of that experience supplies to the question just asked this answer — Intoxication is the hot-bed from which crime springs. Directly or indirectly, all crime is traceable to it, the exceptions being so few as to establish the general rule. If a dray is stopped and robbed on the highway, what is the first object of search?—the keg of spirits. If there be no spirits, the plundered property is converted into cash, speedily to be spent in intoxication. If a store in the country is robbed, the first plunder is that of the cask or the bottle that contains some intoxicating liquor. A quarrel that after a short time, with a little reflection, would be forgotten by sober minds, is renewed and revived with fresh exasperation in the mind at a moment of intoxication, and a thirst created for the most disproportionate and dreadful revenge. At

* Mr. Justice Therry.

such a moment, too, the jealous mind, without any real ground of jealousy, converts remote suspicion into certain conviction, and so on through the whole range of the human passions. Indirectly, intoxication is the cause of crime by producing poverty, for in this country habits of inebriety constitute the main cause of poverty, as no man here is necessitously poor who does not spend in intemperance those means by which he should support his family. Poverty in its turn begets crime, and thus from intoxication, as from a parental source, both derive their existence."

These are wise and weighty words, but happily they are not applicable, at least to any appreciable extent, to the Irish-Australians of to-day. Mr. Justice Therry spoke at a time when colonial society was in its incipient stage of development, and when the more animal type of Australian was in the ascendant. Things have changed considerably since then; civilising influences have been at work; settled and well-organised communities have usurped the place of the wild bush; the higher rational life has the most devotees, and the Calibans are only a small minority of the population.

Through giving way to drink, many a clever Irishman has been constrained to earn a livelihood in some menial subordinate position, entirely out of harmony with his intellectual gifts and attainments. Cases of this kind are very deplorable, and are also at times productive of very comical developments. One of the most amusing scenes ever enacted in a colonial court of justice was the direct result of placing an educated Irishman in an office that is ordinarily filled by an illiterate person. In its early days, the best classical scholar that Melbourne possessed was an Irishman rejoicing in the rolling name of Daniel Wellesley

O'Donovan. He once held a good position in the colony, but he lost it through his fondness for the bottle. He then sank by degrees in the social scale, until finally he became a groom in the stable of Mr. Justice Willis, an irascible gentleman who prided himself on his classical knowledge, and who invariably opened each session of his court with a pedantic address crowded with Latin and Greek quotations. On one of these occasions of state, the ordinary court crier could not attend through illness, and His Honour, seeing that his groom was a good-looking, well-proportioned fellow, called upon O'Donovan to take the vacant high place in court, make the usual official announcements, and preserve order and decorum in the place of justice. O'Donovan did as he was commanded, and all went well until the judge in his scarlet robes commenced to read his usual grandiloquent address in the presence of a crowded court. For the first five minutes he confined himself to the English tongue, but soon His Honour plunged into an unlucky quotation from Horace. Like the war-horse when he hears the sound of the trumpet, so did the temporary crier prick up his ears at the familiar sounds. The judge negotiated four lines successfully, but in the middle of the fifth he floundered; and O'Donovan, forgetting where and what he was for the moment, yelled out in indignation : "See here, your Honour, you are murdering my favourite author, and I will not allow that to be done by either judge or jury. Just listen to me, and I will give you the only true and correct version." Then, to the amazement and the amusement of the whole court, the crier recited a passage of Horace in the most approved academic style. As for the judge, who was so abruptly, unexpectedly, and scandalously pulled up in the course of his address, he was for a time literally speechless with rage and astonishment, but, as soon as he recovered the use of his voice, he roared to the Sheriff to remove "that scoundrel" from the court and lock him up immediately. O'Donovan was thereupon seized, dragged down from his high perch in the court, and placed in one of the prisoners' cells, the innocent expression of his countenance showing all the while that he was utterly unable to comprehend what he had done to deserve such treatment, and that he could not for the life of him see any crime in correcting an obvious Latin misquotation. Until the rising of the court, poor O'Donovan was left in his solitary cell to ruminate over the perils of exhibiting classical knowledge at unseasonable times. Then he was discharged in a double sense—liberated from confinement and commanded by the infuriated judge never to be seen near his private residence or his stable again. This is perhaps the only case on record of a man losing a situation by reason of his being a good classical scholar.

# CHAPTER VIII.

### THE VOYAGE OF THE "ERIN-GO-BRAGH."

IRISH EMIGRATION TO QUEENSLAND—THE LABOURS OF FATHER DUNNE—
OPPOSITION OF THE GOVERNMENT AGENT—THE LAND-ORDER SYSTEM—
CHARTERING OF THE "ERIN-GO-BRAGH"—DESPATCH OF FOUR HUNDRED
IRISH EMIGRANTS TO QUEENSLAND—THEIR SETTLEMENT IN NEW HOMES
—A DIABOLICAL DEED OF A BIGOT—NOVEL METHOD OF SETTLING
DISPUTES—QUESTIONABLE SOUP—A FEMALE PATRICK—OFFICIAL TESTI-
MONY TO THE SUCCESS OF FATHER DUNNE'S EMIGRATION SCHEME—THE
"FIERY STAR"—SUCCESSFUL IMMIGRANTS—PATERNAL ADVICE TO IRISH
YOUTHS AND MAIDENS—SOBRIETY, ENERGY AND PERSEVERANCE.

QUEENSLAND, the youngest of the Australian colonies, had the good fortune, during its infancy and early growth, to receive excellent nourishment in the shape of a steady and systematic supply of Irish emigrants. Through the instrumentality of a devoted Irish-Australian priest, who is now the Very Rev. Patrick Dunne, D.D., Vicar-General of the Diocese of Goulburn, the newly-founded northern offshoot of the parent colony was blessed with many willing Hibernian hearts and hands, that have done much to promote its progress and prosperity, and to accelerate its development in various directions. Soon after the formation of a government in Queensland, the wisdom of fostering and encouraging immigration to so large an unoccupied territory, was immediately recognised and acted upon. An immigration agent (Mr. Jordan) was appointed and despatched to London with instructions to arrange, if possible, for a ship to leave London once a month with emigrants for Queensland. Mr. Jordan experienced some difficulty in securing in England the class of immigrants suitable for the new colony, and it was understood that, in carrying out his mission, he should confine himself almost exclusively to the selection of immigrants from England and Scotland. About this time (1861) there was great distress in Ireland—a partial famine, in fact—and, as usual under such painful and unforeseen circumstances, the heartless landlords were busily engaged evicting and exterminating the poor afflicted people who were unable to pay their rents. On the estate of Lord Digby, near Tullamore, King's County, a large number of families were under notice to quit. Under ordinary circumstances they would, no doubt, like thousands of their compatriots before them, have found new homes and words of welcome across the Atlantic, but America was then the scene of sanguinary strife between the North and the South, and that avenue of escape was thus closed against the persecuted people. There seemed to be no alternative before them but the poor-house, when some of them remembered that Father Dunne was then in the town of Tullamore. Knowing that he had spent some years as a missionary priest in Australia, they came to him in the hour of their affliction, and besought him to obtain passages for them to any of the Australian colonies. Father Dunne communicated at once with Mr. Jordan, the immigration agent of the Queensland Government, but that official's reply was the reverse of encouraging. It amounted indeed to a practical exemplification of a still-cherished maxim in some quarters—"No Irish need apply." Nothing daunted by this rebuff, the good priest lost no time in opening up negotiations with the owners of the Black Ball line of ships, with whom Mr. Jordan had contracted to carry his selected immigrants to Queensland. This immigration was conducted under what was known as the "land order" system, by which every adult paying his or her own passage became entitled to a land order of the value of £20. This order was negotiable and transferable, and could be sold for its market value. The Act further provided that those who paid the passages of others, and landed them safely in the colony, would be entitled to the land orders of such immigrants. Father Dunne at once saw that under this system he could take to Queensland any number of eligible Irish immigrants, if he only had the means of paying their passages. The circumstances of the poor people whom he wished to befriend, could brook no delay. He had recourse to some of his well-wishers in Ireland, and succeeded in borrowing sufficient money to induce him to proceed with his philanthropic scheme. In less than a month he had received upwards of 500 applications for free or assisted passages to Queensland. It was only natural that he should meet with some opposition from Irish priests, who could not but view with sorrow and pain the sad spectacle of their people preparing to leave their native country for a far-distant land. Still, with nothing before them but starvation or the poor-house, it is not to be wondered at that the poor people were ready to fly anywhere in order to avoid the ordeal of choosing between two such dismal alternatives. The landlords, with a few honourable exceptions, were inexorable in their demands for the payment of impossible rents after a succession of bad seasons, and, as a result of their inhuman conduct in this respect, hundreds of unfortunate tenants and their families were bereft of house and home. Most of them willingly embraced the opportunity afforded them by Father Dunne to emigrate to a new country, which freely offered them the means of obtaining that honest livelihood which they were not permitted to earn on the soil of their forefathers. The Queensland Government Agent displayed to the last an ungenerous opposition to Father Dunne's benevolent enterprise, and even went so far as to declare that it was very doubtful if land orders would be given to any immigrants who did not come out under the government regulations and through the accredited agent. Undismayed by this uncharitable threat, the indefatigable priest persevered in his arduous undertaking, succeeded in chartering a ship, gave it the patriotic name of " Erin-go-bragh," and placed 400 Irish immigrants on board at Queenstown. Nor did his pastoral care and oversight cease when he saw them all safely on board the " Erin-go-bragh." Far from it. He accompanied them on the long voyage to their future antipodean home, cheered them with his genial presence and fatherly counsel, shared with them the privations and discomforts of ship life, and, all through the dangers of the deep, showed himself to be a genuine *Soggarth Aroon*. When at last they arrived in Queensland, Father Dunne's living active interest on their behalf was naturally directed into a new channel. He smoothed away all governmental difficulties, set to work energetically to place his people on the road to success and independence, and never left them until every one of the 400 was settled in some industrial occupation in the new land of their adoption.

The voyage of the " Erin-go-bragh " was a memorable one in many respects. It lasted for the long period of five months. The ship, although roomy between decks, was the reverse of a rapid sailer, and this drawback caused a jovial immigrant to suggest to Father Dunne the propriety of re-christening her the " Erin-go-slow." Besides, there was an almost constant succession of head winds and calms throughout the voyage. As there were signs of the water giving out, the ship called in at the Cape of Good Hope, where the tanks were replenished, and a fair quantity of fresh provisions obtained. On setting sail again, the same provoking head winds continued to be encountered, and, what was still more alarming, when the " Erin-go-bragh " was about 300 miles from the Cape, she commenced to leak. The pumps had to be kept working every alternate hour, and, strange to say, the leak appeared to be most troublesome during calm weather, when there was no strain upon the ship. It was afterwards discovered, when the vessel was placed for examination in the dry dock at Sydney, that a large auger hole had been bored through the bottom, which allowed the water to flow in freely when the copper was displaced by the action of the waves. This discovery pointed very plainly to foul play on the part of some bigoted miscreant, as it was well-known in Liverpool that the ship had been chartered for the conveyance of Irish immigrants to Queensland. Moreover, it was remembered, and this intensified the aforesaid suspicion, that a Scotch family, who had taken their passage by the " Erin-go-bragh," were privately warned in Liverpool not to travel by that particular ship, as it was very doubtful if she would ever reach her destination. But a good angel watched over the Irish barque, and the prophecy of evil was not verified by the event. It is true the ship was a long and anxious time on the water, but she reached her destined port at last. Captain Borlase and his mate, Mr. Myler, both Irishmen, were most kind and attentive to the immigrants, whilst commendably strict in preserving due discipline amongst them. There was of necessity some little grumbling and discontent occasionally. Two sturdy immigrants thought one day they would settle their little differences with their own muscular arms, and without troubling any outside tribunal. But the captain decided the dispute for them in a very practical and good-humoured fashion. He called them both on deck, made a ring, and ordered them both to strip and see which was really the better man. At the same time, he quietly told the mate to put on the hose and have the force pumps in readiness. When the combatants made their appearance inside the ring, the captain gave the signal to the mate, the hose was immediately brought into operation, and the would-be fighters received so thorough a drenching that nothing more was heard of such personal quarrels for the remainder of the voyage. Every Friday the passengers were supplied with fish and pea soup. It happened on one day that a piece of pork was found in the soup, and the alarming discovery caused considerable commotion. Some of the immigrants lost all faith in the Friday soup after that little accident, and could not be prevailed upon to taste it again. Indeed, one old woman, in the height of her indignation, went so far as to charge the captain with being a "souper" in disguise, that being the repulsive epithet applied by the people to those aggressive Protestant zealots who, with most unchristian indecency, did their best during the famine years, but with very little success, to pervert and demoralise the starving Irish Catholics by offering them basins of soup on Fridays. As a rule, it took some time to reconcile the Irish immigrants to the ship biscuits and the pea soup. They sometimes imagined that the biscuits were the cause of their sea-sickness, and they could not bear the sight of them. On one of the ships the immigrants rebelled against the pea soup, waited on the captain, and remonstrated with him for offering them such "dirty-looking stuff," and, when the captain answered them it was the same as that used by the ladies and gentlemen in the first cabin, an Irishman made the amusing retort that "it might do very well for the quality and the pigs, but it was not fit for poor people like him." During the voyage there was an outbreak of measles and low fever that caused some mortality amongst the infants. But, if there were some deaths, there were also births on board the "Erin-go-bragh."

One of those interesting domestic occurrences happened on St. Patrick's Night. When Father Dunne was called upon to baptise the child, the usual inquiries were made as to what name should be bestowed on the infant; and, in recognition of the happy coincidence that the child's natal day corresponded with the feast of Ireland's patron saint, Patrick was unanimously selected as a fit and proper title for the baby. Next morning the father of the child came to the priest in an awful state of trouble and anxiety. "Oh, your reverence," said he, "we made a great mistake last night." "How is that?" inquired the priest. "Oh, your reverence, it was all through that ape of a woman who attended my wife. Sure *Paddy is a little girl!*" Here was a truly perplexing state of things. A conference of all interested was held, and the priest eventually pacified all parties with the assurance that the little innocent victim of the baptismal blunder should be registered as "Mary Patrick."

On arrival in Moreton Bay, a large inlet about 25 miles distant from Brisbane, the capital of the new colony of Queensland, the "Erin-go-bragh" was subjected to a short detention in quarantine. When the immigrants were permitted to land, they were taken up the river in a special steamer and heartily welcomed by the Right Rev. James Quinn, the first Bishop of Queensland, and the people of Brisbane. The brother of this energetic and patriotic prelate, the Rev. Dr. Matthew Quinn, of Dublin, afterwards Bishop of Bathurst in New South Wales, followed immediately in the footsteps of the pioneer, Father Dunne, and chartered the "Maryborough" to carry another batch of Irish immigrants to Queensland. The "Maryborough" made a fair passage, and reached Moreton Bay shortly after the "Erin-go-bragh." As soon as the system inaugurated by Father Dunne was found to work satisfactorily, and when it became known that the Queensland Government had decided to offer no positive opposition to the movement, ships conveying a most desirable class of immigrants for a young colony were despatched from Ireland to Queensland month after month in regular succession. Even Mr. Jordan, the government agent, who was so hostile to Father Dunne's scheme at the beginning, completely altered his views afterwards, and bore public testimony to the excellent results it had accomplished. Under the auspices of Dr. Quinn, he went over to Ireland, and lectured in Dublin and Cork on the advantages and prospects of Queensland as a field for emigration.

Having seen his first batch of immigrants comfortably settled on the soil, Father Dunne hastened back to Ireland and safely brought out a second contingent by the "Fiery Star." This vessel had the misfortune to be burned at sea on the return voyage, somewhere between the Auckland Islands and Cape Horn. The passengers and a portion of the ship's crew took to the boats and were never heard of again, whilst the few who remained on the burning hull were luckily rescued at the last moment by a passing barque. The indefatigable priest made still another trip to the old land, and returned to Queensland in the "Sunda," bringing with him a band of Irishmen as noble, as earnest, as intelligent and a industrious as ever quitted the "green shores of holy Ireland," to aid in building up a new colony "by the long wash of Australasian seas." Thus in three short years, and with none of to-day's conveniences for ocean travelling, this intrepid Irish missionary accomplished six of the longest voyages that are possible on this planet for the benefit of his poor, sorely-tried countrymen and countrywomen, many of whom were saved by his splendid exertions from the fearful effects of famine or the dreaded degradation of the poorhouse. Altogether, about 6,000 people were successfully transplanted through his instrumentality from Ireland to Queensland, and it is highly gratifying to be in a position to state, without fear of contradiction, that all of them who permanently settled in the colony, and avoided the curse of their race, strong drink, have prospered to a remarkable degree, and enjoyed the esteem and good-will of their fellow-colonists of other nationalities. Many of them have risen to wealth and opulence, and are to-day familiar, respected figures in the commercial life of the colony; others have devoted themselves with conspicuous success to agricultural and pastoral pursuits, whilst not a few are to be found filling some of the highest positions in the government service. It was unquestionably the fixed intention of the first government of Queensland to exclude the Irish immigrant, and to make the place as far as possible of a Scotch and English complexion, but, thanks to the immigration scheme initiated by Father Dunne, and followed up by the late Bishop Quinn, that narrow-minded policy was wisely abandoned, and the young colony was allowed to assimilate its fair proportion of the Irish element. Before the arrival of the "Erin-go-bragh," one small church—40 feet by 25—sufficed to accommodate the Catholics of the city of Brisbane, and outside the capital there was but one more in the whole of the vast diocese of Queensland, viz. at Ipswich. Not the least important of the good results of Father Dunne's immigration scheme was the planting in the young colony of a good stock of practical Catholics, whose presence soon became manifest in the number of Catholic churches that sprang up all over the country. It was an essential part of Father Dunne's system to make ample provision for the spiritual welfare of his immigrants, and, with that object, free passages for two priests were secured on each of his ships.

Father Dunne not only laboured most devotedly in the work of rescuing thousands of his unfortunate fellow countrymen and countrywomen from the horrors of famine, and of piloting them to " homes and homesteads in the land of plenty," but, with a kindly sympathetic interest in their future, he published for their benefit some weighty words of sterling advice as to the rule of life they ought to follow, and the special dangers they should try to avoid in starting on their colonial career. He warned the young immigrant to guard against allowing the first feelings of disappointment and dissatisfaction to gain upon him, but rather to look forward hopefully to the position he might gain after a few years of perseverance. On no account should he lose that energy which was so essential for the ultimate success of people starting in a new country. Some of the greatest men in Australia, both as regards their social position and their wealth, had to commence their career in the humble capacity of shepherds. The man most respected in Australia was the man who had raised himself to power and prosperity by his own honest exertions. To the young Irish girls who formed so large a percentage of his immigrants, Father Dunne addressed these words of wisdom:

"It is a fact which very few will dispute, that ninety-nine out of every hundred of the single females who emigrate to Australia, are more or less influenced by the hope of getting married as soon as possible after their arrival. I would by no means find fault with their motives, but I would warn them to be very cautious about the selection of a husband. It is on this point that girls should be particularly on their guard, as it is in this they generally make their first false step. They are too ready to accept the first proposal and to run off to get married to a man of whose religion, country, or character they know nothing. In the majority of such cases, the man perhaps has a wife in some other part of the world, or he is a drunkard, or a bad man, and will of course give his wife the worst of treatment as long as they live together, which is generally from six to twelve months, and then she is deserted or discarded, to pine away with a broken heart the remainder of her miserable existence."

Not a few Irish girls, unfortunately, have come to grief in the colonies from the over hasty desire to change their condition in life, and these warning words of a veteran Irish priest will continue to have their full force and application for many years to come. A generous, unthinking impulsiveness of thought and action may be one of the strongest and most characteristic points of the Irish character, but there are occasions when, if not checked in time, it becomes an element of weakness and disaster. It is a quality that has made Irishmen the very best of soldiers, and Irishwomen the most self-sacrificing of heroines, but, on the lower fields of life, and under less heroic conditions, its exercise is calculated to become a source of sorrow and ruin.

After his impressive admonition to young female immigrants, Father Dunne proceeds:

"I will now offer a few words of sincere advice to the young men. In the first place and before all, I would warn them to be careful to shun and repel the snares and allurements of intoxication. Let temperance be their watchword and their guide. If, after having been preserved from the dangers of the sea, the first act, when they have put their foot on shore, is to go to the public-house and get drunk, how can they expect that God will bless their efforts in their adopted country? Such conduct is invariably the starting on the road to temporal and eternal destruction, and Irishmen are, unfortunately, too easily led into the snare. To ensure success, the young man must add energy and perseverance to sobriety. Let him, under every circumstance, pursue an honest and straightforward course, and he need not fear for the result: success, plenty and comfort will crown his career. Those who now hold the highest places of distinction in Australia, to their praise be it said, landed, as most emigrants do, without money or interest. They had to battle against the most adverse circumstances through many anxious years; but they had energy and perseverance, they were sober and honest, and they now enjoy the rewards of their labour."

The motives that actuated Father Dunne in undertaking his philanthropic immigration enterprise have been thus clearly stated by himself:

"In taking the part which I have during the last few years in directing emigration to Australia, let me not be misunderstood. I have neither promoted nor encouraged it. On the contrary, if our poor people had protection and could live at home, I would say, ' Let them remain by all means.' But when they *must* leave, when there is no other alternative except the poor-house or emigration, I am persuaded I could not employ my time better than in directing my countrymen to that part of the world where there is abundance of good land, a salubrious climate, where their faith will not be in danger, and where they can enjoy peace and prosperity after a few years, if it be not their own fault. As soon as I see the priests and the people standing together, and firm in the resolve to demand justice and protection for the farmers and labouring classes of Ireland, I will become the most strenuous advocate to keep the people at home. But I must say with all sincerity, I see no other hope at present for the poor downtrodden people of this country but to fly to the most distant part of the world, where there is perfect equality, civil and religious liberty, no poor-houses to demoralise the people, and no landlords to exterminate them."

Since Father Dunne penned these indignant words, the condition of the Irish peasant has been somewhat improved by remedial legislation, but it is susceptible of further improvement still. Though Irish families may no longer be under the dire necessity of flying for refuge to the most distant part of the world, they have yet many evils to encounter and many trials to endure in the land of their birth. But they are consoled by the hope and the expectation, that the day is not far distant when a domestic Parliament will sit in Dublin, and pass the requisite laws for the rectification of the long-standing evils and abuses of arbitrary power.

To say that one of these poor and friendless Irish emigrants to Queensland rose in a few years to be the chief guide and exponent of the public opinion of his adopted country, seems at first sight a somewhat extravagant statement; but it is nevertheless perfectly true of the late William O'Carroll, in his time the premier journalist of Queensland. A native of Cork, he joined one of the first emigrant bands to the new Australian colony, where he soon found scope for the exercise of his vigorous brain-power and his innate literary talent in the leading journals of Brisbane. For many years, and up to the day of his death, O'Carroll was universally recognised as the ruling literary force in the Northern colony—a lofty altitude for an erstwhile unknown Irish emigrant to attain in a mixed community. "What characterised him above all," said the Brisbane *Courier*, the principal journal of Queensland, whose pages he brightened with his best work and his noblest thoughts, "was the conscience he put into his work. He was never the sort of man who would take up a subject—like a lawyer his brief—and make the best of it without much thought or care concerning the truth of the matter at issue. Truth was the keynote of his nature. The same love of truth made him the most loyal and trusty of comrades to his press colleagues. And there was a strong strain of chivalry in his nature, which found vent in a devotion to his paper similar to that which a soldier bestows upon his regiment. Neither in himself, nor in anyone under his orders, would he tolerate half-hearted service, or anything less than the very best work that could be done. There are men holding high positions in his profession in other countries, who will testify to the value of the sometimes sharp, but always kindly, lessons they received from him when they were among 'O'Carroll's boys.'"

Another brilliant journalist, who was carried away in the very prime of life, was Robert Atkin, a kinsman of Thomas Davis and a member of the Legislative Assembly of Queensland. The monument over his grave by the sea at Sandgate, thirteen miles from the capital, bears the following fraternal inscription: "Erected by the members of the Hibernian

Society of Queensland to the memory of their late vice-president, Robert Travers Atkin. Born at Fern Hill, County Cork, Ireland, November 29th, 1841. Died at Sandgate, Queensland, May 25th, 1872. His days were few, but his labours and attainments bore the stamp of a wise maturity. This broken column symbolises the irreparable loss of a man who well represented some of the finest characteristics in the Celtic race—its rich humour and subtle wit, its fervid passion and genial warmth of heart. Distinguished alike in the press and parliament of Queensland by large and elevated views, remarkable powers of organisation, and unswerving advocacy of the popular cause, his rare abilities were especially devoted to the promotion of a patriotic union amongst his countrymen, irrespective of class or creed, combined with a loyal allegiance to the land of their adoption."

# CHAPTER IX.

## THE MOTHER OF THE AUSTRALIAS.

SYDNEY—THE CENTENNIAL AUSTRALIAN CITY—ITS IRISH MAYOR—ST. MARY'S CATHEDRAL—ST. VINCENT'S HOSPITAL—FOUNDATION OF THE COLONY OF NEW SOUTH WALES—EVILS OF TRANSPORTATION—FORMATION OF THE ANTI-TRANSPORTATION LEAGUE—BOYCOTTING CONVICT SHIPS—EARLY IRISH PRISONERS—THEIR UNDULY SEVERE SENTENCES—HOW THEY PROSPERED IN NEW SOUTH WALES—THE MEN OF '98—A WEALTHY PIKE-MAKER—TWO BROTHERS-IN-ARMS AT VINEGAR HILL—GENERAL JOSEPH HOLT—BRAVE MICHAEL DWYER—OFFICIAL TESTIMONY TO THE GOOD QUALITIES OF THE IRISH—THE STRANGE CAREER OF GEORGE BARRINGTON—HIS CELEBRATED PROLOGUE—SIR HENRY HAYES—HOW HE BANISHED THE SNAKES—A TYPICAL CELT—THE VARIED RESOURCES OF NEW SOUTH WALES.

IN this year of grace 1887, Sydney, the capital of New South Wales, the mother colony of the Australias, has for its municipal governor an active and enterprising Irish-Australian in the person of Alderman A. J. Riley, M.P. And it is only in accordance with the fitness of things, that the honour of the mayoralty of Sydney should be frequently conferred on leading Irish citizens, as a merited recognition of the prominent and laborious part they and their countrymen have played, in building up the greatness of the most historic city of the south. Sydney is now approaching the close of the first century of its existence, and it may be aptly described as a fully-developed antipodean city of great commerce and industrial activity. Situated on the southern shores of Port Jackson, most lovely and capacious of harbours, Sydney is able to welcome the mercantile marine of the world, and to

receive trading representatives of all nations at her very
doors. As the oldest city of the colonies, Sydney presents a
variety of quaint aspects that differentiate it from all its
younger rivals. It is not, for example, laid out on strict
mathematical lines, as are all the recent cities of Australasian growth, but rather rejoices in those narrow, irregular
thoroughfares that characterise primitive cities of the
northern hemisphere. This circumstance necessarily detracts
somewhat from its architectural appearance. Nevertheless,
the churches, public buildings, and business establishments
of Sydney are quite as elegant, as substantial, and as imposing
as those of its great rival Melbourne, despite the fact that
they cannot be seen to equal advantage. St. Mary's Cathedral,
like St. Patrick's, of Melbourne, is an immense, unfinished
memorial of Irish Catholic piety, destined one day to be
the noblest ecclesiastical edifice in the mother colony of
the Australian group. St. Vincent's Hospital, which is
under the kind and Christian management of the Sisters of
Charity, is perhaps the institution that reflects the highest
credit on Catholic Sydney. " Of all our institutions of
charity," says the foremost Irish-Australian statesman, the
Right Hon. W. B. Dalley, "this is the one of which we
have the most reason to be proud. For nearly thirty years
it has been silently and unobtrusively doing a great work.
It has received during that period tens of thousands of
patients suffering from all kinds of diseases, and it has
relieved hundreds of thousands of out-patients. Its doors
are open to those of all religions or of none. Though served
by holy women who have consecrated their lives to the care
of the sick and the relief of the suffering, it is supported by
the entire community. The Catholic Church has the merit
of its foundation, and so far as the nurses are concerned, the

glory of its service; but it has no exclusive claim to its maintenance. I believe its most generous benefactors are not of our communion. Amongst its life-subscribers, I find that some who have purchased that honour and privilege by contributions, are not of the faith of those who serve it. It is thus a standing memorial of that liberality which it is so desirable to cultivate in all the relations of life."

St. John's College, affiliated to the University of Sydney; St. Ignatius' College, Riverview, conducted by the Jesuit Fathers ; and St. Joseph's College, Hunter Hill, under the management of the Marist Fathers, are three educational institutions that reflect the highest credit on the Catholic population of the parent colony.

At the beginning of the century the name "New South Wales" was synonymous with Australia, for no other settlement existed, and its governor exercised jurisdiction over the whole continent. At present, however, its area is restricted to that eastern portion of the continent lying north of Victoria, south of Queensland, and east of South Australia. New South Wales was avowedly founded for the express purpose of relieving the overcrowded gaols of England of their most refractory inmates. The successful effort of the American colonists to assert their independence put an effectual stop to the deportation of English criminals across the Atlantic, and it became necessary to find some other receptacle for them. Eight years previously, Captain James Cook had been sent on a voyage of discovery to the southern seas. He landed on the eastern shores of the Australian continent, at a place whose name has since gained a world-wide notoriety—Botany Bay, so called by Sir Joseph Banks, the botanist of the expedition, on account of the luxuriant vegetation all round it. Landing here he took possession of the continent in the name and on behalf of the then reigning monarch, George the Third. After an extensive voyage, Cook returned to England in June, 1771, and reported his discoveries in Australia. No action, however, was taken in reference to his report, until the loss of the American colonies necessitated the formation of other penal settlements. Then, and not till then, was Captain Cook's report taken from its dusty pigeon-hole and perused with far greater interest than when it was first submitted. To British statesmen it seemed a merciful interposition of Providence, that a new continent in the south was thus rendered available for the occupation of their felonry, so soon after they had forfeited their American possessions by a pig-headed policy and tyrannical dictation. It was immediately decided to found a penal settlement on the delightful shores of Botany Bay. In pursuance of this object Viscount Sydney, then principal Secretary of State for the Colonies in Pitt's administration, recommended the establishment of the colony of New South Wales, and this recommendation was subsequently confirmed by an Order of Council, dated December 6th, 1785. On May 13, 1787, what has come to be historically known as the "First Fleet," consisting of eleven ships, with supplies for two years, sailed from England for the antipodes under the command of Captain Arthur Phillip. The first consignment of prisoners numbered 696 —504 males and 192 females—who were guarded by 212 officers and marines. Captain Phillip, with his living freight of exiles, arrived in Botany Bay on January 20, 1788. But, strange to say, though the name of Botany Bay has ever since been associated with crime and criminals, as a matter of fact the place never was a permanent penal settlement. Two days after landing, Captain Phillip, accompanied by several officers, set out in boats to examine the coast to the north. This boating expedition resulted in the discovery of a harbour, whose praises have since been sounded in every land, and which continues to be the pride and the joy of the Australian native-born population. Entering between two rocky headlands a vision of surpassing beauty burst upon the gaze of the astonished mariners. A noble harbour, dotted with islands, and encompassed by verdant hills, expanded before them, its waters basking in the delights of southern sunshine. As they advanced, each succeeding stroke of the oar opened up new scenes of loveliness and fresh successions of charming inlets all around them. On the shores of this delightful bay they determined to build their little town, which they christened Sydney, in honour of the nobleman already mentioned. The picturesque harbour they called Port Jackson.

For many years the place suffered all the horrors inseparable from a penal settlement under an irresponsible *régime*. Military rule was paramount, and the early annals of the colony literally reek with vice, debauchery and immorality of every conceivable kind. The infant settlement, relying on receiving supplies from the mother country, was once almost annihilated by famine, and an infamous system of traffic in rum, which soon became the recognised currency, was inaugurated. The wholesale saturnalia and indiscriminate intoxication that followed on this miserable state of affairs may be easily imagined. But in process of time these terrible diseases in the body politic found a remedy. As the resources of the colony became generally and better known in the Old World, a gradually increasing stream of immigration began to flow towards the settlement, and this naturally had the effect of purifying to an appreciable extent the moral atmosphere of the colony.

The extraordinary facilities offered by the Australian soil for the rearing of sheep and the production of wool were speedily discovered. John Macarthur, one of the earliest free settlers, imported from the Cape Colony three rams and five ewes—the precursors of the immense flocks of sheep that now roam over the plains of Australia. In 1803 Macarthur brought to England the first sample of Australian wool. In 1834, the year of his death, the quantity of wool, annually exported from Australia, had reached four and a half million pounds. The latest returns show that Australia is now exporting wool to the extent of 410 million pounds annually.

The appointment of a Legislative Council in 1824 did away, to some extent, with irresponsible military rule and its attendant evils, and paved the way for a better state of things in the body politic. The free settlers, becoming emboldened by increasing numbers, and perceiving the horrors inflicted on their adopted country, as well as the evil example placed before their young families, by the transportation system, raised their voices against its further continuance. They organised an agitation and established a league with the object of achieving that desirable result, but the ex-prisoners, many of whom had by this time become wealthy landed proprietors, formed themselves into a counter-organisation called the "Emancipists," and agitated for the perpetuation of the system, so that they might have a constant supply of convict labour. With undeniable truth they urged and contended that the colony was originally founded expressly as a penal settlement, and that therefore the free settlers had come out with a full knowledge of the circumstances, and had no right to object to the conditions of life in which they had found themselves on arrival. The agitation on both sides was vigorously maintained for many years, and it was not until the various colonies had banded themselves together as an "Anti-Transportation League," that the home government was compelled to surrender and find some criminal depôt nearer home. In November, 1849, the colonists at the Cape of Good Hope refused to permit the landing of a cargo of convicts from the "Neptune." John Mitchel gives a lengthy and humorous account of the "boycotting" that ensued, in his "Jail Journal." In June of the same year the "Harkaway," with another cargo of convicts, was refused permission to land them in Sydney. The excitement in Sydney on that occasion was unprecedented. An immense public meeting was held, at which the Ven. Archdeacon McEncroe (a popular Irish priest) declared amidst general applause that, rather than submit to the treatment they were then receiving from the Imperial Government, they would follow the example of the American colonists of 1776 and proclaim their independence. As an evidence of the reluctance with which the Imperial authorities abandoned the transportation system, it may be stated that it was not until the beginning of January, 1868, that the last convict ship quitted the shores of Australia.

In 1843 a liberal concession was made in the matter of representative institutions by the supplementing of the nominee Legislative Council with representatives elected by the various districts of the colony. Twenty-four members were chosen in this manner and twelve were nominated by the Crown. As years rolled on and the colony settled down into a compact community, a still further extension of political privileges was demanded, and eventually this also was conceded in the shape of a full measure of responsible Government. The first fully-endowed Parliament of New South Wales was opened on May 22nd, 1856.

Reference has already been made to the discovery of gold in New South Wales by Hargreaves. As in the case of Victoria, it resulted in a considerable accession of population. At first the eyes of all adventurers were turned towards New South Wales, but when the astonishing yields of the Victorian gold-fields became known, the auriferous regions of the parent colony became comparatively deserted. But in time they again received the attention to which they were justly entitled, and a large area of auriferous country in the south of New South Wales has since been profitably opened up.

Sydney will ever possess an affectionate interest for the Irish heart by reason of its having been the place of banishment of thousands of Irishmen during the early years of the century. These Celtic pioneers, it should be remembered, were transported in convict-ships to Australia for alleged offences that were not crimes at all in the legitimate sense of the word, and now-a-days are never regarded as such. Bishop Ullathorne puts the case very clearly when he remarks:

"The political circumstances of the British Empire were originally to a great degree responsible for the fact of the presence of a large proportion of the natives of Ireland amongst the first inhabitants of Australia. Ignorance or violation of religious principle, the knowledge or habits of a criminal life, were scarcely to any extent recognisable features in this unhappy class of Irish political prisoners. On the contrary, the deepest and purest sentiments of piety, a thorough comprehension of religious responsibility, and an almost impregnable simplicity of manner, were their distinctive virtues on their first consignment to the guardianship of the law. In many illustrious cases, a long and dangerous residence in the most depraved penal settlements was unable to extinguish those noble characteristics."

And the testimony of Sir Roger Therry, who, being an eminent Australian judge of the Supreme Court, is entitled to speak with authority on such a question, is equally explicit and conclusive:

"Very many Irishmen were transported for the infringement of severe laws, some of which are not now in force, and for offences for which a few months' imprisonment would at present be deemed an adequate expiation. In a country where abundant means rewarded industrious habits, these men became prosperous."

As an example of the truth of this latter remark, Sir Roger mentions the case of Edmund Cane, who had been a snug farmer in Ireland, but was transported for complicity in an agrarian disturbance. Cane was assigned to a settler, and became invaluable as superintendent of his master's estate. "From his skill in agriculture, and his good temper in the management of the men, Cane, after having served his seven years' sentence in the settler's employment, became manager of the whole property and received a liberal salary, which was not paid in money, but in cattle and horses. After twenty years of service he thus became a wealthy man. Shortly before his death, his old master had born unto him a son, and Cane was complimented by being appointed godfather to the boy. The old man made a will bequeathing the whole of his property, the accumulated earnings of twenty years and upwards of arduous toil, to the lucky little bantling, who is now the leading gentleman in his district. The stock bequeathed to him greatly increased during his long minority, and, on coming of age, the fortunate godson found himself one of the most extensive stock-owners in New South Wales."

Sir Roger further states that in 1829, many of the men exiled from Ireland for the troubles of 1798 were still living. Amongst them some truly good men were to be found, whose lives were unstained by the commission of any of the ordinary felonies and baser crimes for which convicts were usually transported. On the term of their transportation being completed, they found themselves in the possession of competent means—the saving of wages from indulgent masters during their period of assignment, and their earnings on obtaining tickets-of-leave. Many of these men testified their attachment to their native country in the best practical shape, by sending to their families at home a portion of the fruits of their industry, and frequently defraying the expense of the voyage of other relatives, whom they invited to join them and share their prosperity in the colony. As an illustration Sir Roger cites the case of D———, who was expatriated from Ireland for making pikes in 1798. D——— was a first-rate blacksmith. About the time he became free, the charge for shoeing a horse was from fifteen shillings to a pound. He was an adept in this, as in all other branches of his business, and in the course of a long life of industry, he acquired property to the estimated extent of from £20,000 to £30,000. This was not, of course, the sole result of manual labour. He had, at an early period, made some judicious purchases of land, which in time had greatly increased in value. About two-thirds of this amount, at his death, in 1843, he devoted by will to religious and educational purposes. The remaining third he bequeathed to some relations whom he had brought out at his own expense from Ireland. He was wont to say quaintly that, if he left them more, it might encourage them to an idle life. Being of the humbler class himself, he deemed it was the duty of his relations to earn a livelihood, like himself, by some industrious pursuit. His life was one of simple habits and unselfish prosperity. Nor was this a solitary instance of remarkable success and generous conduct amongst the men of '98. "The oppressor's wrong and the proud man's contumely" drove many of these men into insurrection, and insurrection into exile. "I might easily," says Sir Roger, "enumerate the names of quite a legion of these exiles (for whose errors, on account of the unjust laws that ground them down, no generous mind can refuse sympathy) who became eminently prosperous in New South Wales, and whose children there are now the inheritors of large estates in land, and numerous flocks of sheep and herds of cattle."

On one occasion Sir Roger paid a visit to a little cemetery crowning a gentle Australian eminence, where he came across an humble tombstone, on which was engraved this touching inscription:

"HERE LIE IN ONE GRAVE PATRICK O'CONNOR AND DENIS BRYAN, SHIPMATES IN THE 'BOYD' TRANSPORT FROM IRELAND IN 1799, AND COMPATRIOTS IN ARMS AT THE MEMORABLE BATTLE OF VINEGAR HILL."

And the sympathetic Irish-Australian Judge does not hesitate to give full and open expression to the emotions of pity that he felt for the fate of these exiles, not unmingled with condemnation of the Irish rulers of that time, who were in no small degree responsible for the insurrection and its consequences. "These attached friends," he says, "the

Damon and Pythias of humble life, on becoming free, purchased a valuable farm on the alluvial banks of the Cowpasture River. After the death of one, by arrangement it passed into the possession of the survivor, who bequeathed it for the religious and educational advantage of the religious community, of which he and his compatriot in arms were members.

"On visiting the church of St. Pietro in Montorio, at Rome, many years afterwards, as I stood upon the ornamental and tessellated pavement, and gazed on the spot where repose the ashes of the Earl of Tyrconnell and Baron Dungannon, who died in exile at Rome in 1608, and there read that 'they were brave and valorous men, often engaged in paths of danger, in defence of their patrimony and their faith,' my mind strayed back to the unadorned stone and homely inscription, that marked the humble grave of Bryan and O'Connor in the little cemetery at the antipodes, their fate a common one—exiles from their native land—sufferers alike in the same cause—that cause the resistance to laws which Edmund Burke truly designated as 'the worst and most wicked that ever proceeded from the perverted ingenuity of man.'"

In addition to many of the rank and file, two of the leading spirits in the insurrection of '98 were sent to Sydney at the close of the struggle. They were General Joseph Holt and brave Michael Dwyer. The former received a free pardon in 1814 and returned to die on Irish soil. His life was prolonged for twelve years, during which he prepared his well-known "Memoirs," which were published in two volumes under the editorial supervision of Mr. T. Crofton Croker. Written in a simple homely strain, they contain a large amount of valuable first-hand information, and a variety of shrewd comments on the condition of the colony during the term of his banishment. Heroic Michael Dwyer was not fated to see Ireland once again and to sleep in his native soil. He died in Sydney, and his remains were interred in the Devonshire Street Cemetery, where his resting-place is marked by a stately marble monument. More than half a century has elapsed since he was laid to rest in the far-away land of his exile, but still the patriot chieftain cannot be said to occupy a grave in the land of the stranger, for his grateful Irish-Australian countrymen continue to revere his memory and to make pilgrimages to his shrine, as this little extract from a recent issue of the Sydney *Freeman's Journal* will show: " Sixty years ago there passed away in our city one who, in his own sphere, had led a life as adventurous, heroic, and full of romance as any recorded in the history of struggling nationalities. Michael Dwyer, the insurgent chief of the Wicklow mountains, was exiled by the British Government to this colony in 1803, and now sleeps his last long sleep in Devonshire Street Cemetery, in this city, 'far from the hills of Innisfail.' His descendants are still amongst us, and by them, as well as by his countrymen, the virtues of the dead patriot are kept green and fresh as his own shamrock land; and many years will pass away ere the gallant Kosciusko of Irish history of ninety years ago is forgotten. On Sunday last about a hundred members of the Shamrock Club assembled to pay a tribute of respect to the memory of the departed patriot, and many a Wicklow man's pulse throbbed faster and a flush of pride mantled his brow as he gazed on the grave ' where the hero was buried.'" At the same time Irishmen all over the world cannot help sympathising with the governing thought in the gracefully-touching verses of Miss Katharine Tynan on "The Grave of Michael Dwyer":

> I wish you slept where your kin are sleeping—
> The dove-gray valley is sweet;
> And the holy mountains their strange watch keeping
> Would love you lying still at their feet,
> The dewy grass for your winding sheet.
>
> You would sleep sweet with your sad lips smiling,
> Dreaming, and hearing still
> The bonny blackbird with songs beguiling,
> The rain's light feet on the hill,
> The children's laughter merry and shrill.
>
> I have a fern that hath waved above you,
> Just at your gray grave's head,
> Sent to me by one who doth love you,
> Bitter the tears she shed
> Praying long by your lonely bed.
>
> And now I weave of my idle fancies,
> All for the love of you,
> A wreath of passion flowers and of pansies
> To lay on the grave I never knew,
> And tears are thick on its leaves for dew.

There is a remarkable official testimony to the good qualities of the Irishmen who were exiled to Australia in the early days, that deserves to be dug out of the musty blue-book in which it has long been buried, and to be placed on permanent record. In 1819 Mr. John Thomas Bigge visited Australia in the capacity of special commissioner from King George III. to investigate the practical operation of the transportation system. He spent three years in making full and exhaustive inquiries into every phase of the question; and in his final report, dated May 6th, 1822, occurs this significant and noteworthy passage:

"The convicts embarked in Ireland generally arrive in

New South Wales in a very healthy state, and are found to be more obedient and more sensible of kind treatment during the passage than any other class. Their separation from their native country is observed to make a stronger impression upon their minds, both on their departure and during the voyage."

Amongst the remarkable Irish convicts who were shipped to Sydney by the home authorities was Edward O'Shaughnessy, a man of conspicuous ability. He was a graduate of Trinity College, Dublin, and, in his new sphere at the antipodes, his talents advanced him to the position of editor of the official journal of the colony, the *Sydney Gazette*. Mr. Flanagan\* describes him as "an effective political writer, and endowed with considerable poetical talent, which he employed for some years in cultivating a taste for literature amongst the colonists." As showing the shameless severity of the laws during the early years of the century, Major Marjoribanks mentions the case of an Irish gentleman who died in New South Wales some years ago worth a quarter of a million of money. And yet this gentleman, who accumulated such vast wealth in the colonies by honest industry, was transported from home in his youth for the alleged offence of taking a handkerchief out of the pocket of a pedestrian. But the cleverest and most celebrated pocket-picker that ever landed on the shores of Australia, or the shores of anywhere else, was George Barrington, the name by which he is generally known, or George Waldron, to give him his baptismal title. His remarkable achievements have furnished many themes for literary and dramatic treatment, and quite recently

---

\* "History of New South Wales."

he has received from Mr. Leslie Stephen the crowning honour of a place in the "Dictionary of National Biography." A native of Maynooth, County Kildare, Barrington's precocious talents gained him the favour and the patronage of a sympathetic clergyman, through whose interest he was placed in a boarding-school at Dublin. Here he remained until his sixteenth year, when, having been severely flogged for a violation of scholastic discipline, he ran away, after revenging himself by stealing twelve guineas from the master of the establishment and a gold repeater from that gentleman's sister. He turned his steps towards Drogheda, where he fell in with a company of strolling players, to whose ranks he became a welcome acquisition by reason of his handsome stage presence, and his marvellous memory. But the company got into financial difficulties at Londonderry, and Barrington resolved to replenish his empty purse by pocket-picking. He succeeded beyond his most sanguine anticipations, Cork and Dublin being his favourite and most lucrative fields of operation. Ireland becoming at length too hot to hold him, Barrington crossed the Channel and made his appearance in London fashionable society as a handsome young gentleman of good family, a character which he was naturally well qualified to play to the life. His ready assurance and his polished address enabled him to fraternise on the most familiar terms with noblemen and gentry, and to explore their well-lined pockets with an easy grace and a boundless self-confidence, that almost inspire a feeling of admiration at the perverted abilities of this accomplished adventurer. Once he actually attended a Royal reception, and succeeded in the difficult feat of cutting off the collar of an Order of the Garter, besides appropriating many snuff-boxes and purses from the pockets of the distinguished company. He then attempted a still higher flight of villany by trying to seize the diamond snuff-box presented to Prince Orloff by the Empress Catherine, and valued at £30,000. Barrington made this daring attempt in Covent Garden Theatre. He contrived to get a seat next to that of the Russian Prince, and succeeded in snatching the snuff-box, but it was soon missed, and the culprit was caught before he had time to get away from the theatre with his splendid prize. After a long career of undetected pocket-picking, Barrington was now bowled out for the first time, and just as he was essaying the most ambitious of his exploits, but his cool self-possession did not desert him in the hour of trouble. When brought before the court and charged with the crime he had so nearly consummated, Barrington spoke so effectively, and concocted such a plausible defence, that the Russian Prince, relenting, refused to prosecute, and the prince of pickpockets was discharged with a caution to be more careful in his handling of other people's property for the future. The publicity that this little incident acquired necessitated Barrington's retirement for a season from fashionable and exclusive circles, and he had to be content with exercising his talents in the humbler and less remunerative walks of life. He made a professional tour through Ireland and Scotland, and after this eclipse, he returned to aristocratic society and shone with even greater brilliancy than before. But, unrivalled artist as he was, continued success had the natural result of making him less cautious in his operations, and one day Barrington was caught picking a pocket on a racecourse. He was tried, convicted, and sentenced to seven years' transportation. Barrington bade good-bye to the old world in this clever and characteristic little speech from the dock: "My Lord—I have a great deal to say in extenuation of the crime for which I now stand convicted at this bar; but upon consideration, I will not arrest the attention of the honourable Court too long. Among the extraordinary vicissitudes incident to human nature, it is the peculiar and unfortunate lot of some devoted persons to have their best wishes and their most earnest endeavours to deserve the good opinion of the most respectable part of society frustrated. Whatever they say, or whatever they do, every word and its meaning, every action and its motive, is represented in an unfavourable light, and is distorted from the real intention of the speaker or the actor. That this has been my unhappy fate does not seem to need much confirmation. Every effort to deserve well of mankind, that my heart bore witness to, its rectitude has been frustrated by such measures as these, and consequently rendered abortive. Many of the circumstances of my life, I can, without any violation of the truth, declare to have therefore happened absolutely in spite of myself. The world, my lord, has given me credit for abilities, indeed much greater than I possess, and therefore much more than I deserved; but I had never found any kind hand to foster those abilities. I might ask, where was the generous and powerful hand that was ever stretched forth to rescue George Barrington from infamy? In an age like this, which in several respects is so justly famed for liberal sentiments, it was my severe lot that no noble-minded gentleman stepped forward and said: 'Barrington, you are possessed of talents which may be useful to society. I feel for your situation, and as long as you act the part of a good citizen, I will be your protector; you will have time and opportunity to rescue yourself from the obloquy of your former conduct.' Alas, my lord, George Barrington had never the supreme, felicity of having such comfort administered to his wounded spirit. As matters have unfortunately turned out, the die is cast; and as it is, I have resigned to my fate without one murmur of complaint."

On the voyage to Australia, Barrington was the means of saving the ship from being captured by his fellow-prisoners. A few of the most desperate convicts on board plotted to seize the vessel that was bearing them into exile, and to steer for America and freedom as soon as they had got rid of their gaolers. Availing themselves of the first favourable opportunity, they made a rush for the deck, but found an unexpected opponent in one who was wearing their own uniform of crime, for Barrington stood at the hatchway wielding a handspike, and kept them at bay until the officers appeared on the scene and quelled the mutiny. The two ringleaders were executed on the spot, and their followers were punished in a minor degree. For the great and important service he rendered at this critical moment, Barrington naturally received a large measure of liberty and indulgence during the remainder of the voyage; and, when the ship arrived at Sydney, the officers warmly commended him to the generous consideration of the governor of the colony, who not only gave him a full and immediate emancipation, but appointed him to the lucrative office of superintendent of convicts. Ever afterwards he was a changed man. He kept religiously to the straight path of duty, and his facile fingers were never known to stray into a strange pocket at the antipodes.\* He settled in the mother

---

\* One exception must be made to this remark. When Barrington was a very old man, he heard that a certain lady, who held a high position in Sydney society, had been talking about him in an objectionable manner, and saying that, for her part, she would never believe he was such a fine gentleman in his youth, neither would she believe any of those silly stories about his marvellous

colony of the Australias, wrote its history in two bulky volumes, and lived to be a patriarch in the land of his exile. But Barrington's " History of New South Wales," dedicated to His Gracious Majesty George the Third, is not the literary monument that will transmit his name to an admiring posterity. He will be best and longest remembered by the audaciously witty prologue which he wrote and recited on the occasion of the first dramatic performance that was given in the city of Sydney by a company of convicts:

> From distant climes, o'er widespread seas we come,
> Though not with much *éclat*, or beat of drum ;
> True patriots all, for, be it understood,
> We left our country for our country's good ;
> No private views disgrac'd our generous zeal,
> What urg'd our travels, was our country's weal ;

skill in pocket-picking. A few days after she had been speaking in this slighting strain, an elderly gentleman, of dignified bearing and affable manners, called at her mansion and inquired if her husband was in. "He would be presently," the lady replied; "and would the gentleman come in and take a seat?" The gentleman did so, and made himself so agreeable that the lady took him round to see the pictures and *curios* of her house. The husband not having arrived in the meantime, the gentleman expressed his regret, but he really could not wait any longer. After a graceful good-bye, he suddenly retraced his steps as if he had forgotten something, and, putting his hand into his pocket, drew out two gold pendants of ear-rings and a massive gold locket. "I think, madam, these are your property," he remarked, with a serio-comic smile, as he handed them back to the lady. "Kindly tell your husband that Mr. Barrington called," and, with a profound bow, he vanished. The lady could hardly believe her eyes, but one glance in the mirror was sufficient. There were no pendants to her ear-rings, and the chain around her neck had no locket attached to it. They had been deftly removed by the former prince of pickpockets whilst she was amiably showing him around, and, so skilfully was the difficult feat accomplished, that she had not the slightest suspicion of her loss. Barrington had a twofold object in perpetrating this practical and rather risky joke. It was both a rebuke and an experiment. He wanted to mildly punish the lady for her derogatory remarks about him, and he wished to ascertain whether both his hands still possessed their cunning after thirty years of abstinence from pocket-picking.

And none will doubt, but that our emigration,
Has proved most useful to the British nation.
But, you inquire, what could our breasts inflame
With this new passion for theatric fame;
What, in the practice of our former days,
Could shape our talents to exhibit plays?
Your patience, sirs, some observations made,
You'll grant us equal to the scenic trade.
He who to midnight ladders is no stranger,
You'll own will make an admirable Ranger.
To seek Macheath we have not far to roam,
And sure in Filch I shall be quite at home.
Unrivalled there, none will dispute my claim,
To high pre-eminence and exalted fame.
As oft on Gadshill we have ta'en our stand
When 'twas so dark you could not see your hand,
Some true-bred Falstaff, we may hope to start,
Who, when well bolstered, well will play his part.
The scene to vary, we shall try in time
To treat you with a little Pantomime.
Here light and easy Columbines are found,
And well-tried Harlequins with us abound;
From durance vile our precious selves to keep,
We often had recourse to th' flying leap;
To a black face have sometimes owed escape,
And Hounslow Heath has proved the worth of crape.
But how, you ask, can we e'er hope to soar
Above these scenes, and rise to tragic lore?
Too oft, alas! we've forced th' unwilling tear,
And petrified the heart with real fear.
Macbeth a harvest of applause will reap,
For some of us, I fear, have murdered sleep;
His lady too, with grace will sleep and talk,
Our females have been used at night to walk.
Sometimes, indeed, so various is our art,
An actor may improve and mend his part;
"Give me a horse," bawls Richard, like a drone,
We'll find a man would help himself to one.
Grant us your favour, put us to the test,
To gain your smiles we'll do our very best;
And without dread of future Turnkey Lockits,
Thus, in an honest way, still pick your pockets.

It may be doubted whether Richard Brinsley Sheridan

himself could have bettered this original and historical prologue.

But convictism, as an institution, has long since passed away in the parent colony, and nought remains to tell of its organised existence save an occasional suggestive name, that has survived the process of modern transformation into prettily-sounding titles. In Sydney harbour, for example, there stands a small rocky islet that still bears the expressive name of Pinchgut Island. In that unpleasing and somewhat vulgar appellation is embalmed the story of the prisoners who were caught in the act of pilfering provisions from the government stores in the early days of the colony, and who were dramatically punished, as a warning to the whole community, by being left without food for several days on this solitary rock, round which the sharks were continually circling.

Vaucluse, one of the prettiest spots on Sydney Harbour, has a curious and romantic history. At the beginning of the century it was chosen as his place of residence by Sir Henry Hayes, an Irish baronet, who had the misfortune to be transported for abducting the lady on whom he had set his affections, but who did not see her way to reciprocate his tender passion. Though technically a prisoner, Sir Henry's rank and social position caused him to be treated by the authorities as a privileged person, and he was allowed a full measure of freedom on his giving his word of honour that he would make no attempt to leave the colony and return to Ireland. Sir Henry accepted his fate with philosophical resignation, and commenced to build a new home for himself on the beautiful estate which he had purchased and called Vaucluse. But though the place was, and still is, one of the loveliest spots on earth, it had at that time one serious and annoying drawback. It was infested with snakes. One day, however, a bright idea struck Sir Henry as he was cogitating on the subject, and wondering if there were any practicable means of ridding himself of these unwelcome intruders. He resolved to try a bold and remarkable experiment. He would see whether the virtue of St. Patrick's prohibition of snakes on Irish soil would extend to the same soil if transferred to the other side of the world. He accordingly sent home for a number of barrels of Irish soil, and they arrived in Sydney in due course. Sir Henry then spread this imported earth as far as it would go around his residence, with the result, very gratifying to himself, that his domestic precincts were never afterwards troubled by snakes, although the other portions of the estate continued to be infested by the reptiles. Succeeding occupants of Vaucluse, amongst them the distinguished statesman, W. C. Wentworth, all agree in testifying to the singular fact that a snake was never known to cross the charmed circle of Irish earth.

The "well-known and highly popular alderman and member of the Legislative Assembly, and of genially Milesian extraction," whom Mr. George Augustus Sala met in Sydney and thus described, is Mr. Daniel O'Connor, a typical specimen of the industrious and unconquerable Celt. He told the story of his life at a banquet given last year in his honour, when he assumed office as Postmaster-General in the Ministry of Sir John Robertson. It is worth quoting as a characteristic specimen of the ups and downs of colonial life, and as showing how a brave-hearted Irishman can triumph over all the obstacles that ill fortune may cast in his path. Mr. O'Connor informed a distinguished company on that occasion that he commenced to earn a livelihood for himself at the early age of ten. In 1865 he started business for himself in the city of Sydney, and he worked with such industry and perseverance that he realised a considerable fortune in six years' time. In 1871 he was the possessor of fourteen houses, and had over £7,000 to his credit. Then he launched into mining speculations, with the result that in five months he lost everything he possessed. He sold all his houses, and although he paid every man as far as the money went, he was still left very largely in debt. But he did not lose heart at this sudden revolution in his fortunes. He set to work again at his legitimate avocation, and, at the end of seven years, he was in the proud position of paying everybody twenty shillings in the pound, besides being in receipt of a clear income of £1,000 a year—the reward of untiring industry and dauntless courage in fighting the up-hill battle of life.

Sydney has of late years made such rapid strides in population and commercial importance that it is now almost on an equality with its great southern rival, Melbourne; and the competition between these two chief centres of colonial life is now characterised by the keenest intensity. Political considerations enter largely into this struggle for supremacy, for at Sydney free-trade is the orthodox gospel; whereas, at Melbourne, protection to native industries has been the settled fiscal policy of the country for years by the deliberate vote of the great majority of the people. Time alone will tell which of these opposing systems is the best adapted to the development and the material well-being of the colonies. Besides Sydney, there are several other prosperous cities and towns in the parent colony—notably Newcastle, Maitland, Bathurst, and Goulburn—all largely peopled by the industrious Irish, who constitute a third of the general population of New South Wales. In the rural districts also are numerous agricultural and pastoral settlers, either of Irish birth or of Irish parentage, the possessors of smiling, productive homesteads, and members of a free and independent yeomanry.

There cannot be the slightest doubt that New South Wales contains within her wide domain all the elements of permanent prosperity. Her mineral resources are both extensive and valuable. Her coal mines in the basin of the Hunter river will be a source of industrial wealth for many years to come, as on them the sister colonies are mainly dependent for a supply. Her gold-fields are by no means yet exhausted, and the richness of her pastoral resources is unsurpassed. Wool is her staple product, and, as is well known, it commands a high price in the home markets. She has acquired to a great extent the large and growing river trade of the Murray and its tributaries, and is pushing her railways in every direction with commendable vigour and enterprise. It is no wonder, therefore, that her people now confidently predict that she will soon overtake the haughty Victoria, and once more wear the laurels of colonial supremacy.

# CHAPTER X.

## FOUR OF THE FAMILY.

SOUTH AUSTRALIA—A NOVEL EXPERIMENT IN COLONISATION—RICH COPPER MINES—WHEAT-GROWING CAPABILITIES—IRISH EMIGRATION TO SOUTH AUSTRALIA—ADDRESS OF ST. PATRICK'S SOCIETY TO THEIR COUNTRYMEN AT HOME—WESTERN AUSTRALIA—ITS IMMENSE EXTENT AND UNDEVELOPED RESOURCES—THE LAST OF THE PENAL SETTLEMENTS—FENIAN EXILES—JOHN BOYLE O'REILLY—J. K. CASEY—DR. R. R. MADDEN, COLONIAL SECRETARY—TASMANIA—ITS EARLY DEGRADATION—ITS DELIGHTFUL SCENERY—THE TRANSPORTED MEN OF '48—SMITH O'BRIEN—THOMAS FRANCIS MEAGHER—TERENCE BELLEW McMANUS—JOHN MITCHEL—JOHN MARTIN—KEVIN IZOD O'DOHERTY—NEW ZEALAND—MAORI WARS—CAREER OF TE KOOTI—A COURAGEOUS IRISHWOMAN—ACTIVITY AND ENTERPRISE IN THE COLONY—MINERAL WEALTH—LIBERAL IMMIGRATION POLICY—IRISH SETTLEMENT IN THE ISLANDS.

So much of what has been said in previous chapters, concerning the progress of colonisation in Victoria, New South Wales, and Queensland, and the concurrent advance of the Irish citizens of these states, applies with equal force and truth to the other four colonies in the Australasian dominion, that, to avoid recapitulation, it will be most convenient to place South Australia, Western Australia, Tasmania and New Zealand under a general heading, and regard them as forming an harmonious family group at the antipodes. The colony of South Australia was founded almost simultaneously with Victoria, but in a far different manner. In 1836 an English enthusiast, Edward Gibbon Wakefield, propounded a new and fantastical scheme of colonisation, which, as is usually the case, attracted many by its novelty

13—2

alone. The scheme, viewed as a theory, looked very sound
and substantial, but, as not unfrequently happens with
brilliant theories, it failed miserably when put into
practice. Briefly summarised, Wakefield's scheme consisted
in placing a high value on land, in order to attract a socially
superior class of intending colonists, and thus forming a
fund by which labour, both skilled and unskilled, could be
obtained at low rates. On this novel principle it was proposed to form a model community of labourers, artisans,
and land-owners. The waste land of New South Wales
could be purchased without difficulty at the rate of five
shillings per acre, but, in order to carry out the rose-water
theory of Wakefield, the land of the proposed new colony
was valued at twelve shillings per acre, or 120 per cent.
above its presumably actual value. Surprising as it may
appear, it is no less true that this chimerical project
made numerous converts throughout England, and received the support of many eminent men, who afterwards
no doubt wondered exceedingly what on earth induced
them to lend their names to such a hare-brained scheme.
The promoters, amongst whom were Grote, the historian
of Greece, and Henry Bulwer, had no difficulty in forming
the South Australian Association on the principles laid
down by the sanguine Wakefield. Dr. Whately was one o
the most enthusiastic advocates of the scheme, and, on one
occasion, he waxed eloquent in describing its splendid ad
vantages. "A colony so founded," he said, "would fairly
represent English society. Every new-comer would have hi
own class to fall into, and to whatever class he belonged, he
would find its relations to the others, and the support de
rived from the others, much the same as in the paren
country. There would be little more revolting to the feel

ings of an emigrant than if he had merely shifted his residence from Sussex to Cumberland or Devonshire." It is a great pity that this clerical orator did not accompany those to whom he addressed these delusive words. Had he done so, he would have discovered the enormous gulf that separates theory from actuality, and would have been furnished by experience with material for an additional chapter to his well-known treatise on "Logic." Had he voyaged to the antipodes with the Wakefield pioneers, he would have come in contact with a great many things " revolting to the feelings of an emigrant." However, until the bubble burst, all went merry as a marriage-bell. The association progressed splendidly in public confidence, the prospectus of the new colony was everywhere perused, and the scheme was puffed into a feverish existence by the promises of promoters and the frenzy of reckless speculators.

The first practical step towards the formation of the new colony was taken in May, 1836, when a heterogeneous collection of surveyors, clerks, architects, engineers, teachers, lawyers and clergymen, was despatched to the new land of promise. All these accomplished gentlemen were devout believers in the Wakefield theory, but they would have been the last people in the world chosen by a common-sense leader for the rough-and-ready work of pioneer colonisation. As they afterwards learned to their cost, it would have been far better for them if they had had less book-knowledge and more hand-skill before starting on their wild-goose expedition to the other side of the globe. They found on landing, that the place of which they had heard and read such glowing accounts, was wholly unfit for purposes of settlement. All their delicious old-world dreams were rudely dispelled by the hard realities that stared them in the face. They set out in search of a suitable site for a settlement, and after exploring St. Vincent Gulf chose a position on its eastern shore, a large fertile plain bounded on the east by a mountain range, and traversed by a small river, on the banks of which they settled down, and named their infant city Adelaide, in compliment to the Queen of William the Fourth.

Whilst the first settlers were thus contending with the unexpected difficulties of their position, the London promoters of this ill-digested scheme continued their policy of puffing its alleged advantages, with the result that large numbers of deluded individuals were despatched to the antipodes before any adequate preparations had been made for their reception. These unlucky people were discharged at Port Adelaide as so much human freight, and found themselves compelled to drag their luggage and merchandise after them to the little settlement. To add to the difficulties of the situation, a most pernicious system of gambling in land orders sprang up, and to such an extent did this mischievous speculating proceed, that the future city was actually mapped out as consisting of nine square miles. It would be impossible in a cursory sketch to refer in detail to the numerous absurdities that were perpetrated by the pioneer colonists of South Australia.

Suffice it to say that the reign of speculation came to its inevitable and inglorious collapse in a very short space of time, and the usual unhappy consequences ensued. The unfortunate victims of the broken-down Wakefield theory found that they had been living all the while in airy castles of their own imagination, and had been trading on fictitious capital. They were literally reduced to the direst extremities of poverty. In the excitement of the speculation mania, the natural fertility of the soil was lost sight of, and had it not been for the assistance rendered by the adjacent colonies of Victoria and New South Wales, the Wakefield settlement would have been involved in all the horrors of famine. Thus ended this celebrated attempt to found a colony on abstract scientific principles, and without reference to the suggestions of common sense. The Wakefield experiment, like all other socialistic enterprises of the kind that have been once tried, was never repeated.

Consequent on the collapse of the Wakefield scheme, a general exodus ensued, and Adelaide, the city of nine square miles on paper, ceased for a time to have any actual existence. A happy accident, however, saved the place from complete and utter abandonment. This was the discovery of copper, a discovery that caused a revolution in the fortunes of the colony, and served in a great measure as an antidote to the evils of fantastical colonisation. Mine after mine was opened up, and it was soon ascertained that the settlement had permanent mineral resources of great value. The most famous mines are the Burra Burra, the Kapunda, the Wallaroo and the Moonta. From the Burra Burra mine copper to the value of £5,000,000 sterling has been raised, and the quantity of ore obtained from the Wallaroo is represented by a still higher amount. When the excitement that followed the discovery of copper cooled down, a new source of wealth was found in the agricultural resources of the soil, and South Australia has ever since ranked amongst the finest wheat-growing countries on the face of the earth.

On July 7th, 1849, the members of the St. Patrick's ociety of South Australia issued an address to their countrymen at home, expressive of gratitude to God for the prosperity with which their labours in the southern land had been rewarded, and of commiseration for the dire distress and suffering with which it had pleased Providence to afflict their brothers in blood and affection in the old country. It was their anxious desire, they said, to make an effort to lighten the sorrow, to cheer the hopes and to invigorate the energies of their suffering brethren by making known to them a "land flowing with milk and honey," a land of refuge from the political and social evils under which Ireland groaned, a land of rest for their weary spirits, and of promise for their rising sons and daughters.

In this fraternal address, the colony of South Australia was described as "a country where the reward of steady industry, prudence, and sobriety, is certain, where the labour of comparatively few years will ensure a homestead and a competence to the working man and his family—even wealth, abundance, and social advancement to many; where the climate is generally salubrious and agreeable, and where none but freemen tread the soil." But every picture must have its due proportion of shade, and in accordance with that universal principle, the succeeding paragraph of the address intimates to the intending emigrant that "You must be prepared to labour hard, to endure privations, to toil occasionally under a burning sun and a scorching wind, and to suffer loneliness in the bush (for there you must rear your home or work out the means of purchasing one)." A rich recompense is predicted for the Irish emigrant who possesses the manly qualities of resolute perseverance, sobriety, and frugality. An Irishman of determination, undaunted by the inevitable difficulties of a newly-settled land, would be sure in the course of time to accumulate means, create a property, and attain a position of security and comfort, that would enable him to cheer the hearts, and close in comfort the eyes, of his aged parents, besides offering unthought-of advantages to his little ones. That this is no exaggerated statement is proved by facts within the personal knowledge of the writers of the address. "We are happy to state that a large portion of the Irish labourers who have arrived in this province, have, within a period of a few years, been enabled to withdraw themselves from the labour market, to become proprietors of land and stock, and employers of labour. The man who on his native soil was a careworn, toilworn being, living in a wretched hovel, without a chance of improving his circumstances, ill-clad, hungry, hopeless, with no motive for exertion, no work for more than half the year, getting a pittance of sixpence to tenpence a day, yet paying a high rent for his miserable holding, and competing to the death for its possession—this man of despair, transferred to a land of peace, with hope before him to stimulate his energies, and lead them into a right direction, here at length finds his services valuable and well remunerated; and learning for the first time in his life the luxury of feeling that he too can earn something to save, and that he occupies a higher position in the social scale, unfolds qualities that never seemed to belong to the national character."

This inspiriting address was signed by the Hon. Major O'Halloran, President of the St. Patrick's Society; Mr. R. R. Torrens, Collector of Customs, Vice-President; Sir George Kingston; the Hon. Captain Bagot, M.L.C., and a number of other representative Irish colonists. Its publication in Ireland naturally induced many intending emigrants to select South Australia as their future home, but the Imperial authorities seemed to still cling to the old unfortunate Wakefield idea that this particular colony must be kept socially superior to all the rest. Acting under this excessively stupid notion, they did their best to discourage Irish immigration, and the local St. Patrick's Society was compelled to send home a remonstrance against the unfair distinctions that were being made in the choice of immigrants. Under date "Adelaide, July 14, 1849," Sir Henry E. F. Young, governor of South Australia, wrote to Earl Grey, Secretary of State for the Colonies, commending to his favourable notice a memorial from the St. Patrick's Society of the colony, praying that Irish labourers might be shipped from Ireland direct, by the Land and Emigration Commissioners, in equal relative numbers to the English and Scotch labourers who were brought out at the expense of the colonial funds. In the memorial referred to, the members of St. Patrick's Society directed Earl Grey's attention to the fact that their countrymen, who were desirous of proceeding to South Australia, were not receiving a fair share of the facilities and encouragement to which they were entitled at the hands of the home authorities. In proof of this statement, statistics were quoted, showing that the proportion of English to Irish emigrants was as twenty to one. The memorialists further declared that it had come to their knowledge that English agents had in various instances refused to give passages to Irish emigrants, qualified in all respects, solely because they were Irish. And they concluded with a direct intimation to his lordship that they were prepared to prove that the Irish emigrants of South Australia were as orderly, industrious and thrifty as their brethren of England and Scotland, and made equally good colonists.

On December 15th, 1849, Earl Grey replied to the effect that he thought it right to refer the questions raised in the memorial, for the consideration of the Land and Emigration

Commissioners, a copy of whose report he enclosed. The Commissioners admitted that taking South Australia by itself, it had not received its equitable proportion of Irish emigrants, a state of things which they attributed to the peculiar circumstances under which that particular colony was founded. "The first settlers," they remarked, "were, with few exceptions, English capitalists, who had acquired by purchase the right of nominating emigrants for free passages and who chiefly selected English labourers." Taking the Australian colonies as a whole, the Commissioners alleged that Ireland had received ample justice in the matter of emigration.

The effect of this energetic remonstrance was that something more closely resembling fair play was afterwards meted out to intending Irish emigrants to South Australia, and a goodly number of them were brought out and satisfactorily settled on the land. Adelaide, the capital of the colony, grew apace, and is now a handsome, well-planned, and well-regulated city of 120,000 inhabitants.

Western Australia enjoys the curious distinction of being at the same time the largest and the least populous of the Australian colonies. It is eight times as large as Great Britain and Ireland, and comprises the immense tract of country lying between the 13th and 35th parallels of latitude, and stretching from the 129th meridian to the Indian Ocean. Its area is estimated at 975,920 square miles or 625 millions of acres, whilst, in striking contrast to this immensity of space, the population does not exceed forty thousand souls. A considerable portion of this huge expanse is not yet thoroughly explored, and the population is practically limited to a small sea-coast area on the south-western side. A "French scare" was the moving impulse that led to the foundation of this colony. In 1829 the Sydney governor, Sir Ralph Darling, heard a rumour that the French intended establishing a colony on the western side of the Australian continent, and forthwith resolved to checkmate the audacious foreigners by anticipating them. An expedition was accordingly fitted out, a landing was effected at the mouth of the Swan River, and the colony was duly proclaimed. However, the French never put in an appearance in the neighbourhood, and the settlement until quite recently had but a very precarious sort of existence. In 1849, at a critical period in the history of the place, the colonists took the extraordinary course of petitioning the Imperial authorities to send out a consignment of prisoners. This reads strangely by the side of what has already been said concerning the herculean efforts made by the other colonies to put a stop to transportation, but the fact was that labour was absolutely unprocurable at that time in Western Australia, and the colonists saw clearly that the settlement would have to be abandoned unless labour of some description, free or bond, was speedily introduced. The authorities at home were only too glad to comply with a request to send out a cargo of first-class felons and enterprising burglars. With a celerity and promptitude they never exhibited in redressing the substantial grievances of the colonists, they despatched upwards of ten thousand convicts, whose labour is described as being of incalculable benefit to the settlement, and to have actually proved its salvation. When, in consequence of the pressure brought to bear by the other colonies, transportation was entirely abolished, the Western Australians went so far as to petition against the cessation of the system as likely to prove prejudicial to their material interests. Fortunately for their neighbours, this selfish prayer was not granted. Amongst the convicts transported to Western Australia were several of the Fenian prisoners of twenty years ago, one of whom, John Boyle O'Reilly, after successfully escaping to America, published an interesting story of Western Australian life, under the title of "Moondyne." Mr. O'Reilly has since achieved a series of literary successes in the United States, and now stands in the front rank of American writers. J. K. Casey (Leo), the author of the popular poem, "The Rising of the Moon," was another of the Fenian prisoners deported to Western Australia. Dr. R. R. Madden, the writer of that splendid monumental work, "The Lives and Times of the United Irishmen," also spent some time in this colony, though not as a captive of the Crown. For three years the industrious historian of '98 filled the office of Colonial Secretary of Western Australia.

It is only within the last few years that the resources of this vast territory have come to be estimated at their right value. The explorations of Giles and Forrest have brought to light millions of acres of rich pastoral country, most of which has been taken up and occupied by enterprising capitalists from the adjoining colonies. Gold, too, has been discovered in considerable quantities, and what is known as the Kimberley district of the colony has been rushed by adventurous diggers from all parts of Australasia. Railways have been started in various directions; public works have been commenced on an extensive scale, and a liberal system of immigration has been adopted with a view to supplying the colony with its greatest need—a population in some measure proportionate to the vastness of its area and its undeveloped resources. The olive, the vine, and the orange grow with the greatest luxuriance, and, in the immense forests of jarrah timber, with which the country is studded, a valuable article of export is found. If only she can induce a full tide of immigrants to flow to her shores, Western Australia will, before long, rank amongst the richest provinces to the south of the equator.

Tasmania, the smallest but prettiest of the colonies, was, up to the date of the abolition of transportation, known as Van Diemen's Land—the title bestowed upon it by its discoverer, Abel Jansen Tasman. But, when the colony decided on turning over a new leaf and getting rid of the unpleasant associations of convictism, it was deemed advisable to re-christen the island, and thus it is now named after the enterprising Dutch navigator by whom it was first descried. Tasmania is a small but beautiful island situated to the south of Victoria, from which it is separated by Bass Straits. It has an area of 26,375 square miles. Its history is almost a counterpart of that of New South Wales, as it was colonised from the parent settlement for the express purpose of forming a second penal colony. This took place about the beginning of the century, and from that time up to the year 1854, the lovely island was a theatre on whose stage were enacted all the horrors incidental to the presence of rampant convictism. In some respects the picture is even blacker than that of New South Wales during the same period, the daughter revelling in greater infamy than the mother. It would be impossible for any pen to adequately describe the frightful excesses of the early days of Tasmania, but the condition of the island may be conjectured from the following words of Sir James Mackintosh in the House of Commons: "The settlement can never be worse than it is now, when no attempt towards reformation is dreamed of, and when it is governed on principles of political economy more barbarous than those which prevailed under Queen Bess." A government inspector of public works describes the moral depravity as "unparalleled in any age," and one horrified historian sums the island up as "that den of thieves, that cave of robbers, that cage of unclean birds, that isthmus between earth and hell." Sales of wives, public and private, were occurrences so common as to cause not the slightest comment. Several authenticated records of such transactions are still extant in the colonial archives. One lady of some personal attractions was publicly sold in the streets of Hobart, the capital of the island, for fifty ewes; another charmer changed hands for five pounds and a gallon of rum; whilst a third accommodating lady was disposed of for twenty ewes and a gallon of rum. The present Roman Catholic Bishop of Birmingham, Dr. Ullathorne, who was one of the earliest missionaries to the island, in his evidence before a parliamentary committee on transportation, horrified that body with the startling picture he presented of the frightful immoralities connected with convict life in Tasmania.

But this terrible state of things has entirely passed away. The dead past has buried its dead; the island is now purified; as in the parent colony, free immigration has gradually extinguished the evils and almost the remembrance of the convict days, and a new Tasmania has arisen on the ruins of the old penal Van Diemen's Land. As the island has one of the finest climates in the world, it is a favourite resort for excursionists during the summer season. On the subject of the enchanting scenery of Tasmania, many writers have exhausted the vocabulary of praise. John Mitchel's "Jail Journal," in particular, contains some exquisite descriptions of the loveliness of the interior of this "isle of beauty." And his brother-exile, Thomas Francis

Meagher, has written on the same theme in this rapturous strain: "So far as heaven has ordered, and the Divine Hand has blessed it, it is a beautiful, noble island. In most, if not all, of those gifts which constitute the strength, the true wealth, and grandeur of a country, it has been beneficially endowed. The seas which encompass it, the lakes and rivers which refresh and fertilise it, the woods which shadow, and the genial sky which arches it, all bear testimony to the bounteous will of its Creator; and, with sights of the brightest colouring, and sounds of the finest harmony, proclaim the goodness, munificence and power of God in its behalf. The climate is more than healthful: it is invigorating and inspiring. Breathing it, manhood preserves its bloom, vivacity, and vigour long after the period at which, in other lands, those precious gifts depart, and the first cold touch of age is felt. Breathing it, age puts on a glorious look of health, serenity, and gladness; and even when the gray hairs have thinned, seems able yet to fight a way through the snows, and storms, and falling leaves of many a year to come. Oh, to think that a land so blest, so rich in all that renders life happy, bountiful and great—so kindly formed to be a refuge and a sweet abiding place in these latter times for the younger children of the old, decrepid, worn-out world at home—to think that such a land is doomed to be the prison, the workshop, and the grave of the empire's outcast poverty, ignorance and guilt! This is a sad, revolting thought, and the reflections which spring from it cast a gloom over the purest and the happiest minds. Whilst so black a curse lies on it, no heart, however pious, generous, and benignant it may be, could love this land, and speak of it with pride. May that dark destiny of hers be soon reversed! From the pillar to which she is bound; from the derision and the contumely; from the buffeting and the blows she is doomed to bear in this her night of weakness and humiliation; from the garments of scorn, the crown of torture, and the gall they have given her to drink; may the brave spirit of her sons decree to her a deliverance—speedy, blissful and eternal!"* As every one knows, it was to Tasmania that some of the most prominent leaders of the Young Ireland party were expatriated at the close of the State trials of '48. William Smith O'Brien, Thomas Francis Meagher, Terence Bellew McManus, and Patrick O'Donoghue reached Hobart, the capital of the island, on October 27, 1849, in Her Majesty's steamer "Swift." Four days afterwards the "Emma" arrived, having John Martin and Kevin Izod O'Doherty on board, and the "Neptune" followed with the most belligerent and irreconcilable State prisoner of all— the ex-editor of the *United Irishman*, John Mitchel. On landing in their place of exile, the Irish leaders were offered tickets-of-leave, under which they would be severally assigned to different districts as their place of abode, and by the acceptance of which they would be giving their word of honour not to leave their respective localities without having previously given due notice of their intention to the authorities. As the alternative to this arrangement was rigorous imprisonment, with the repulsive prospect of forced association with the vilest of criminals, the exiled chiefs, with one exception, very naturally and properly accepted the proffered indulgence and comparative liberty. McManus was sent to the Launceston or northern district of the colony; Meagher was appointed to reside in the neighbourhood of Campbell-

---

* Meagher to Duffy. *Nation* Correspondence.

town; Mitchel and Martin were allowed to live together at Bothwell; O'Donoghue was assigned to New Norfolk, and O'Doherty, being an incipient doctor of medicine, was retained in Hobart, where his professional services were utilised on the staff of St. Mary's Hospital. The men of '48 were thus carefully dispersed through the island in a manner that prevented anything like social friendly intercourse, except on those rare and stolen occasions so sympathetically described by Mitchel in his "Jail Journal." "I do complain," wrote Meagher, "that having separated us by so many thousand miles of sea from all that was dear, consoling, and inspiring to our hearts, they should have still further increased the severity of this sentence by distributing us over a strange land, in which the best friendship we could form would compensate but poorly for the loss of the warm, familiar, gay companionship we so long enjoyed together." *

The exception to the general rule was Smith O'Brien, whose stern and uncompromising adherence to what he conceived to be the right course under the circumstances, precluded him from giving a pledge of any sort to the colonial representatives of the British authorities. The Tasmanian Government had therefore no option but to specially guard their iron-willed State prisoner, and they treated him like another Napoleon. Maria Island, a lonely, cheerless spot, was made a prison for his special benefit, and the vigilance with which he was guarded, was redoubled and rendered more painful than ever to the high-born captive after an unlucky and unsuccessful attempt to escape. Smith O'Brien did eventually, and after protracted sufferings accept a ticket-of-leave like his comrades in exile, and

* Meagher to Duffy. *Nation* Correspondence.

it is greatly to be deplored that he could not see his way to do so in the first instance, as his refusal was a source of considerable pain, humiliation, and annoyance to himself, and of no little embarrassment to the colonial authorities. After five years' banishment, Smith O'Brien, Martin, O'Doherty, and O'Donoghue received a conditional pardon from the Crown, the proviso being that they must not set foot within the United Kingdom, an unworthy disqualification that was subsequently removed. Meagher, McManus, and Mitchel had, in the meantime, succeeded in escaping to America, and were in consequence not named in the Queen's proclamation of clemency. The delicate question, as to whether the mode in which Meagher and Mitchel effected their escape from Tasmania was in harmony with the conditions on which they enjoyed a comparative degree of liberty, has been a subject of discussion for many years. That the point should be a debatable one is solely due to the different interpretations placed upon the spirit of the parole. Meagher and Mitchel believed, and their belief is shared by the majority of their countrymen, that the requirements of honour and of conscience would be satisfied by giving fair notice to the local authorities of their intention to surrender the comparative liberty which had been extended to them, and by affording these said authorities an opportunity to take them into custody if they were so disposed. Smith O'Brien put the case very clearly in his speech at the banquet given in his honour by the Irishmen of Melbourne, on July 22nd, 1854,* when he was passing through that city, after his

* On this occasion Smith O'Brien was presented with a splendid vase of native gold, the gift of the Irishmen of Victoria "as a trifling testimony of our appreciation of the disinterestedness and devotion by which your past

release from captivity. "I have been complimented in the House of Commons," he said, "at the expense of my fellow-prisoners who have escaped to America, and a cheer was raised on the occasion. I trust that there are reporters now present who will convey to the world that I accept no such compliment. (Cheers.) Previously to his escape, Mr. Mitchel consulted me, and I then gave it as my opinion that if he adopted the course which he ultimately did adopt, there would be nothing dishonourable in it. If, therefore, Mr. Mitchel were guilty of having sacrificed his honour, I am equally guilty. The treatment which he had received at Port Arthur, and elsewhere, was sufficient to destroy health, and it may be a question for casuists whether, under the circumstances, a prisoner is bound by his parole. Nevertheless, he and his fellow-prisoners agreed to be bound by that parole —but not beyond the letter of the parole (cheers). There has also been some question regarding the propriety of Mr. Meagher's escape. I offer no opinion on that subject, for I was not consulted in the matter. But this I know, that Thomas Francis Meagher would never have escaped in any way that he did not deem honourable. So jealous was Mr. Meagher of his honour that, rather than suffer any imputation on it, he had actually taken his passage in a vessel bound from California to Australia, in order to deliver himself again into the hands of the British Government, and he was only restrained from his purpose by the remonstrances of his friends, who represented to him its Quixotic nature. As re-

career has been distinguished in endeavouring to promote the amelioration of the country of your birth." As a special gift from themselves, the Irish diggers on the Sandhurst gold-field sent the patriot chief a beautiful nugget of their own gold, nine pounds in weight. His two fellow-exiles, John Martin and Dr. O'Doherty, were at the same time presented with purses of two hundred sovereigns each.

gards Mr. McManus, there could be no question of parole, as he had escaped when in custody, and when a writ of Habeas Corpus had been issued to bring him before a judge. There are thus no grounds whatever for the imputations cast on my fellow-prisoners, or for the compliments paid to myself."

In his "Jail Journal," Mitchel has told the full story of his escape, of the galling disappointments he had to endure, and the numerous perils he had to evade, before he could contrive to get clear of his island prison. Meagher's flight from captivity was a more lucky, neat, and expeditious performance. In his own vindication he supplied the *New York Herald* (June 6, 1852) with the facts in these terms:

"In consequence of some misstatements regarding my escape which I have just seen in two or three of the European newspapers, and which appear to have been copied from an Australian paper, I think it right to set the true facts before the American public, to whom alone I now hold myself responsible. The remarkable kindness I have received from the press and the public generally, ever since my arrival in this noble country, and the anxiety I feel to have it understood that I am not deficient in the honourable spirit which qualifies a stranger to become its citizen, compel me to break the silence which no act or word on the part of my enemies could disturb. The facts are these: In the month of April, 1851, I was called upon to renew my parole. I did so in writing in the following words : 'I hereby pledge my word of honour not to leave the colony so long as I hold a ticket-of-leave.' I handed this pledge to the police magistrate in the open court. Any one can see it who wishes to refer to it. Towards the end of December, the same year, I came to the determination of attempting my escape. Accordingly on January 3rd last I sent the following letter to the police magistrate of the district in which I resided: 'Lake Sorrell, District of Campbelltown, Saturday, January 3rd, 1852.—Sir, Circumstances of a recent occurrence urge upon me the necessity of resigning my ticket-of-leave, and consequently withdrawing my parole. I write this letter, therefore, respectfully to apprise you that after 12 o'clock to-morrow noon I shall no longer consider myself bound by the obligations which that parole imposes. In the meantime, however, should you conceive it your duty to take me into custody, I shall, as a matter of course, regard myself as wholly absolved from the restraint which my word of honour to your government at present inflicts. I have, &c., T. F. MEAGHER.' The police magistrate received this letter at eleven o'clock the same morning. I remained in my cottage at Lake Sorrell until seven o'clock that evening. A few minutes after that hour, four of my friends arrived on horseback and communicated to me the intelligence that the police were coming up to arrest me. I went out with them into the bush and remained there about 300 yards from the cottage, until my servant brought the news that the police had arrived and were sitting in the kitchen. We mounted our horses immediately and rode down to the cottage. 100 yards from it my friends drew up. I rode on until I came close to the stable, which was within pistol-shot of the kitchen door. I drew up there and desired him to go in and tell the police I was waiting for them. He left me at once and entered the cottage. Two or three minutes elapsed—the police appeared. The moment they appeared I rose in my stirrups, called out to them that I was the prisoner they came to arrest, and defied them to do so. The challenge was echoed by my friends with three loud hearty cheers, in the midst of which I struck spurs to my horse and dashed into

the woods in the direction of the coast. Accompanied by
my generous and courageous-hearted friends, I reached the
sea-shore on Monday afternoon at a point where a boat was
in readiness to receive me. I jumped from my horse, got
into the boat, put off to sea, and beat about there for a few
days until the ship came up which, thank God, bore me at
last to a free and hospitable land. In plain words these are
the plain facts of the case, as I have written them here.
They were written by one of my friends at the house where
we changed horses on our way to the coast. The manu-
script containing them was forwarded the next morning to
the editor of the leading journal of the colony, and bore the
names of my friends, written by their own hands in attes-
tation of the truth. The men who vouched with signatures
for the truth of the statement they made, and now repeated,
are men of considerable property and highly creditable
position in the colony, and no one there would be rash
enough to speak a single word derogatory of their honour."

Of the little group of illustrious Irishmen who were
exiled to Tasmania forty years ago, there is now but one
remaining in the land of the living. Dr. O'Doherty, still
hale and vigorous, continues in the practice of his profession
at Sydney, and, by the unanimous wish of his Australian
countrymen, holds the office of president of their National
League. The stern and unbending Smith O'Brien died whilst
travelling in Wales; Mitchel returned to his native land after
an absence of a quarter of a century, and expired just after
having been elected to the House of Commons by the men of
Tipperary; he was followed to the unseen world in a few days
by his old friend and fellow-sufferer, John Martin; General
T. F. Meagher, with conspicuous bravery, led the Irish
Brigade through the great American civil war in defence of

the Union, and, by a deplorable accident, lost his life in the dark waters of the Missouri; and McManus, having died in San Francisco, was buried with national honours, his body having been conveyed across the American continent, and over the Atlantic, to the Irish metropolis, from which he had been sent into captivity thirteen years before.

The material resources of Tasmania are varied and abundant, though but inadequately developed. Its tin mines have been a source of considerable profit for years, and latterly its gold deposits, after long neglect, are being scientifically and systematically worked to advantage. In making the best use of the mineral wealth at their doors, the Tasmanians, who are said by their neighbours to be constitutionally lethargic, have an extensive field for the exercise of any latent energy and industry they may possess. At present they are principally engaged in agricultural pursuits, and Tasmanian produce always secures good prices in the home and colonial markets.

New Zealand—the "Great Britain of the South," as Captain Cook termed it—would probably object to be classed with the Australian colonies, for it has always professed a lofty and sturdy independence of the big continent in its vicinity. It consists of three islands, originally named after three of the four provinces of Ireland. North Island, or New Ulster, has an area of 44,000 square miles; Middle Island, or New Munster, is somewhat larger, having 55,000 square miles; whilst Stewart Island, or New Leinster, is very small, consisting of only 1,000 square miles. The islands are situated in the South Pacific, at a distance of 1,200 miles from the nearest part of New South Wales. They were discovered by Tasman in 1642, but were not again visited by Europeans until Cook took possession of them in 1769 in the name of the British sovereign. Numerous whaling stations were first established along the coast by enterprising Sydney merchants, and a permanent settlement was eventually effected on the site of Wellington, in the extreme south of the North Island. Wellington is now the official and political capital of the colony, having superseded its more northerly rival, Auckland, which nevertheless continues to be the larger and more populous city of the two. In 1848 a Scotch settlement was founded at the southern extremity of the Middle Island, now known as the province of Otago, whose chief city is Dunedin, the largest, most populous, and most commercial city in the group. Almost contemporaneously, the province of Canterbury, on the eastern coast of the same island, was colonised under the auspices of the Church of England, a fact sufficiently denoted by its name and that of its capital, Christchurch, one of the finest and wealthiest of the New Zealand cities.

The history of New Zealand presents a violent and startling contrast to that of the other antipodean states. In the work of colonising the mainland of Australia, no opposition worth mentioning was manifested by the natives to the coming of the whites. The aborigines retired before the new-comers without striking one combined blow. As time passed on, the white man's brandy-bottle did its silent work of destruction and extermination so effectually that now, with the exception of the remote districts of the interior, scarcely a solitary pure black is to be met with on the continent of Australia. Not so in New Zealand. There the whites found a warlike, active, intelligent, and high-spirited people in possession. The Maories declined to surrender their lands at the bidding of the invaders; a bad feeling was thus at the outset engendered between the two races, and boat-loads of the early immigrants were surprised and massacred as they stepped on the beach. Reprisals ensued, and, for a series of years, the northern island was the scene of some of the most sanguinary native wars that stain the annals of colonisation. These were in a great measure provoked by the stupidity and arbitrary conduct of the colonial authorities. On one occasion 200 Maories were seized as suspected persons, and without trial, evidence, or any form of law, banished to a penal settlement on a neighbouring small group, called the Chatham islands. Amongst them was Te Kooti, a young, brave, and daring man, whose name was in after-years a name of terror to the New Zealand settlers.* Lieutenant Gudgeon, the historian of the New Zealand wars, candidly declares it as his conviction " that all the after atrocities committed by Te Kooti or by his orders were dictated by a spirit of revenge and retribution against those who had caused his deportation." Te Kooti, by his innate military genius and natural force of character, soon became the leader of the Maori exiles. By a well-planned and skilfully-executed scheme, a Government vessel that had brought provisions for the prisoners, was captured by Te Kooti and his confederates on the morning of July 4th, 1868. He immediately released his fellow-prisoners and placed them on board the vessel. The white men that constituted the crew, were allowed by Te Kooti to take their choice between two alternatives—instant death or the navigation of the vessel to Poverty Bay, the place from

* "Te Kooti was not committed for trial, but, having been thus arrested without warrant, was shipped off to the Chatham Islands by Mr. Stafford's Government, without writ or authority of any kind, and the wrong done to him was to be written a few years later in terrible characters of blood."— "History of New Zealand," by G. W. Rusden, vol. ii. page 321.

which the Maories had been so illegally and unjustifiably transported. Naturally they chose the latter, and worked the vessel in safety to Poverty Bay. Te Kooti landed, and immediately commenced his terrible career of fanatical butchery and indiscriminate slaughter. Having defeated the colonial forces that were sent against him, his ranks were joined by other Maori tribes hostile to the British. Thus recruited, Te Kooti, one night in November, 1868, descended like an avalanche of fire on the unfortunate settlers in the district of Poverty Bay. So well was the murderous secret kept, that not the slightest precautions had been taken to guard against a Maori surprise. With the stealthy step of the tiger, Te Kooti and his bloodthirsty band surrounded house after house, shooting down the men without an instant's warning, and despatching the women and children with bayonets and tomahawks. Whole families, refusing to come out when called upon by Te Kooti, perished miserably in the flames of their burning houses. And not only the white settlers, but a number of friendly natives, who had accepted the inevitable, and had settled down to live, as they hoped, in peace with the conquerors, were surprised and slaughtered without mercy. Indeed, throughout his campaign, Te Kooti evinced an undying hatred towards those tribes of his countrymen that had become friendly to the British, and he never spared any of them when taken prisoners. The morning after the Poverty Bay massacres dawned on a desolated country. Where on the previous day there had been smiling homesteads and fertile farms, the pleasant surroundings of rustic toil and the cheerful prattle of innocent children, blackened ruins and mutilated corpses now told their silent tale of savage frenzy and ruthless destruction. As Lieutenant Gudgeon truly remarks in his history of the war, the narrow escapes of that dreadful night would fill a volume. One Irishwoman, whose husband happened to be away from home, whilst lying awake in bed, fancied she heard the firing of guns. Her suspicions being aroused, she immediately got up, and one glance at the horizon, glowing with the reflection of the incendiary fires, was sufficient to convince her of the imminent danger in which she stood. Hastily collecting her children, she slipped over the steep bank of an adjacent river, and literally crawled for miles under the shadow of the precipitous cliffs until she arrived with her children in safety at the nearest town, where she was the first to give the alarm. Many other anecdotes of that terrible time might be narrated from contemporary evidence. This massacre, it is needless to say, sent a thrill of horror through the community. Operations directed by English military officers, and supported by the colonial militia, were commenced against Te Kooti, who, during several engagements, displayed a surprising natural knowledge of military science. He understood thoroughly the advantages to be gained by rapid movement and sudden surprise, and it was on this principle that he invariably acted. No part of the northern island felt safe from a sudden attack, and every settlement was required to look to its defences. But, however successful Te Kooti might be in prosecuting this guerrilla sort of warfare, he was occasionally brought face to face with the British trained soldiers, and compelled to fight a pitched battle. Though manifesting the same stubborn and fanatical courage, he was on most of these occasions under the necessity of retreating before the steady battalions of disciplined men arrayed against him. In these engagements he lost many of his finest warriors, and, as the conflict proceeded, his little army gradually melted away, whilst the ranks of his enemies received regular accessions. Still he continued to prosecute with success his favourite Napoleonic plan of swift and sudden attack; but eventually his losses in the field reduced his devoted followers to little more than the strength of a body-guard. With this trusty few, he commenced his retreat to the Waikato, the military and a large body of friendly natives following with all possible rapidity, in the hope and almost certainty of effecting the capture of the redoubtable Maori leader, for whose body, dead or alive, the Government had offered a reward of £5,000. At this critical stage of his career, Te Kooti seemed to possess a charmed life. There were times when his camp was completely surrounded by his enemies, when he himself was recognised sitting in front of his tent, and yet, when the volley was fired, and soldiers rushed from every side, and the camp was taken by assault, Te Kooti was never amongst the slain or captured. He had escaped, no one knew how or whither. Several of the minor rebel chiefs were caught and executed, but the arch-rebel himself—the perpetrator of the Poverty Bay massacre—was never taken. Hunted over mountain and glen, with the bloodhounds ever at his heels, this extraordinary savage, after enduring every privation and escaping every peril, succeeded at length in reaching the iron fastnesses of the Waikato, where he has ever since remained, secure under the protection of the Maori King.

This latter remark demands a little explanation. New Zealand is classed as a British colony, but there is a portion of it over which neither the Queen of Great Britain nor her representative, the local governor, can be said to exercise any actual jurisdiction. This district is situated in the centre of the North Island, and is known as the Waikato, or "King Country." After a long and brave, but unsuccessful, resistance against the encroachments of the whites, a number of the leading Maori Chiefs met, and with a view to the erection of a last barrier against the invaders of their soil, resolved to proclaim the mountainous Waikato country as their sacred territory, to elect a king of their own, and to make all necessary laws for themselves. The agitation was sedulously promoted by the more turbulent and warlike chiefs, and the result was the election and proclamation of a Maori King, who took up his residence at the Waikato. The colonial authorities at first did not know how to regard this unexpected movement on the part of the Maories, and the mischief was all done before they had recovered their wits. They then saw that a fatal mistake had been committed in tacitly consenting to this assumption of independent power within the confines of the colony. Ever since, this portion of New Zealand has been a sort of *refugium peccatorum* for Maori offenders. The present Maori King—Tawhiao—has dwelt there for years in sullen seclusion, surrounded by the surviving veteran war chiefs. Here Te Kooti is somewhere concealed from the vengeance of the colonists. As long as he remains within the charmed circle of the King Country he is perfectly safe; but once he steps outside, is recognised and captured, a swift and summary penalty will be exacted in atonement for the lengthy and diabolical catalogue of crime attached to his name. It is characteristic of the dare-devil disposition of the man that, with a full knowledge of the fate in store for him, he has occasionally ventured out into the settled districts, and regained his retreat before a pursuit could be organised.

However, Te Kooti has now eluded justice for so many
years that, unless some radical change should come over
New Zealand affairs, the murderer of so many innocent men,
women and children will in all probability never expiate his
crimes on the gallows.

The "native difficulty" in New Zealand is by no means
permanently settled. It has a disagreeable habit of forcing
its way to the front when least expected; still, there is very
little probability of actual war again arising between the
Maories and the whites. The former are now too diminished
to endanger the public peace. Settlers in New Zealand are
now to all intents and purposes as free from peril as those
who have chosen homes for themselves and their families in
Victoria, New South Wales, or South Australia—colonies in
which the "native difficulty" has never been experienced.
Since the cessation of hostilities between the two races,
New Zealand has made rapid strides in material progress.
Railways and public works have been prosecuted on a very
extensive scale. Indeed, in proportion to population, this
active and enterprising colony has a greater mileage of railways than any other of the antipodean states. There are
lines of well-appointed steamers maintaining regular communication with the ports of all the islands, as well as with
Melbourne and Sydney. The exports and imports amount
to £15,000,000, and the population of the three islands now
exceeds 600,000. In addition to large droves of cattle and
horses, there are 12 millions of sheep in the colony. Official
statistics go to show that the average production of wheat is
no less than 27 bushels to the acre. In mineral resources
New Zealand has been specially favoured. Three provinces—
Otago, Westland, and Nelson—have yielded large quantities
of gold, the soil of Otago in particular being wonderfully

rich in deposits of the precious metal. There was what is colonially known as a "rush" when the news of the Otago discoveries was circulated. Crowds of Victorian miners filled the steamers *en route* to New Zealand, and, in the excitement of the moment, hundreds of educated men threw up good remunerative situations and joined in the exodus. Many of them afterwards had reason to regret their unthinking impulsiveness in preferring the pick and shovel to the pen, but most of the experienced miners did remarkably well and settled down as permanent residents. In addition to gold, almost every known variety of iron ore has been found in New Zealand, and there are also numerous coal measures continuously and profitably worked. The New Zealand Government has ever pursued a wise and liberal policy in regard to immigration, and, thanks to the commendable facilities that have been afforded, a large number of Irish families have been enabled to found new homes in the South Pacific. All honour to the men who received with open arms and words of welcome the victims of landlord oppression on the other side of the Equator, who raised no objection on the score of country or creed, but took the honest new-comers by the hand, placed them securely on the land, and formed them into happy, industrious, and contented colonists.

## CHAPTER XI.

### THE CHURCH IN THE COLONIES.

DEVOTED IRISH PRIESTS—FATHER WALSH, OF OSSORY—THREE UNJUSTLY TRANSPORTED PRIESTS, FATHERS DIXON, O'NEIL, AND HAROLD—TYRANNICAL POLICY OF THE EARLY GOVERNORS—ARRIVAL OF ARCHPRIEST O'FLINN—HIS ARREST, IMPRISONMENT, AND EXPULSION FROM AUSTRALIA —INTERVENTION OF BISHOP ENGLAND—APPOINTMENT OF FATHERS THERRY AND CONOLLY AS THE FIRST COLONIAL CHAPLAINS—ANECDOTES OF "THE GOOD FATHER THERRY"—ARCHDEACON McENCROE AND HIS LABOURS—DR. ULLATHORNE—HIS ORGANISING WORK—SIR RICHARD BOURKE AS GOVERNOR—REVERSAL OF THE OLD ANTI-CATHOLIC POLICY— ESTABLISHMENT OF RELIGIOUS EQUALITY—ARRIVAL OF THE FIRST BISHOP, DR. POLDING—ARCHBISHOP VAUGHAN—CARDINAL MORAN—ARCHBISHOP GOOLD—THE BISHOP AND THE BUSHRANGERS—DR. GEOGHEGAN— BISHOP REYNOLDS—THE SISTERS OF ST. JOSEPH—THE REV. JULIAN E. TENISON-WOODS—BISHOP WILLSON, "THE APOSTLE OF PRISON REFORM" —DR. MURPHY, THE AUSTRALASIAN NESTOR—DR. CROKE AS BISHOP OF AUCKLAND—THE FIRST AUSTRALASIAN PLENARY COUNCIL—TRIUMPH OF CATHOLICITY IN THE COLONIES.

JUST as in other distant parts of the world, the light of the Gospel has been principally spread and preserved throughout the Australian colonies by the apostolic zeal and energy of Irish priests. True sons of St. Patrick, they triumphed over the grievous official persecution of the early days, they overcame the prejudices of race and creed, and they established themselves in the land by the main force of personal merit, generous self-sacrifice, and unceasing labours for the moral and spiritual welfare of their Catholic countrymen. The governmental policy at the period of the colonisation of Australia, and for a generation afterwards, was openly and avowedly to refuse to recognise the Catholic religion at all, and to regard everybody in the settlement as belonging to the Church of England, whether he liked it or not. It was in pursuance of this shameful policy that the request of Father Walsh, of the Diocese of Ossory, Ireland, to be permitted to accompany the "first fleet" to Australia a century ago was churlishly refused by the reigning powers. Nothing but blind bigotry could have suggested such a refusal, for the request was an eminently reasonable one in the circumstances, and should have been conceded, not so much as a favour, but as a matter of strict right, and a plain duty towards the Catholic members of that pioneer band of exiles, going forth to found a new nation in an unsettled land 12,000 miles away. It was not until 1799, twelve years afterwards, that the Catholic population of the infant settlement were gratified with the sight of three ordained clergymen of their church. But it was not as clergymen that the home government had sent them out, but as convicted prisoners. Father Dixon, Father O'Neil, and Father Harold, along with the Reverend Mr. Fulton, a Protestant minister, were transported for their alleged complicity in the Irish rebellion of 1798. It has since been proved, beyond the shadow of a doubt, that these three pioneer priests of Australia were unjustly convicted, and compelled to submit to the indignity of transportation. Father Dixon was a Wexford priest and had a brother who did engage in the rebellion, but he himself exercised all his influence to keep his people within the limits of the law. Nevertheless, he had a rebel brother, and that was sufficient to condemn him in those dark days of unchecked martial law. The case of Father O'Neil was harder still. His treatment throws a lurid light on the unprincipled and unscrupulous measures that found favour in Irish governing circles towards the close of the last century. A soldier happened to be murdered in the neighbourhood of Youghal, and, as the actual culprit could not be discovered, the authorities resolved that some one must suffer for the deed, and accordingly made an indiscriminate arrest. They seized an idle, worthless scamp, and threatened him with a flogging if he did not give information as to the perpetrator of the murder. Under the influence of this threat, he promised to disclose everything, and he actually had the sacrilegious audacity to name the parish priest of Youghal, Father O'Neil, as the murderer. On the strength of this reckless assertion, and with nothing more substantial to go upon, Father O'Neil was arrested, and, horrible to relate, was cruelly flogged in the vain hope of compelling him to confess the crime or give information concerning it. After being kept in prison for a time, Father O'Neil was sent away in a felon-ship to the new convict settlement at the antipodes, but in less than a month after his departure from Ireland, his innocence was completely demonstrated. He was at once liberated by order of the Crown, brought back from Australia, and re-appointed in his old parish of Youghal, but no recompense or apology did he receive from the government for the harsh, unjust, and scandalous treatment to which he had been subjected. The impious scoundrel who bore false witness against him was subsequently convicted of heinous crimes and executed in Cork.

The case of Father Harold, though not so painful, was equally unjust. He was a hard-working priest in the parish of Dublin, and, because some of his people joined the rebels in '98, he was arrested and transported on the mere gratuitous supposition that they had taken that course with his knowledge and by his advice. After Father O'Neil's departure from the penal settlement in Sydney, his brothers in misfortune—Fathers Dixon and Harold—remained there as prisoners until April 19th, 1803, on which date the Governor of the colony, Captain P. G. King, of the Royal Navy, was pleased to issue a proclamation granting "unto the Reverend James Dixon a conditional emancipation to enable him to exercise his clerical functions as a Roman Catholic priest, which he has qualified himself for by the regular and exemplary conduct he has manifested since his residence in the colony." Father Dixon of course availed himself of this permission to resume his sacred functions in a place where they were so sadly needed, the more especially as he had received faculties from his ecclesiastical superiors at home to officiate at the antipodes as soon as he was allowed to do so. At about the same time, Father Harold's clerical status was recognised by the government, and he was placed in charge of the Catholic prisoners at Norfolk Island, a delightful spot a thousand miles away in the Pacific, which had been profaned and degraded by being perverted into a prison for the worst and most irreclaimable of convicts. Fathers Dixon and Harold were thus the first duly-appointed Roman Catholic clergymen in the Australian colonies. The former laboured devotedly for several years amongst the Catholic population of Sydney and its vicinity, but, as an historian of the era has truly remarked, "the hatred, bigotry, and jealousy with which he was surrounded, soon found a pretext to deprive him of the power of doing good." This pretext was found in certain malicious and groundless reports that reached the ears of the authorities, to the effect that Father Dixon's congregations at Mass on Sundays were in reality meetings of rebels and traitors, and that the peace of the settlement would be endangered by their continuance. Without holding any inquiry into these spiteful allegations, the Governor jumped to the conclusion that they must be correct, and, by an order in the *Government Gazette*, he suppressed the public celebration of the Mass throughout the colony. There was not a shadow of justification for this high-handed proceeding, which was only possible under a system of military despotism such as then prevailed in New South Wales. It is quite true that a convict outbreak had to be suppressed soon afterwards, but the disturbance had no connection whatever with the meetings of the Roman Catholics for public worship. Indeed, Father Dixon accompanied the commanding officer and exercised all his influence on the side of order and humanity. Nevertheless, the story that this was an attempted repetition under southern skies of the Irish insurrection of '98 received the stamp of official approval, and has been accepted as gospel by several historians who did not care to inquire too closely into the facts. But nobody believes that silly story now, for direct appeals to contemporary evidence have shown conclusively that the "Colonial Vinegar Hill," as it was long the fashion to call this convict outbreak, was not traceable either to race or creed, but was the immediate and natural result of the tyranny and the brutality of heartless overseers towards the prisoners in their charge. Father Dixon tried every possible means to obtain the removal of the governmental interdict, but without the slightest success. He was forbidden to offer up the Holy Sacrifice, to preach, to baptise, or to visit the sick. The good priest soon found his position to be intolerable, and he applied for leave to return to Ireland—a permission which was granted with a readiness and an alacrity that showed pretty plainly how the wind was blowing in high quarters. Father Harold, hearing of the sad turn affairs had taken on the continent, left his little island prison in the Pacific, in the hope of being allowed to minister to the spiritual wants of the larger Catholic population around Sydney; but, immediately on his arrival, he was suppressed and interdicted like his predecessor; and like him, too, he refused to remain in a place where his hands were tied, his mouth closed, and his eyes bandaged by order of an autocratic governor. With Father Harold's departure for Ireland, the Australian continent was left without a solitary Catholic priest, and it continued in that hapless condition of spiritual destitution for no less than nine miserable years. During the whole of this terrible time, the country was compulsorily Protestant, that is to say, prisoners of every religious belief were obliged to attend the service of the Church of England. The penalty for refusal was a flogging of twenty-five lashes. A second refusal was visited with fifty lashes, and a third would have to be expiated in the chain-gang or in the solitude of the prison cell. In these latter days, Australian Anglicans have frequently laboured hard to whitewash this foul page of their history by contending that the foregoing penalties were never actually enforced, and they have been considerably aided in this contention by the care and completeness with which the compromising records in relation to this unpleasant business have been committed to the flames. But the first quarter of our century is not so remote from our day as to preclude the possibility of reliable evidence on the point being forthcoming; and whenever the allegation has been made in the press or on the platform that the penalties for staying away from the Church of England service were not enforced, witnesses were not wanting to come forward and declare, either from their own personal knowledge or on the solemn testimony of departed friends and relatives, that these abominable penalties were enforced, and in a merciless manner too. Mr. James Bonwick, himself a Protestant, and one of the most industrious investigators into the facts of early colonial history, does not hesitate to say, in speaking of this persecuting era :

" All had to go to church; they were driven as sheep to the fold. Whatever their scruples, they had to go. Fallen as many were, they were not to be regarded as aliens altogether in principle and indifferent to faith. In some the very consciousness of crime had developed an eagerness after faith, and that the faith they had known, the faith of a mother. But expostulations were unheeded. If a man humbly entreated to stay behind because he was a Presbyterian, he incurred the danger of a flogging. It is said that upon a similar appeal from another, who exclaimed, 'I'm a Catholic!' he was silenced by the cry of a clerical magistrate, 'Go to church or be flogged!'"

In several places in his "Memoirs," Joseph Holt, or "General" Holt, as he was most frequently styled, from his being one of the chief leaders in the rebellion of '98, mentions the shocking brutality with which his fellow Irish-Catholic prisoners were treated in those dismal days. Here is one harrowing instance out of several that might be quoted: "I marched to Toongabbee, where all the government transports were kept, who were called out to witness the punishment of the prisoners. One man, Maurice Fitzgerald, was sentenced to receive 300 lashes, and the method of punishment was such as to make it most effectual. The unfortunate man had his hands extended round a tree, his two wrists tied with cord, and his breast pressed closely to the tree, so that flinching from the blows was out of the question, for it was impossible for him to stir. Two men were appointed to flog, namely Richard Rice, a left-handed man, and John Johnson, the hangman from Sydney, who was right-handed. They stood on each side of Fitzgerald, and I never saw two thrashers in a barn move their flails with more regularity than those two man-killers did, unmoved by pity, and rather enjoying their horrid employment than otherwise. The very first blows made the blood spout from Fitzgerald's shoulders, and I felt so disgusted and horrified, that I turned my face away from the cruel sight."

After nearly a decade of attempted wholesale Protestantising through the agency of the lash and the dungeon, a cheering and most welcome ray of light to the sorely-afflicted Catholics appeared on the horizon. Their pitiful condition had been made known in the centre of Catholicity, and relief was at hand. In 1817 there arrived in the settlement at Sydney the Very Rev. Jeremiah O'Flinn, with the jurisdiction of an archpriest—the first ecclesiastic who came to Australia with a direct commission from Rome. But he soon found that something more than a Papal commission was necessary for his protection in a despotically-ruled penal colony. It had struck him before sailing from Ireland that it would be well to obtain a permit of some sort from the British Government, and he forwarded an application to that effect; but he made the mistake of not waiting for a reply, and this mistake was the source of all his subsequent misfortunes. He, in fact, regarded this permit as a mere formality, and, asking a friend to forward it to him when it was prepared, he set sail in the first ship for Australia.

When he arrived in Sydney and took a survey of the situation, he realised the supreme importance of the absent document, and wisely concealed himself until it should come to hand, as he expected, in a few months' time. While he was in hiding, the leading Catholics and the liberal Protestants presented a memorial to the Governor of the day, General Macquarie, stating the circumstances of the case, and respectfully asking him to recognise the newly-arrived archpriest. True to the discreditable traditions of his office, the General's only reply to this very reasonable request was that the memorialists were guilty of a gross piece of presumption.

This answer sufficed to show what would be the fate of Father O'Flinn if his hiding-place became known to the authorities. The secret was well kept for a couple of months, during which the Catholics of Sydney, in regular batches, enjoyed the unwonted and unspeakable blessing of assisting, though by stealth, at the celebration of the holy sacrifice of the Mass. Father O'Flinn also succeeded in baptising hundreds of young Catholics who had grown up in the ten years of spiritual darkness that had covered the land. Getting bolder by degrees, he ventured into the out-settlements, collected his scattered people, celebrated mass for their benefit, and gave them instructions both in the English and the Irish language. Long years afterwards, a venerable old man told Dr. Ullathorne, now Bishop of Birmingham, that Father O'Flinn " had the sweetest and the swiftest tongue of Irish that ever I heard." The same aged colonist gave an additional significant piece of information, viz.: that he " never spoke a word of English himself until it was made fifty lashes to speak a word of Irish." When, in his zeal to remedy the mischief of the past, Father O'Flinn ventured out into the open and went about doing good, he ran the risk of arrest at any moment ; and it was not long before the priest-hunters laid their impious hands on this inoffensive clergyman and lodged him in the common gaol. There he was kept a close prisoner until a ship was about to sail for England, when he was escorted on board and sent back across the seas by the arbitrary act of a despotic governor. Thus, once again were the hopes of the Australian Catholics dashed to the ground, but they had one great consolation in their distress. Father O'Flinn had left the Blessed Sacrament in the house of one of their number, Mr. James Dempsey, of Kent street, Sydney ; * and there, in the Divine presence, the bereaved flock reverentially met on Sundays and holidays, practised the simple devotions of their Church, and kept the lamp of faith steadily burning. Worthy descendants these of the steadfast men and women of an earlier generation, who, throughout the long dark night of the penal code, worshipped and prayed in the caves and on the hillsides of Holy Ireland! As Dr. Ullathorne has sympathetically said: "It was remarkably beautiful to contemplate these men of sorrow round the Bread of Life, bowed down before the Crucified; no voice but the silent one of faith ; not a priest within ten thousand miles to offer them that pledge of pardon to repentance, whose near presence they see and feel." †

* Traditions differ on this point. Some accounts state that the house in which the Blessed Sacrament was preserved was occupied by Mr. William Davis, and that it stood in close proximity to the present site of St. Patrick's Church, Sydney.

† " Father O'Flinn was the first clergyman who came to the colony expressly with the view of ministering to the spiritual wants of the Roman Catholic part of the population. He occupied in his church the position of archpriest, an office which enabled him to perform some of those higher functions which ordinarily belong to a bishop. This, among other circumstances, made it clear that his coming was directly influenced by the great and pressing wants of that large section of the population, both free and bond, who professed his faith.

When the banished Archpriest returned to Ireland, the illustrious Dr. England, Bishop of Charleston, in the United States, happened to be on a visit to his native land, and to this able and accomplished prelate, Father O'Flinn narrated the ill-treatment and the injustice he had received at the hands of the governing powers in distant Australia. Intense was the bishop's indignation at the recital of the persecution to which the good priest had been subjected, and of the grievous wrongs inflicted on the Catholic population of the colony through being deprived of the ministrations of a clergyman of their faith. Dr. England brought the case under the notice of Lord Donoughmore, then member for Cork, by whom it was ventilated in the House of Commons, with the result that the grievance under which the Catholics of the colony had so long laboured was fully recognised, and an act of tardy justice was performed by the Imperial Government in becoming responsible for the sending out to Australia of two salaried and accredited priests. The Rev. John Joseph Therry and the Rev. Philip Conolly were the clergymen who offered to devote their lives to the service of their exiled countrymen at the antipodes. Father Therry, whose long and laborious career amidst many dangers and difficulties has justly won for him the high title of the " Apostle of the Australias," was a native of Cork, like Bishop England, the Apostle of the American Church. He entered Carlow College in his seventeenth year, and had the good

The compulsory retirement of this clergyman is the greatest, if not the only slur on the administration of Macquarie. The proceeding adopted by the authorities in forcing him to quit a community where his ministrations would have been not less valuable in a social than in a religious point of view, was the more inexcusable, inasmuch as the character and conduct of Father O'Flinn, alike as a priest and a subject, were irreproachable."—" History of New South Wales," by Roderick Flanagan, vol. i. page 215.

fortune of studying for the priesthood under the famous theologian and controversialist, Dr. Doyle, more widely known under his episcopal initials "J. K. L." Ordained in 1815, Father Therry was appointed to a curacy in his native city of Cork, and it was there he met the returned Archpriest O'Flinn, the victim of governmental intolerance at the antipodes. This memorable meeting was the turning-point in the young priest's career. He listened with intense interest to the sad account of oppression and cruel wrongs in a faraway land, and his sympathies were powerfully excited on behalf of his suffering countrymen in Australia, whom he pictured in his mind as holding out their hands, like the vision of St. Patrick of old, and crying out in piteous accents, "Come and abide with us!" Having got the consent of his bishop, and being provided with the necessary credentials from the Imperial Government, the devoted missionary, in company with his colleague, Father Conolly, sailed from the Cove of Cork in the ship "Janus" on December 5th, 1819. They arrived safely in Sydney Harbour at the beginning of May, and presented their credentials to General Macquarie, the same governor who had behaved so badly towards Archpriest O'Flinn. Commissioned as they were by the home authorities, the governor had no option but to receive and recognise Fathers Therry and Conolly, but he showed that his prejudices were as strong as ever by sending them a series of dictatorial written instructions for their guidance. The two newly-arrived priests were warned on their peril "not to try to make converts from the members of the Church of England or from Protestants in general." They were enjoined not to celebrate Mass publicly "except on Sundays and the holidays of the Church of England." But the most outrageous restriction of all was that Fathers Therry and Conolly "were not to interfere with the religious instruction of the Catholic children in the orphan schools, all the inmates of which are to be instructed in the faith and doctrines of the Church of England." Father Therry never lost an opportunity of protesting with all his might against this tyrannical and infamous decree. In punishment of his pertinacity, he was once suspended from his clerical office by the government for a considerable period, and it was only after an appeal to the Imperial authorities that he was reinstated. It is needless to say that the indomitable priest triumphed eventually, and vindicated the right of the Catholic Church to the spiritual control and training of her own children.

Soon after their arrival, the two priests resolved to separate in order that they might achieve a maximum of good, Father Conolly taking charge of the growing settlement in Van Diemen's Land in the far south, whilst Father Therry remained in the parent settlement at Sydney. He lost no time in setting about the erection of a suitable church, for, up to that time, the Catholic population of Sydney, though numbering 10,000, had no ecclesiastical edifice they could call their own. So much success attended his exertions that, in the year after his arrival in the colony, the foundation-stone of the old St. Mary's Cathedral—the precursor of the present noble structure—was laid amidst great congratulations and rejoicings. For five long years did Father Therry labour devotedly, without the assistance of a brother priest, amongst the Catholics of the settled districts of New South Wales. Many are the anecdotes related of his uncompromising zeal, energy, and determination in the discharge of his sacred duties. Mr. Bonwick records that on one occasion the good priest received a message that a convict, who had been sentenced to death, had expressed a desire to see him and make a last confession. The time was short; a long distance had to be traversed; the roads were in a very bad condition, and the rivers were flooded. After a weary day's ride, Father Therry found his progress barred in the evening by a raging torrent, into which his horse could not possibly go, and on which no boat could live. But the brave priest was determined to reach his destination, and carry succour to a departing soul at all hazards. Seeing a man on the opposite side of the torrent, he asked him for help in God's name. The man, understanding the urgency of the case, procured a rope, and by means of a stone attached to a cord, threw it over to Father Therry, who hesitated not an instant, but tying the rope around his body, jumped into the swollen stream and was dragged across through the foaming waters. Without stopping for rest or changing his clothes, the *Soggarth Aroon* mounted another horse, and arrived just in time to give absolution to the doomed convict on the scaffold.

At another time, during the period of his unjustifiable suspension by the reigning governor, Father Therry was informed that a Catholic was dying in a prison hospital. It was late at night, and, when he came to the door, an armed sentry opposed his entrance. "I must come in," said the zealous priest. "My orders; I cannot permit you to pass," was the soldier's reply, as he brought his weapon into position. "But," Father Therry persisted in tones of anguish, "a Catholic is dying within—I am the priest—his eternal loss or salvation may depend on you—now which is your first duty?" The soldier was unable to resist this pathetic appeal. He clapped his musket to his side, and Father Therry walked in to give consolation to a departing soul.

A contemporary of this distinguished Irish-Australian missionary has summed up his character and career in a sentence: "Neither time, nor distance, nor danger—and his duties were often performed at the real peril of life—ever impeded or obstructed him in the zealous performance of the sacred duties of his mission." It was his custom on Christmas-day to celebrate his midnight mass in Sydney, a second mass in Liverpool, and a third at Campbelltown, spending the whole of the subsequent week amongst the scattered Catholic families in the interior. Wherever he went, every door was ready to receive him, and Protestants vied with Catholics in extending assistance and hospitality to the general favourite. Disputes arising between neighbours were as a rule referred to him for arbitration, and Father Therry's decision was invariably accepted as final by both parties. Truly has it been said of him that " in the days of transportation he was the chief comforter and friend of the convicts of his creed, and no minister has enjoyed, in a larger measure than this truly reverend man has done throughout his long career, the confidence and affection of both bond and free."

In 1826 Ireland sent the indefatigable pioneer a helper in the person of Father Daniel Power, and, a few years afterwards, a still more important acquisition arrived, the Rev. John (subsequently Archdeacon) McEncroe. A native of Rathsalla, near Cashel, in Tipperary, Father McEncroe devoted the early years of his priesthood to missionary work under Bishop England in the United States. There for seven years he preached and lectured, established a Catholic newspaper, and combated the now overthrown institution of slavery with a vigour and determination that made him an object of numerous threats from the exasperated dealers in human flesh. Unceasing work at high pressure almost ruined his health, and he was forced to return to Ireland. After an interval of comparative repose, he was nominated to a vacant bishopric in the United States ; but, acting on a providential inspiration, and with the approval of the then Archbishop of Dublin, Dr. Murray, he declined the proffered well-earned promotion, and accepted the hard lot of an humble missionary amongst his exiled countrymen in Australia. Years before, he had seen in Clonmel, Tipperary, a prison-van full of unfortunate fellows about to be transported to the antipodes. Running into a neighbouring bookseller's shop, the thoughtful priest soon emerged with three dozen Catholic prayer-books, which he threw into the van as so much spiritual bread upon the waters. Years afterwards, he had the supreme satisfaction of seeing several of these identical prayer-books in the houses of prosperous settlers in the far interior of New South Wales—a remarkable transformation of that dismal and discouraging scene in Clonmel, when he first saw the men and handled the books. Apart from his conspicuous services on behalf of the moral and spiritual elevation of the Catholic prisoners that were sent to Australia, Archdeacon McEncroe will long be remembered for the prominent part he played in the establishment of the leading charitable institutions of Sydney. He was also the founder of the Sydney *Freeman's Journal*, a high-class literary weekly newspaper, which, together with the Melbourne *Advocate*, has for many years ably and consistently upheld and defended Irish and Catholic interests in the southern hemisphere. During his lifetime he was himself the chief, the most scholarly, and the most extensive contributor to its columns. One of its editors was a distinguished member of an Irish literary and patriotic family, viz., Richard O'Sullivan, a brother of that lamented orator, author, and journalist, A. M. Sullivan, and of that, happily, still living devoted Nationalist leader and patriotic poet, T. D. Sullivan, M.P., editor of the *Nation*. When he revisited Ireland in 1859, he brought back with him to Australia the Rev. Dr. Forrest as the first rector of the now-flourishing St. John's College, affiliated to the University of Sydney. In short, Archdeacon McEncroe is fully entitled to share with Archpriest Therry in all the posthumous honours that are justly due to the self-denying, successful pioneer, each having been largely instrumental in laying the sure foundation on which the imposing edifice of the Australian Catholic Church of to-day is built. The Right Hon. W. B. Dalley, soon after the decease of the twin founders of Catholicity on the southern continent, reminded a large gathering of his co-religionists in Sydney of "the privilege of having possessed two such pure, simple, heroic confessors as the two great priests whose memory we wish to perpetuate. They are endeared to us by lives as blameless as they were beautiful, and identified with everything of interest in our ecclesiastical history."

With the arrival in Australia, more than half a century ago, of Dr. Ullathorne, now the aged Bishop of Birmingham, in England, another important stage of Church development was reached. Dr. Ullathorne, then an active young man of twenty-six, came out in the capacity of Vicar-General of the Bishop of the Mauritius, who at that early period exercised a sort of nominal jurisdiction over the whole of Australia and the South Sea Islands. The organising faculty was possessed in no small degree by Dr. Ullathorne, and he was fortunate in receiving material assistance from the new Governor, Sir Richard Bourke, who, though not a Catholic himself, had sympathies in that direction by reason of his many Catholic relatives and friends around his native city of Limerick. The coming of Sir Richard Bourke was coincident with a complete reversal of that avowed anti-Catholic policy, which previous governors took a shameless delight in administering. A powerful despatch of his to the Right Hon. E. G. Stanley, Secretary of State for the Colonies, under date September 30th, 1833, dealt a knock-down blow to the pampered little state Church which his predecessors had laboured so hard to erect on Australian soil. He pointed out with clearness and effect the grossly unfair manner in which the annual grant from the public treasury for Church purposes was distributed, £11,500 being grabbed by the Church of England, whilst the Roman Catholics, notwithstanding their large numbers, received only £1,500, and the Church of Scotland £600. "The chaplains of the Church of England," he proceeded, "are provided with glebes of forty acres each, or with a money allowance in lieu, and with houses or lodging money. No advantage of this kind is possessed by the clergy of the Church of Scotland, or by the Roman Catholics. Such an unequal distribution of support cannot be supposed to be acceptable to the colonists, who provide the funds from which this distribution is made. Accordingly, the magnitude of the sums annually granted for the support of the Church of England in New South Wales, is very generally complained of, and a petition to the governor and the Legislative Council has been lately prepared at a public meeting, and very numerously signed, praying for a reduction of the expenditure. In a new country, to which persons of all religious persuasions are invited to resort, it will be impossible to establish a dominant and endowed church without much hostility, and there is great improbability of its becoming permanent. The inclination of these colonists, which keeps pace with the spirit of the age, is decidedly adverse to such an institution; and I fear the interests of religion would be prejudiced by its establishment. If, on the contrary, support were given as required to every one of the three great divisions of Christians indifferently, and the management of the temporalities left to themselves, I conceive that the public treasury might in time be relieved of a considerable charge; and, what is of much greater importance, the people would become more attached to their respective Churches, and be more willing to listen to, and obey the voices of, their several pastors."

This brave and statesmanlike description of the situation, Sir Richard Bourke followed up with a plan of his own devising for the future equitable distribution of the Government grant for religious and educational purposes. The Imperial authorities in London took some time to digest the most momentous despatch they had yet received on Australian affairs, but at last came the reply from Lord Glenelg, the Secretary of State for the Colonies in Lord Melbourne's Administration. It bore the date of November 30, 1835, and was a complete and highly satisfactory endorsement of the broad liberal views that had been enunciated by Sir Richard Bourke. Writing on behalf of his colleagues in the cabinet as well as for himself, Lord Glenelg thanked Sir Richard for the "full and clear statement" which he had transmitted to them, with respect to the existing means of religious instruction and education in New South Wales, and for the suggestions with which that statement had been supplemented. "I am disposed," his lordship continued, "to commit to the Governor and the Legislative Council the task of suggesting and enacting such laws and regulations for the distribution and appropriation of the funds applicable to the general purposes of religion and education, as they consider best adapted to the exigencies of the colony. In the general principles upon which your plan is founded as applicable to New South Wales, His Majesty's Government entirely concur. In these communities of the Australian colonies, formed and rapidly multiplying under most peculiar circumstances, and comprising great numbers of Presbyterians and Roman Catholics, as well as members of the Church of England, it is evident that the attempt to select any one church as the exclusive object of public endowment, even if it were advisable in every other respect, would not long be tolerated. To none of the numerous Christians of those persuasions should opportunities be refused for worship and education on principles which they approve."

This unmistakable official sanction cleared the path for local legislation. The Church Act, establishing religious equality on the lines laid down by Sir Richard Bourke in his despatch, was speedily introduced and passed by the Legislative Council. It came into operation on July 29, 1836, a red-letter day in the annals of Australia, for it witnessed the close of the long, dark, and sanguinary era of ecclesiastical supremacy and intolerance, and the beginning of the benign reign of religious liberty throughout the Australian dominions. It is true that a few years later, when the first Roman Catholic prelate, Dr. Polding, arrived in Sydney and assumed his legitimate title, the local head of the Church of England, Dr. Broughton, made one last desperate attempt to reanimate the ashes of sectarian strife, and to regain his vanished position of pre-eminence in the religious world. Standing on the north side of his altar and surrounded by his clergy, the Anglican prelate made a public and somewhat theatrical protest, "that the Bishop of Rome has not any right or authority, according to the laws of God and the canonical order of the Church, to institute any episcopal or archiepiscopal see or sees within the diocese of Australia and the province of Canterbury." This silly performance produced a little temporary turmoil, and that was all. It did not alter the opinion of the general community in the least, but rather confirmed the majority in the wisdom of their action in placing all denominations, without exception, on an equal footing in the eye of the law. In after years the two Sydney prelates—Roman Catholic and Church of England—entertained laudable feelings of mutual respect and esteem, and contrived to work harmoniously within their respective spheres of action.

It was during the governorship of Sir Richard Bourke that large numbers of free immigrants from Ireland and England commenced to pour into New South Wales, and to remove the hitherto conspicuous convict element into the background of affairs. In other words, the country was emerging from the sullen, chilly gloom of the penal settlement, and advancing rapidly into the bright sunshine of a free state. This happy change in the condition of the colony was reported to the Roman authorities, with the result that Dr. John Bede Polding was delegated and appointed as the first Roman Catholic Bishop of the Australian continent, with Sydney as his cathedral city. He was subsequently elevated to the dignity of Archbishop, and, for the long period of forty-two years, he was a commanding force in the fostering and development of the Australian Church. And yet so scrupulous was he in avoiding even the appearance of offence to his fellow-colonists of other beliefs,

that he became one of the most popular and universally
respected of the leading men at the antipodes. When he
passed away in March, 1877, at the patriarchal age of
eighty-three, all Sydney turned out to honour his remains
with a public funeral. He was succeeded by his brilliant
young coadjutor, Dr. Vaughan, whose episcopal career in
Sydney, though short, was distinguished for bounding ecclesiastical progress and the greatly-increased influence of
Catholicism in the land. Dr. Moran, Bishop of Ossory, Ireland, was called to be the third occupant of the primatial
see of Australia, and on him the present Sovereign Pontiff,
Pope Leo XIII., has conferred the highest of honours, the
dignity of the Cardinalate. His Holiness, by that generous
act, lifted the young Church of Australia to the same level
with those great historical churches of the old world, that
can gaze back through long centuries of growth and vicissi-
tude, of faith and fidelity, of triumph and toil.

As the Catholic population of New South Wales increased,
three provincial sees were constituted—Maitland, which is
governed by the Right Rev. James Murray, formerly private
secretary to the late Cardinal Cullen, in Dublin; Goulburn,
which continues to be administered by its first diocesan, Dr.
Lanigan, from Cashel, Tipperary; and Bathurst, which was
organised by the late Dr. Matthew Quinn, and is now presided over by the Right Rev. Dr. Byrne, one of its pioneer
missionaries.

One of the first duties that Dr. Polding discharged on his
arrival in Sydney was the dedication of a church to St.
Patrick at Parramatta. Finding intemperance to be lament-
ably prevalent amongst the colonists, the Bishop availed
himself of this opportunity to preach a powerful sermon on
the subject. In the name of their glorious St. Patrick, he

entreated his people to show forth the power and the purity of their faith in the propriety of their conduct, to shun all excess and drunkenness as most offensive to the Almighty, derogatory to the memory of a saint distinguished for his abstemiousness, and degrading to the descendants of those noble men whose holy lives obtained for Ireland that most cherished title of the Island of Saints. This advice was urgently needed, for the free immigrants who were constantly arriving were in great danger of being demoralised by the scenes of debauchery they were compelled to witness in the streets of Sydney. But, fortunately, the best friends and protectors of the Irish Catholic immigrant were simultaneously making their presence felt in the now growing community. Dr. Ullathorne, who assumed the office of Vicar-General on the arrival of Dr. Polding, made several voyages to the home country, and returned on each occasion with a further supply of Irish missionary priests, several of whom were destined to fill high places in the Church of the future. Thus it was that, wherever a settlement was formed, the priest was soon on the spot, collecting the Catholic people together, building a modest little church, and establishing a school for the young ones. Many now prosperous and populous cities and towns in New South Wales, having large and wealthy congregations and numerous Catholic institutions, began life in this humble fashion under the presiding care of a pioneer Irish missionary priest.

One of the young clergymen, into whom the untiring Dr. Ullathorne infused some of his own abounding enthusiasm for the promotion of the cause of Catholicity in the colonies, was the Rev. James Alipius Goold, a member of an old Cork family, who had been educated for the priesthood on the continent. Meeting him one day on the steps of the church of St. Augustine in the Piazza del Popolo in Rome, Dr. Ullathorne pourtrayed so vividly the need of labourers in the distant Australian mission-field, that Father Goold did not hesitate to volunteer his services on the spot. It was this providential rather than accidental meeting in the Eternal City, that gave to the Church in Victoria its pioneer bishop. For, when in the course of a few years the Port Phillip district of New South Wales became prominent and promising, the Holy See, on the recommendation of Dr. Polding, decided to erect it into the bishopric of Melbourne, and to appoint Father Goold as its first prelate, though he was then but thirty-six years of age. After his consecration in St. Mary's Cathedral, Sydney, Dr. Goold undertook the long drive of 500 miles through the roadless bush to Melbourne, and accomplished the distance in nineteen days. He will live in history as the first man who had the hardihood to essay that then perilous, but now comparatively easy feat. Many Catholic citizens of Melbourne went a long way into the country to meet their new bishop, and he was escorted into his cathedral city by an imposing cavalcade. He found his diocese extending from the River Murray to the Southern Ocean, manned with less than half a dozen priests, and possessing but a few scattered places of worship to meet the requirements of so large a district. He immediately commenced the work of organising the church in a land that, he foresaw, was destined to make marvellous strides in the immediate future. In the early years of his episcopate, he did an enormous amount of rough bush travelling, the era of roads and railways not having yet arrived, sleeping out at night camped under the gum-trees, officiating in primeval huts during the day, and personally visiting the most distant and outlying portions of his diocese.* The fact so frequently noted and commented on by literary travellers, that in almost every Victorian city and town the Roman Catholic Church occupies the premier site, is an evidence of the activity and the shrewdness with which Bishop Goold in those early days gauged the probabilities of the future, and made ample provision for the populous times to come. The golden discoveries of 1851, the consequent vast influx of people from all quarters of the globe, the bursting into existence of new centres like Ballarat, Sandhurst, Castlemaine, &c., considerably enlarged the sphere of the Bishop's activity, and found him equal to the unexpected and extraordinary emergency that had arisen. A large percentage of the diggers, he knew, was composed of Irish Catholics, and in order to minister to their spiritual necessities, he speedily planted priests on each of the permanent gold-fields, and sent to Ireland for more clergymen to keep pace with the urgent requirements of the new colony of Victoria, into which the Port Phillip district had now bloomed. Dr. Goold was in short the pioneer prelate that was demanded by the difficult circumstances of the time ; and the host of

* A venerable Australian missionary writes : "In 1850 and part of 1851 Father Dunne had the whole of the Geelong district to attend, the nearest priests being at Warrnambool on the one side and Melbourne on the other. Archbishop Goold was then in the prime of life, and besides his episcopal duties, he did as much clerical duty as any priest in his diocese. When visiting the remote districts, he often had to be content with the accommodation of a shepherd's hut. There were no railroads in these days or even passable roads after heavy rains in winter. On one occasion when his lordship and Father Dunne were returning from Colac to Geelong, they were overtaken by a severe storm, and had to take shelter in the hut of a Tipperary man named John Ryan. There was only one bedroom, which was given up to the bishop and Father Dunne. The Bishop, of course, got the bed, Father Dunne slept on the boards, and Mr. Ryan and his family sat up all night at the fire drying the bishop's and priest's clothes."

churches, schools and religious houses for which he secured sites all over Victoria, and which, thanks to his keen and intelligent prevision, are flourishing institutions to-day, will be long-standing memorials of his organising and administrative abilities. His Honour Judge Quinlan, an old Victorian colonist, has supplied some interesting reminiscences of Dr. Goold's early episcopal career. "I had the good fortune," he says, " of making his lordship's acquaintance in the latter part of the year 1853. He was a bishop whose duties can never be equalled, by reason of their inseparable association with the circumstances of the early days. The whole face of the colony is now changed, and the circumstances of the diocese have so altered, that it is impossible that any of his successors can labour in his footsteps. The reason is this. He came at a time that was most exciting in the history of this colony, when people were pouring in at the rate of a thousand a week. He had to supervise a territory of enormous extent, teeming with human souls that wanted saving, and with children that wanted education. It was a task for a Hercules, but he did it. He was obliged to do all his travelling on horseback, and he did it. I remember his excursions through the bush in the olden times. How unostentatious he was! How zealous! How indefatigable! How under his mild bland exterior he carried the heart of the Christian warrior! I remember his coming to Ballarat at the time of the Eureka riots and I know for a fact that his presence and influence there had more effect in upholding law and order than all the soldiers and police put together. I remember when he went to Mount Eversley during the disturbances in that neighbourhood, and can recall the enthusiasm of the people—how they determined to build a church, and that the only place where the church should be built was Tipperary Flat. I have a vivid recollection of the kindness and courtesy with which he was treated by the English officers in the camp, and of their anxiety that the bishop should stay with them, but his lordship politely but firmly declined their kind invitation, remarking, " I must go to my own people." And he went to his own people, and slept that night amongst them in a little tent. On the following morning I was present when he spoke. A more unobtrusive orator I never heard, and yet I do not think I ever heard one more effectual. I was assured by the officers and others that Dr. Goold's advice and exhortation to the people effected a revolution for good, and they personally expressed their gratitude to him for his timely visit and his tranquillising words." In those early days referred to by Judge Quinlan, Dr. Goold could easily have become a millionaire, or, to use the words of the Hon. John Gavan Duffy, "the richest bishop in the Christian world," had he preferred to place in his private purse the golden gifts that were showered upon him by lucky diggers during his periodical visits to the gold-fields, when they were at the height of their splendour and productiveness.* But all the riches he acquired were utilised in the building up of the Church throughout the extensive district that had been committed to his pastoral charge; and, after governing his Victorian diocese for thirty-eight years, he passed away in June, 1886—the Archbishop of Melbourne—leaving an honoured memory, but little of worldly wealth beyond a few thousands of pounds to be

* The Rev. Dr. Backhaus, the priest whom Dr. Goold placed in charge of the Sandhurst gold-field, died a few years ago, leaving £250,000 for the building of a cathedral and the endowment of the newly-created diocese of Sandhurst.

devoted to works of religion and charity. His mortal remains fittingly rest within the walls of that noble Cathedral of St. Patrick in Melbourne, of which he was the founder and the chief builder in life. An able and accomplished member of the Irish hierarchy, the Most Rev. T. J. Carr, Bishop of Galway, has been appointed as his successor in the see of Melbourne.

The Rev. John Brady, a brother Irish priest, who was a fellow-voyager with Dr. Goold to Australia, also became a pioneer bishop, the scene of his labours being the vast and remote colony of Western Australia. Two Spanish prelates —Drs. Serra and Griver—succeeded him in the administration of a diocese almost equal in area to half the size of Europe; but now the Western Australian Church is once again ruled by an Irish ecclesiastic in the person of Dr. Matthew Gibney, the recently consecrated Bishop of Perth. His name is associated with one of the most heroic incidents recorded in colonial history. An orphanage near Perth having been almost destroyed by lightning, Father Gibney was deputed to collect in the neighbouring and richer colonies sufficient money for its restoration. Whilst he was engaged in this duty in Victoria, a band of outlaws—"bushrangers," as they are colonially termed—who had long defied capture, and had carried on a career of murder and robbery, descended from their haunts in the mountain ranges and took possession of the village of Glenrowan, in north-eastern Victoria, making all the inhabitants prisoners. They cut the telegraph wires and tore up the railway track; nevertheless the authorities in Melbourne were apprised of the daring outrage, and despatched a large force to the locality. The bushrangers, taken by surprise, threw themselves into the village hotel, which they defended against the besiegers for the greater part of the day. Father Gibney, who happened to be in the neighbourhood at the time, hastened to the scene of strife, so that the services of a priest would not be wanting, if required. At an early stage of the conflict, he endeavoured to advance through the open to the hotel, and exert his influence with the besieged bushrangers to induce them to surrender, and thereby avert further bloodshed. He was confident that even such desperadoes as they would not fire upon a priest, but the officers in command thought differently, and declined to allow him to place his life in jeopardy. When, however, late in the afternoon, the hotel was seen to be in flames, the brave priest refused to be kept back any longer, and rushed across to the burning building in the hope of still being able to administer the last sacraments of the Church to any surviving bushrangers within. He was watched with eager and breathless attention as he crossed the open space in front of the outlaws' citadel, the general fear being that he would be shot down before he reached the house. A cheer went up from the excited spectators as they saw him rush through the flames into the interior of the hotel, and a number of them were emboldened to follow in his footsteps. When Father Gibney got within the blazing building, he saw the bodies of the bushrangers lying on the floor, they having apparently preferred to shoot themselves or each other, rather than fall into the hands of the authorities. He had just time to touch their bodies and ascertain that they were lifeless, before the advancing flames compelled him to beat a hasty retreat in order to save his own life. The courage and intrepidity displayed by Father Gibney on this occasion won universal admiration, and the news of his elevation to the mitre was received with cordial approval by the press and the public of all the colonies.

The South Australian Church has had three Irish bishops during the forty-five years of its existence, and is now governed by a fourth accomplished prelate of the same nationality. The first Bishop of Adelaide was the Right Rev. Francis Murphy, who had well earned the distinction by the ardour and activity with which, in the home country, he had seconded the efforts of Dr. Ullathorne to obtain a supply of missionaries for the colonies. It was one of his little band of pioneer priests, the Rev. Patrick Bonaventure Geoghegan, who succeeded him as second Bishop of Adelaide. Dr. Geoghegan was the first resident priest in Melbourne, and was highly esteemed by all sects and classes in the capital city of Victoria. After wearing the mitre in honour for six years, he died in Dublin, to the intense regret of thousands of antipodean admirers of his many sterling qualities of head and heart. Dr. Sheil, who was called to fill his vacant chair in the Adelaide cathedral, was also a Victorian ecclesiastic. He had creditably filled the positions of president of St. Patrick's College in Melbourne, and archdeacon of the Ballarat district. Dr. Reynolds, the present occupant of the see, laboured long and devotedly as a missionary priest in the diocese, before he was chosen as its ruler, and, |under his vigorous administration, the Church in South Australia has become remarkably well officered and equipped. The contrast with the circumstances of its birth is striking and instructive to a degree. This is how Dr. Reynolds recently described the state of affairs when the first bishop, Dr. Murphy, came to Adelaide: "His episcopate was an arduous one, his congregation was struggling; he had no help from the State, no church, no school, no home, and only two priests. An old cottage that was used as a public-house, became his episcopal residence. An old store was hired and fitted up as his cathedral, and here he commenced his self-denying labours as Bishop of Adelaide."

South Australia enjoys the unique distinction of being the only colony that has so far given to the Church a religious order peculiar to the southern hemisphere. This order is known as the Sisters of St. Joseph, and is mainly composed of the daughters of Irish families, who have devoted their lives to the education of the poor. The sisters conduct schools in all the leading centres of South Australia, and have latterly been extending their field of duty to the neighbouring colonies as well. At the inception of the order, they had a hard struggle to maintain a footing in their own colony, for they were assailed by slanders and misrepresentations, and for a time they were suppressed and disbanded, on prudential grounds by Dr. Sheil, the then Bishop of Adelaide. An appeal to Rome ensued, and Pope Pius IX. reversed the bishop's decision. The order was thereupon re-established, and it has ever since nobly vindicated its right to exist, and effectually silenced the voice of calumny, by the earnest, self-denying labours of its members throughout the colonies in the cause of Catholic primary education. Its founder, the Rev. Julian E. Tenison-Woods, has gained a widespread reputation as perhaps the most eminent scientist in the southern hemisphere; but many who have read his numerous works on the geology, botany, and natural history of the Australian continent, are, perhaps, not aware that his real vocation is that of a hard-working missionary priest, and that his scientific studies have been for the most part pursued in the brief intervals of leisure allowed him by the calls of sacred duty.

It is related that a little over forty years ago a few priests ventured northwards from New South Wales to what was then called the Moreton Bay district, in the hope of being able to plant the Church in that newly-settled quarter. But, to borrow a Biblical phrase, they could find no rest for the soles of their feet at that early period, and they were under the necessity of retreating to Sydney in a little boat. And, yet, in the comparatively few years that have elapsed since this abortive attempt was made, the Moreton Bay district has developed into the fine and populous colony of Queensland, with an Irish Catholic bishop enthroned in its capital city of Brisbane. And spread over its ample surface are scores of towns, each with its resident priest and its Catholic congregation. Bishop James Quinn was sent from Dublin in 1859 to take charge of the newly-formed diocese of Brisbane and for twenty years he spent himself in the up-hill work of its organisation. Before he passed away, and before resigning his episcopal charge into the hands of his vicar general, the present bishop (Dr. Dunne), he had the satisfaction of seeing many of the fruits of his prudent and energetic administration. More than once was Bishop Quinn called upon to calm the angry passions of excited bands of Orangemen and Catholics, ready to fly at each other's throats; and his good-humoured advice, added to his general popularity, was always effectual in dispelling the impending storm, and restoring peace and good-will to the previously agitated community.

In referring in a preceding page to the arrival of the two duly-accredited pioneer priests, Fathers Therry and Conolly, it was stated that, whilst the former made Sydney his headquarters, the latter established himself in the new settlement at Van Diemen's Land, the "isle of beauty" lying to the south of the Australian continent, and afterwards christened under its present sweeter and shorter name

Tasmania. Father Conolly landed at Hobart, the capital
of Tasmania, in 1820, and, during the succeeding fifteen years,
he was the only resident priest and Catholic chaplain on the
island. At first his congregation assembled in the store of
the leading Catholic of Hobart, Mr. Edward Curr, but, after
a few months' trial of this temporary expedient, Father
Conolly resolved to approach the governor (Colonel Sorrell)
with a request for a grant of land, on which to commence
the building of a permanent church. "The regulations
allow me to grant land only to those who bring capital into
the colony," was the governor's answer to the priest's request.
"Well," replied Father Conolly, "when I landed, I had just
£14 in my pocket." "Then I regard you as a capitalist,"
said the governor, with a merry twinkle in his eye, "and
will give you a grant in proportion. You may have fourteen
acres of land." Father Conolly lost no time in selecting a
site and erecting the first modest little Catholic church on
Tasmanian soil, the precursor of the present spacious and
beautiful St. Mary's Cathedral of Hobart. Year after year,
he lived and laboured by himself amongst the few free
settlers of his faith in Tasmania, and the Catholic convicts
who were being annually expatriated from the old country.
On behalf of the latter, he had to fight the same battle that
Father Therry successfully waged in the parent colony, in
order to relieve the Catholic prisoners from compulsory
attendance at the Church of England services. "Many a
poor fellow had the punishment of fifty lashes inflicted
on him for not going to the Protestant church on all
occasions," writes one of the oldest and most respected
dignitaries of the Church in Tasmania.* It was not until

* The Ven Archdeacon Hogan, of Westbury.

the arrival of the first Roman Catholic Bishop of Hobart, Dr. Willson, in May, 1844, that this gross abuse of power became entirely a thing of the past. John Francis Maguire, in his well-known work on "Rome : Its Ruler and its Institutions," mentions that the feelings of the late Pope Pius IX.—himself a great prison reformer—"were touchingly expressed on the occasion of his giving a final audience to the late Bishop Willson, when that prelate was about to return to his distant diocese: 'Be kind, my son,' said the Pope, 'to all your flock at Hobart, but be kindest to the condemned.'" These weighty words from the lips of the Sovereign Pontiff made a deep and lasting impression on the newly-consecrated prelate, and, during the whole of his subsequent episcopal career, Dr. Willson was the best friend of the banished prisoners of the United Kingdom, the "Apostle of Reform," in the words of Sir Charles Trevelyan. It was his regular practice to board every convict ship immediately on its arrival in Hobart. Then he would single out the Catholic convicts, give them a wholesome practical address, telling them what they should avoid, and pointing out to them the path of righteousness and reform. Many are the testimonies to the beneficial effects of "good Bishop Willson's" earnest endeavours to ameliorate the hard lot of Great Britain and Ireland's transported prisoners. Here is an official one out of several of the like character that might be quoted: "I can affirm," writes Mr. James Boyd, the commandant of the prison at Port Arthur for a long series of years, "from personal observation and the abundant voluntary testimony of the prisoners themselves, that but one sentiment animates them towards his lordship's person, viz., that of mingled gratitude, respect, and affection. Many a hardened, reckless convict has, through Bishop Willson's missionary zeal and Howard-like philanthropy, been awakened to a sense of his unhappy position, and induced to enter upon an amended career, whereby he has manifested a disposition to act rationally and conform to discipline whilst he remained under my charge, and has ultimately become a respectable member of society." And Colonel Champ, the head of the Tasmanian Convict Department, bore further testimony to the " constant and unwearied exertions of Bishop Willson in administering to the spiritual needs of the convict population, and the success with which those exertions have been attended." Sir William Denison, the Governor of Tasmania, wrote in these terms on the eve of the Bishop's departure for a brief visit to Europe in 1852 : " If the government owe you much, so do the convicts; and they, I am certain, will participate in those feelings of regret, with which every one who has had the pleasure of your acquaintance will hear of your approaching departure."

Like all the other pioneer prelates, Bishop Willson threw himself on the generosity of the Irish Church, in the full assurance that his appeal for more missionaries to man his island diocese would not be fruitless. There were only three priests and three churches in the whole of Tasmania at the time. The Rev. Thomas Kelsh, the biographer of Bishop Willson, describing his visit to Ireland, states that " though great difficulties prevented his getting the supply of priests he had hoped for, some ecclesiastical students, quite captivated by his venerable appearance and address, volunteered for the distant colony as soon as their studies were completed." They kept their promise, came out to Tasmania, were ordained by Bishop Willson, and were established in various parts of the island, where their presence was sorely needed. Having provided his diocese with a fresh contingent of clergy, the bishop proceeded to the erection of St. Mary's Cathedral in Hobart, which he was enabled to do through the princely generosity of a local Irish Catholic, Mr. Roderick O'Connor, who gave him the noble sum of £10,000 for the purpose. The spirit in which the bishop set about this great undertaking is shown by his own words, expressing an earnest desire for "an humble revival of that taste and skill which influenced our forefathers in the faith, when erecting St. Peter's in Canterbury and York, St. Patrick's in Dublin, St. Canice's in Kilkenny, St. Finbarr's in Cork, and the many glorious churches, the pride of our land." Dr. Willson was not spared to see the completion of the cathedral in whose erection he took so laudable a pride, but the structure has been finished under the supervision of his successor, the Right Rev. Daniel Murphy, the present venerable Bishop of Hobart. Dr. Murphy is the Nestor of the Australasian prelates, having worn the mitre for more than forty years, first under the burning sun of India, and afterwards under the beautiful skies of temperate Tasmania.

France is entitled to the honour of having planted Catholicity in New Zealand, but, just as in the other Australasian colonies, the working of the Church is now almost entirely in the hands of Irish ecclesiastics. Dr. Pompallier, the first bishop of New Zealand, landed there in 1838, accompanied by one priest and a lay brother. He, and the clergy who followed in his footsteps, made many converts to Christianity amongst the high-spirited Maories, and a large percentage of the present, but rapidly-vanishing, generation of New Zealand natives, is thoroughly and devotedly Catholic. One priest in particular, the Very Rev. Walter McDonald, has laboured for many years so successfully in their midst as to earn for himself the high title of the "Apostle of the Maori Race." He speaks the Maori language as fluently as a native; he has made a complete study of their intricate national character; he is thoroughly acquainted with all their tribal customs and peculiarities, and has gained their absolute confidence and affection. It is of him that this pleasant little anecdote is told: "Father Walter is well known as a flute-player of more than ordinary ability; but few of the large audience assembled within the walls of the Panmure Hall, on the occasion of the concert recently held in the village, were prepared for the treat which was afforded them by the worthy parish priest, who contributed a flute solo, playing in his best style. On one occasion, in Auckland, when summoned on a sick call, Father Walter, having ministered to the spiritual wants of the patient, was chatting in his genial way, just prior to his departure, when his eye caught sight of a flute lying near by, and, taking it up, he surprised and delighted his hearers by 'rattling off' in great style 'Haste to the Wedding,' 'The Wind that Shakes the Barley,' 'The Pigeon on the Gate,' and many other old-fashioned but charming airs so dear to every Irish heart, and which have been played 'many a time and oft,' and will be played to the end of the chapter, at the 'harvest home' and merrymakings in the South of Ireland. Probably the most delighted of those present was the patient himself, who rapidly recovered, and was quite well again within a short time, such was the efficacy of Father Walter's novel prescription."

Father Walter's ecclesiastical superior for some years was the distinguished prelate who now rules the Archdiocese of Cashel, in Ireland. Dr. Croke's first episcopal appointment was that of Bishop of Auckland, a diocese that comprises the greater part of the North Island of New Zealand, and embraces within its bounds nearly the whole of the Maori population. His administration of ecclesiastical affairs was characterised by great vigour in the building of churches and the establishment of schools. Dr. Croke ever manifested the deepest interest in the spiritual and temporal welfare of the native population, and it was with the object of securing a supply of Irish priests to take charge of the Maori missions, that His Grace returned home in 1874. But Ireland would not allow one of the best and bravest of her sons to go abroad again. She kept him at home and made him Archbishop of Cashel, and, in that wider, loftier, and more responsible arena, Dr. Croke has become a trusted beacon-light to his countrymen throughout the world, a valiant defender of Irish rights, and a foremost champion of the national cause.

Besides Auckland in the far north of New Zealand, there is the diocese of Dunedin in the extreme south. This extensive district is under the spiritual supervision of the Right Rev. Patrick Moran, a fearless prelate of the controversial order, whose voice and pen have been actively employed for more than thirty years in the defence and assertion of Catholic rights. Midway between Auckland, the old capital of New Zealand, and Dunedin, the most populous city and the great commercial centre of the colony, is Wellington, the political capital and the residence of the governor. Wellington constitutes a third diocese, which is ruled by the Right Rev. Francis Redwood, who, by general consent, stands in the front rank of the pulpit orators of Australasia.

In casting a retrospective glance at the foundation and

growth of the Church in the colonies, and in summarising
the ecclesiastical history of the Australasian dominion, one
cannot help being struck by the extraordinary rapidity
with which the complete organisation of to-day has been
evolved from the small and unpromising beginnings of
half-a-century ago. The now flourishing condition of the
Australian Church affords another signal illustration of the
utter futility of trying to impede the growth of Catholicity
in young countries. An unworthy policy of that sort may
have a little temporary success, but the eventual triumph
must always rest with the Church. The failure that attended
the efforts of the early Australian governors to make
Anglicanism the State Church in the colonies, as in the
mother country, is now regarded with openly expressed
satisfaction by colonists of all classes and creeds. An
established religion in these free, self-governed democratic
communities would not be tolerated for an instant, and the
principle that every denomination stands on a perfect
equality from a State standpoint, receives full recognition
throughout the whole of Australasia. In such a fair and
open field the Catholic Church can always advance by leaps
and bounds, as the wonderful strides it has made in the colonies
during recent years abundantly testify. Well and truly did
the Bishops of Australasia, assembled in Plenary Council for
the first time in Sydney, at the close of 1885, under the
presidency of Cardinal Moran, refer to the present and the
past in their joint Pastoral Letter in these mingled terms of
pride and pathos:

"The prevalent impression on our minds during these days of our council is one of intense thankfulness to God, who has so blessed the mustard seed of the faith in the Church of Australasia. At a date so recent as to be quite within the lifetime of men still moving amongst us, there was not one priest, or one single altar, in all these southern lands. It is not simply that the ministration of the Church was poor and scant; but, as a matter of fact, it did not exist. Children came into the world and there was no Catholic clergyman nearer than the northern hemisphere to baptise them. Old men were dying on the scaffold, or in their beds, but the Indian and Pacific Oceans, and the coral seas of the north, lay between them and all the sacraments of the dying. Within sight of where we are now assembled the mystery of our faith, the most Holy Sacrament, was preserved by stealth in a poor man's house. It and its few faithful lay worshippers were the whole of God's Church in this part of the world at the beginning of the current century. At the present hour the priests in the colonies number several hundreds; the churches are among the most beautiful in Christendom; and there is scarcely a religious community in the old world which is not largely represented in our midst. Every town has its convent and Catholic schools; and an assembly of 18 Australasian prelates meets here in this capital of New South Wales. A Cardinal is Archbishop of Sydney, and presides over such meetings. Such a contrast between the beginning and the close of a century is unexampled in history. Such a blessing of fruitfulness is unparalleled since the early ages of the Apostles.

# CHAPTER XII.

#### A GROUP OF STATESMEN.

SIR JOHN O'SHANASSY—ORANGE OUTRAGES—RIOTING IN MELBOURNE—ST. PATRICK'S SOCIETY—SIR CHARLES GAVAN DUFFY—HIS ENTHUSIASTIC WELCOME TO AUSTRALIA—THE FATHER OF AUSTRALIAN FEDERATION—SETTLING THE PEOPLE ON THE LANDS—THE DUFFY LAND ACT—A SERIES OF STRIKING LECTURES—SIR BRYAN O'LOGHLEN—HIS RAPID POLITICAL PROMOTION—WILSON GRAY, PRESIDENT OF THE LAND CONVENTION—MICHAEL O'GRADY—THE GLENVEIGH EXILES—A BENEFACTOR TO HIS RACE—THE HON. NICHOLAS FITZGERALD—WILLIAM CHARLES WENTWORTH, "THE AUSTRALIAN PATRIOT."

THE somewhat remarkable and frequently quoted fact that Irishmen attain the most exalted positions in every country save their own, has been consistently exemplified throughout the Australian colonies, and nowhere more strikingly than in the career of the late Sir John O'Shanassy, thrice Prime Minister of Victoria. For more than thirty years he was the commanding figure of Victorian public life—brilliant in speech, ready in debate, able in administration, skilful in organising, a popular leader of his countrymen, and an ardent defender of Catholic rights. His first appearance on the scene of his future energetic and useful life is thus graphically narrated by his old and intimate friend, Mr. W. H. Archer:

" When John O'Shanassy sailed from Plymouth in the 'William Metcalf' on July 26, 1839, he never thought of settling in Melbourne. A near relative of his had already emigrated to New South Wales, and had induced him to go out to Sydney. The voyage was a long one, and it was not till nearly four months afterwards—that is, on November 15— that the ship cast anchor in the bay of Port Phillip. The young emigrant, who had barely reached man's estate, was noticeable not only for his fine manly bearing, but for his peculiarity in dress. It was also observed that among his several hundred fellow-passengers he was very reserved, and that, book in hand, he generally kept retired from all. His favourite practice was to climb up high in the rigging, and thus secure his studies from interruption. He was arrayed in a blue swallow-tailed coat adorned with brass buttons; and his garb and position must have often stimulated the curiosity and the gossip of those beneath him. Among the first of the visitors to the ship was a Catholic priest. As soon as he stepped on board, he called on all who might be Catholics to come forward. The most stalwart of the group of emigrants advanced at once and grasped the hand of paternal welcome held out by Father Geoghegan. That meeting was the commencement of a lifelong friendship. The discerning eye of the wise ecclesiastic took in at a glance the promising look of the new arrival; and his satisfaction was not lessened when he learned that the young emigrant had brought with him a young wife. Long years afterwards, Dr. Geoghegan told me how he was struck by the appearance of them both. As he gazed upon the young man, who was tall, athletic and of intelligent appearance, and on the young girl, who had more than an ordinary share of good looks, and whose face was beaming with hope and gladness, he felt instinctively that those two were cut out by nature to help in making a new community prosperous, and he lost no time in trying to persuade them to cast their lot on t' e banks of the Yarra Yarra. He told them that Sydney overdone, and Melbourne would prove a richer field for young folk such as they. In the end he prevailed, and they permanently united their fortunes with the few hundred persons who had already settled in the straggling township which is now a great metropolis."

He had no sooner settled down in his new home, than his success in business and his innate capacity for public life made him a man of mark. In all the great movements of the early days, such as the agitations for the legislative independence of Victoria, and the abolition of the transportation of British criminals to the colonies, he bore a leading part; but it was not until Victoria was granted a parliament of its own, that an opportunity was afforded of bringing his great statesmanlike abilities into play. As one of the members for Melbourne in the first Legislative Council, he gave abundant evidence of his intellectual qualifications for popular leadership. He was one of the committee who drafted the constitution under which the Government of Victoria has ever since been administered, and to his wise suggestions many of its most admirable features are to be attributed. As soon as it came into operation, he was elected to the popular chamber by Melbourne and Kilmore simultaneously. He chose the latter seat, to the great delight of its warm-hearted Hibernian electors, who continued for years to return him whenever he presented himself for re-election. O'Shanassy was the first Victorian member of parliament to hold office as Premier by a vote of the majority of the people's representatives. The three governments, of which he was the head, have been credited by friends and foes alike with placing on the statute-book some of the most beneficial and enduring pieces of legislation, notably the Local Government Act and the Crown Lands Act of 1862. To O'Shanassy himself be-

longs the credit of successfully negotiating the first public
loan (eight millions) that the young colony asked from the
capitalists of the old world. He was mainly instrumental in
securing the simplification of official oaths, and the recognition of the equal rights of all classes of colonists, irrespective
of religious belief. As an Irish-Catholic leader, it could
hardly be expected that he should escape calumny and mis-
representation. At the very outset of his public career, the
report was industriously circulated that he was working to
become President of an Australian republic, and that he was
in reality a Jesuit whom the Pope had allowed to marry, as
a convenient cloak for the concealment of his diabolical
designs. The Orange Society in Melbourne assumed a.
first a very aggressive and deliberately offensive attitude
and it required the exercise of all O'Shanassy's personal
influence, together with that of the zealous and patriotic
Father Geoghegan, to prevent bloodshed. Collisions between
the insulted Catholics and the overbearing Orangemen were
not unknown; and at one Twelfth-of-July demonstration
serious rioting was the result of a premeditated display of
Orange banners and emblems from the upstairs windows of
the hotel, in which the disciples of King William were toast-
ing the "pious and immortal memory." Impulsive Irishmen
indignantly heard the news, and hurrying to the scene from
all quarters, surrounded the hotel, and succeeded in forcing admission. In the meantime Father Geoghegan had been informed of the disturbance, and, dashing into the hotel, he endeavoured to separate the combatants, who were by this time
fighting in close quarters. One scoundrel deliberately fired at
the heroic priest. Providentially, he missed his aim, but the
bullet struck and wounded David Hurley, who, with O'Shanassy
had just rushed in to the protection of the *Soggarth Aroon*

Eventually the military put in an appearance; the combatants were separated, and the Orange leaders arrested. The Catholics withdrew to the north of the city, and the Orangemen to the south. Martial law was proclaimed, and the military encamped for the night in the heart of Melbourne, midway between the two forces. Fortunately, the influence of Father Geoghegan and John O'Shanassy prevailed, and the exasperated Irish Catholics were induced to return to their homes and their distracted families. The result of that day's work was disastrous to the influence of the Orange Society in Victoria. It never raised its head in public afterwards. The Peace Preservation Act was passed for the express purpose of proclaiming the illegality of displaying Orange flags and emblems, and, though attempts have now and again been made to repeal that wise enactment, they have all deservedly failed, because the commonsense of the community was opposed to giving any secret society the power of making itself offensive and provoking breaches of the public peace. By a strange irony of fate, the hotel which was the Orange head-quarters, and the scene of the riot just described, is now, and has been for several years, known as the "Harp of Erin," with a pronounced Parnellite as its proprietor.

On only one occasion afterwards were these arch-disturbers permitted to resort to their traditional tactics. Forbidden by law to show themselves as an organisation in public, they built a Protestant Hall, and within its walls they were, of course, free to meet, drink, and talk as much and as often as they chose. But, on the evening of November 27, 1867—twenty-one years after the riot just referred to—all Melbourne was illuminated in honour of the visit of His Royal Highness the Duke of Edinburgh, second son of Queen

Victoria; and the followers of King William, under the pretence of demonstrating their ultra-loyalty, seized the opportunity to once more outrage the feelings of Irish Catholics. Outside their hall they exhibited a most offensive design, which naturally provoked a counter demonstration. This was resented by the Orangemen within the building, and the murder of an inoffensive boy was the result of their indiscriminate shooting amongst the crowd below. By a regrettable miscarriage of justice, the ringleaders in this disgraceful affair escaped the punishment they so richly deserved. The Protestant chaplain who accompanied the Queen's son, was himself deeply disgusted at the misconduct of the Orangemen on this occasion. At the 245th page of his narrative of the Prince's travels, he thus severely comments on the occurrence, and shrewdly philosophises on the evil results of the Orange organisation from its beginning:

"A serious disturbance, resulting in the loss of life, too place in front of the Protestant Hall in the course of the evening. On the night of illumination the front of the hall had been decorated with a large transparency, representing William III. crossing the Boyne, with a figure of Britannia on one side, and the motto, 'This we will maintain.' The exhibition of a design of such a decidedly party character had been generally condemned as likely to provoke the animosity of an opposite faction, and the authorities tried, but without success, to prevail upon the Orangemen not to exhibit it. On the night that it was lit up a few of the more excitable Ribbonmen loudly expressed their indignation at the party emblem, and threatened to destroy it, but contented themselves with throwing a few stones and slightly damaging it. On Wednesday night, however, a large crowd collected in front of the building, abused the Orangemen and their picture, sang 'The Wearing of the Green,' and ended by throwing a shower of stones at the obnoxious device. The people within the building immediately fired an indiscriminate volley in amongst the crowd. Two men and a poor boy were seriously wounded, and the boy eventually died from the effects of his wound. One man was arrested as he was escaping from the building, and others were subsequently captured who were known to have been inside at the time when the shots were fired. They were tried some weeks afterwards, but, for some reason or other not ascertained, were acquitted. Nothing can excuse the Orangemen for having in the first instance exhibited a party device, which they knew would provoke retaliation and lead to a breach of the peace. Amongst the numerous causes which may have combined to produce Fenianism, it becomes a question whether the constant irritation and annoyance inflicted on their enemies by Orangemen, in their noisy celebration of the 'Battle of the Boyne,' for the last two hundred years, have not had a much greater effect than all other grievances, fancy or real, put together. It is scarcely possible to conceive that even less excitable people than the Roman Catholic population of Ireland would tamely submit to incessant taunts and most provokingly contrived devices and emblems to remind them of defeat and subjection."*

Reverting from this digression to the career of Sir John O'Shanassy, it has to be recorded of him that no man in his lifetime laboured more earnestly or more successfully to build up a new Ireland at the antipodes. Seeing around him a wide expanse of rich undeveloped country, he wisely encouraged emigration from the oppressed old land to the

* "Cruise of the Galatea in 1867-8," by the Rev. John Milner, chaplain of the expedition.

free and hospitable soil of Victoria; and, as Prime Minister of three Victorian governments, he facilitated, by every means in his power, the transit of Irish families over twelve thousand miles of water to the homes and homesteads that awaited them in the land of plenty. Thanks to the system of open competition for appointments in the Civil Service, thousands of young Irishmen were enabled to out-distance all competitors at the prescribed examinations; and, whenever John O'Shanassy was in power, they had not long to wait for the prizes to which they were entitled. Nothing pleased him more than the satisfaction he felt in being instrumental in advancing young Irish-Australians who exhibited ability and promise. One of the last acts of his busy life was to preside at a convention of delegates (of whom the present writer was one) which was held in St. Patrick's Hall, Melbourne, for the purpose of drawing up a scheme of federation for the Catholic Young Men's Societies of Victoria. All who were present at that gathering could not fail to be impressed with the deep sympathetic interest evinced by the veteran statesman in the welfare of the young Catholics of his adopted land, and with the sound practical advice embodied in his presidential address.

No higher compliment has ever been paid to an Australian statesman than the large gathering, representative of all classes and creeds in the community, which entertained Sir John O'Shanassy in St. George's Hall, Melbourne, when he was about to revisit the land of his birth, and seek the restoration of that once robust health which had become shattered in the service of his adopted country. Accompanying a munificent public testimonial was an address, signed by the foremost men of the colony and couched in these most appreciative terms: "Whatever differences o opinion may divide us—differences perhaps incidental to the working of constitutional government in a young community—we must all concur in testifying our admiration of a gentleman who has dedicated to the honourable, but arduous and unthankful, labours of political life, great abilities, vigorous thought, anxious study, and long experience, unquestionable honesty of purpose, indomitable energy, and a resolute devotion to what he believes to be the true and permanent interests of the country. In proportion to the rarity of such efforts as these must be the sincerity of our acknowledgments. To have spent the best years of existence in the service of the State, and to have done so at a time when innumerable avenues to fortune were opening on every side, and when comparatively few were found capable of exercising the self-denial implied in remaining faithful to the duties of a political leader, would alone constitute a strong and lasting claim on our esteem. As one of the principal framers of our constitution, and of a system of administration on the gold-fields, under which disaffection was replaced by loyalty and order; as the strenuous opponent of transportation to Australia, and the earnest friend and zealous promoter of the principle of local self-government, and of every undertaking calculated to advance civil and religious liberty, sustain the reputation and accelerate the progress of the colony of Victoria, we offer to you this sincere expression of our regard, and express the hope that we may soon have the pleasure of welcoming your return to a country which can ill afford to be deprived of the services of such an experienced and able politician."

From the earliest period of his colonial career we find Sir John O'Shanassy consistently fostering the sentiment of

Irish nationality, and eloquently advocating the claims of every philanthropic movement that was originated in the old land of his birth. As one of the founders and first members of the St. Patrick's Society, he was the moving spirit in organising one of the strongest and most representative bodies of Irishmen in the world. His thoughtful, racy speeches at the banquets that have been regularly held by that society for many years past in St. Patrick's Hall on the evening of the national anniversary, have a high educational value for his countrymen, and would, if collected, form an appreciable addition to our already rich stores of Irish oratory. Of his services to Catholicity, and the great cause of Catholic education many pages might be written, but it will suffice to summarise them in the words of the Rev. Thomas Cahill, S.J., as spoken, in the presence of an immense and sorrowing audience, over the mortal remains of Sir John O'Shanassy as they lay in St. Patrick's Cathedral, Melbourne, on the morning of May 7, 1883 : " I deem it unnecessary to speak of his career as a politician, as a legislator, as at times the head of the government in this colony. His name and his merits are well known, and throughout his whole career not only his friends who agreed with him, but those who differed with him, found a man faithful in all things, faithful to his principles. But it is when I think of him as a Catholic that the words, 'Be thou faithful unto death, and I will give thee the crown of life,' are in a more marked manner verified. When I look back to the past I see him, as I heard him sometimes describe himself, standing on the spot where now stands St. Francis' Church, forming one of a congregation of three, when for the first time the Holy Sacrifice was offered in Melbourne. I see him bear the banner of St. Patrick's Society, as was his pride and privilege, when the first stone of this great cathedral was laid—that banner a symbol of the faith which he loved and kept to the end. I see him throughout life faithful to his duties as a Catholic. In every year, and throughout his life, he was the true and consistent Catholic, a man who gloried in his religion and never had the weakness to be ashamed of it."

Sir Charles Gavan Duffy is a familiar name in both hemispheres. As the founder and editor of the *Nation;* the lieutenant and coadjutor of Daniel O'Connell; the organiser and biographer of Young Ireland; the compiler of the "Ballad Poetry," and himself the author of a number of vigorous popular poems, Gavan Duffy belongs to Irish history; but as Victoria's successive Minister of Lands, Prime Minister, and Speaker of the Legislative Assembly, the founder of her National Picture Gallery and the most earnest worker in the cause of colonial federation, he stands in the front rank of the representative Irishmen of Australia. It was in November, 1855, that Mr. Duffy, heartsick at the numerous defections from the Tenant League, and seeing no ray of hope in the political future of Ireland, voluntarily expatriated himself and sought a new home thousands of miles away at the antipodes. To use his own mournful language on bidding farewell to the familiar scenes of Dublin, he left Ireland "a corpse on the dissecting-table." On arriving in Melbourne, in the early part of 1856, he was accorded a most enthusiastic reception at the hands of his fellow-countrymen. He was entertained at public dinners in Melbourne, Geelong, Ballarat and Sydney. At the time of his arrival, the election of the first Victorian Parliament under the new constitution was in progress, and there was a universal desire to see Mr. Duffy returned as a member.

But a property qualification was necessary, and immediately committees were formed throughout the colonies, and, in a remarkably brief space of time, the sum of £5,000 was raised. With this a property in Hawthorn, a pretty suburb of Melbourne, was purchased, and Mr. Duffy entered the first Parliament of Victoria as member for the combined counties of Villiers and Heytesbury. The presentation of the title-deeds of his Hawthorn property was made the occasion of a grand demonstration in Mr. Duffy's honour. It took place in Melbourne on August 20th, 1856. Mr. (afterwards Sir John) O'Shanassy presided, and made a graceful reference to the enthusiastic manner in which Mr. Duffy had been welcomed to the colonies, and how he had been everywhere spoken of as a valuable acquisition to the ranks of their public men. The large gathering of that day was meant to testify their regard for genius, talent, honour and fidelity shown in a good cause. It was their object in making that presentation to endeavour to attach Mr. Duffy to Victorian soil. All parties, all creeds and all classes had united in doing honour to their guest, and wishing him many happy days in his new home.

The speech that Mr. Duffy delivered on this occasion is of historical value, as it sounded the key-note of his future honourable and lengthened political career in Victoria. He said, and said truly, that such a generous gift as a freehold estate to a man in his position had no parallel for munificence in the history of Australia, but its weight in solid gold was not its chief value. The immense constituency it represented, in upwards of 100 districts of Victoria and New South Wales, made it a political demonstration of peculiar weight and significance. He trusted he would never forget, as a stimulus to worthy courses, that he had had the happiness to possess, and must be careful not to forfeit, the widespread confidence of which it was the token. His new home would remind him habitually that he could not become slothful or selfish, or embark in any slothful or selfish cause, without base ingratitude to the men of many nations and creeds who had opened its doors to him. He accepted the gift as frankly as it was given; he would accept it as a noble retaining-fee to serve the interests of Australia according to the best of his abilities. He had hoped that night to speak of the future destiny of the Australian colonies, not only of the political liberty in store for them, but of the precious opportunity they enjoyed in the new social experiment of adopting whatever was best in the habits of kindred nations, and rejecting whatever was deleterious or dangerous, till a national Australian character would grow, which, once created, would probably prevail on the shores of the Southern Ocean after the last stone of the city of Melbourne had crumbled into dust. They might imitate the energy and decision of America, which exhibited themselves as much in the arts of locomotion and commercial enterprise as on the battle-field, and their love of simplicity, which had given them codified laws and cheap effective government, without adopting the servile fear of the majority and the indifference to spiritual aims which seemed to be the dry rot of their system. From the old country they carried whatever was best, and, he feared, often whatever was worst. Let them be careful not to revive its parliamentary system steeped in corruption, its government by one favoured class, its bigotry which taught men to hate their neighbours and to love themselves, nor to perpetuate its northern life under southern skies. What good was it to them that their soil teemed with gold if it would not purchase settled liberty and the rational enjoyments of life? These were the topics on which he had proposed to address them that night, but he had a nearer duty to discharge. One of the duties he owed to the mixed community from whom that splendid gift had come, was to protest against the attempt visible in several places to introduce religious feuds and distinctions. He could not see what any man, high or low, wise or foolish, hoped to gain by setting Protestant against Catholic, and Catholic against Protestant. They might destroy peace and prosperity in their country, but they could not possibly destroy one another. After a generation of bad blood and wasted energies, the struggle would end in leaving every one who outlived it in a worse position than if it had never taken place. The rival creeds had quarrelled in Canada for twenty years, and with what result? The prostration and the provincialisation of that fine country. But they gave up the contest, united on terms honourable to both, and the country commenced to outrun the neighbouring great republic in growth from that hour. In the name of common-sense, what justification was there for raising the anti-Catholic cry in Victoria? If the Catholics were aiming at some undue or unreasonable power, he could understand it, but no one could pretend that such was the case. Since he had landed on Australian shores, he had constantly urged that it was the interest and duty of all classes to fuse into one common Australian nationality. No men were better disposed to do so than the men of his own race and creed, but they were not members of the Peace Society, and if they were misrepresented and assailed without cause, they would naturally stand on the defensive. If they were threatened with political extinction, they were entitled and bound to answer, and all fair men of whatever creed would applaud them for answering: "To make Helots of us is what you cannot do and shall not do." A fair field for each man according to his capacity was all they demanded. It had been insinuated indeed that Catholics should be deprived of political power, because political and religious liberty had been denied in Catholic countries. That meant repealing the Emancipation Act. For his part he would as soon sell his children as slaves, as allow them to live in a country where such a doctrine prevailed. But was it true that political and religious liberty had been denied in Catholic countries? It was as true as that witches ride on broomsticks, that one Englishman could beat five Frenchmen, or any of the hundred other fables of ignorance and prejudice. There had been bigotry and cruelty wherever uncontrolled power had existed, no matter to what creed it belonged. But he could answer unhesitatingly for the Catholics of Ireland and affirm that they never denied civil and religious liberty. When anyone spoke to an Irish Catholic of his creed being the symbol of persecution, and Protestantism the symbol of liberty, he might well think the speaker mad. Why, in the reign of Queen Mary, English Protestants fled to Dublin and were sheltered in that Catholic city, and in the reign of Queen Victoria, a large number of Catholic constituencies elected Protestants as their chosen representatives. For 300 years the Irish Catholics had been robbed and oppressed because they were Catholic, down to that very hour when they were compelled to support the richest church in the world for a handful of the population.* It was realising the fable of the wolf and the lamb to raise the cry of intolerance against

* Happily Sir Charles Gavan Duffy has lived to see that monstrous injustice swept away by the disestablishment of the State Church in Ireland, thirteen years after these words were uttered.

those who had not inflicted but endured the pains of ascendancy. A ludicrous charge had been made against himself, that he had come to Australia to promote sectarian triumphs. He would not descend into the kennel even to defend himself, but let his life answer it. There were ten thousand Irish Protestants in that country, who were his contemporaries at home. They were to be found at the bar, in the church, behind the counter, and in the workshop. Let them answer it. Their opinion, whatever it was, would infallibly prevail in the end, and he was content to abide by the verdict. When canvassing in the west a few weeks previously, a local bigot had raised the same cry, and he answered him by appealing to his career in Ireland. Three gentlemen, then unknown to him, at once came forward and confirmed his words. The first declared that he was one of the young Protestants of Dublin, whom the *Nation* had won to nationality. The other two were the resident Presbyterian ministers, who declared that they were among the Ulster clergymen who had acted on the Tenant League, of which he was one of the founders. He was perfectly satisfied to leave his character to witnesses of that sort scattered over Australia. They could tell how the main part of his life in Ireland had been spent in combining hostile sects into a national party, and how in furtherance of that object he had co-operated with men of honour, wholly irrespective of creed. They must not shrink from the work before them, if they would not have that fine country swayed by the narrow spirit of a parish vestry, instead of the generous ambition of a young nation.

The above is only a summary of a very notable speech—the forerunner of many others based on the same theme, and preaching similar noble sentiments—compiled from the newspaper reports of the day; but it is sufficient to show that, even at this early period of his colonial career, the grand idea of a federated Australia was occupying a large place in Sir Gavan Duffy's thoughts. For the practical realisation of that idea, he worked consistently and well for many years at the antipodes, and, though he has not yet had the satisfaction of seeing a second Dominion of Canada established in the south, he has the satisfaction of knowing that, through his instrumentality, many preliminary difficulties have been removed, many intercolonial jealousies smoothed down, and the way paved for a United Australia in the near future. In a special manner has he exerted himself to put down that curse of all new countries, the revival, or the attempted revival, of those bitter feuds and religious prejudices that have worked so much mischief in old and historic lands. Mr. Duffy's arrival was most opportune and beneficial to the newly-born colony of Victoria. He was the only member of its first Parliament who had sat in the House of Commons, and the knowledge and experience he had thus acquired naturally gave him a preponderating influence and *prestige*. It was owing to his advice and suggestions that the Victorian Legislative Assembly was made almost an exact counterpart of the House of Commons. The painful recollection of the terrible evils of unbridled landlordism in Ireland, determined Mr. Duffy to do all in his power to prevent the possibility of such inhuman scenes being re-enacted on the colonial soil of his adoption. From the first he was a vigorous land reformer, and he laboured with might and main to destroy the monopoly of the pastoral tenants, and settle the people on the lands. To him the colony was indebted for its most liberal land law—the Land Act of 1862—a measure which, if it had only been accorded fair play, and administered in accordance with the wishes of its framer, would have opened up the country in all directions, and planted a prosperous agricultural population on the soil. But, unfortunately, the monopolists' gold and the cupidity of the people whom the Act was intended to benefit, defeated in a measure the statesman's magnanimous design. Bribery was resorted to on an extensive scale, with the result that a large part of the finest agricultural land in the colony—the western district—fell irrevocably into the hands of the monopolists. In the east these unworthy influences were less actively at work, and the success of the Duffy Land Act was unequivocal in that quarter. Describing, in April, 1877, a tour through the vast and still undeveloped province of Gipps Land, which occupies the south-eastern portion of Victoria, Sir Gavan Duffy thus spoke from the platform:

"I travelled from Briagolong to Maffra, and thence to Cowwar, a district justly called the granary of the East; I afterwards visited Bruthen and Lindenow Flat, at the other end of the electorate, which rivals the Farnham Survey in fertility, and in all these places I had the inexpressible pleasure of being assured by legions of prosperous farmers who possess the soil, that they obtained their homesteads under what has been named the Duffy Land Act. All the unaccustomed toil of a long journey was repaid by the picture I had imagined long ago, realised under my eyes— the picture of happy homes possessed by a free, manly, yeoman proprietary. And why have we not Maffras and Lindenows in the West as well as in the East? Because the very class for whom we legislated, sold their inheritance for some paltry bribe."

As a leading member of the three O'Shanassy Ministries, Sir Gavan Duffy proved himself an administrator of the first order, and when, in 1871, he became Premier himself, he formed a government that would have indubitably exercised a lasting influence for good on the progress of Australia, had it not been stopped short in its career by an unprincipled parliamentary combination. The Duffy Ministry held office for a year in the face of such virulent and factious opposition as was unparalleled in the political history of Victoria. A perusal of the parliamentary debates of the period will afford ample corroboration to every unprejudiced mind of the truth of Sir Gavan's remark: "They hated the Ministry mainly because I was an Irishman and a Roman Catholic." These rabid opponents of a clever Irish-Australian Premier pretended to believe, and tried their little best to make the public believe, that the patronage of the government was exclusively conferred on Fenians—a name that was as continually in their mouths as the catch-word of a play. One appointment in particular—that of Mr. John Cashel Hoey to a position in the office of the Victorian Agent-General in London—was made the battle-ground of a most bitter and acrimonious discussion, for no other reason than that the gentleman appointed was at one period of his life connected with the staff of the *Nation*. According to the logic of the bigots, he was therefore necessarily a self-condemned Fenian. On a motion of want of confidence, Sir Charles exploded this ludicrous charge, and thus narrated the circumstances under which he first became acquainted with Mr. Cashel Hoey:

"It is said by the hon. member for Williamstown: 'Was not Mr. Cashel Hoey engaged in stimulating rebellion in Ireland?' Sir, for the *Nation* newspaper which existed before the attempted insurrection in 1848, I may be held responsible, and I never did shrink from the responsibility.

But for that insurrection Mr. Hoey is no more responsible than the hon. member for Williamstown, because he was then a boy at school or a lad at college. I never set eyes upon him till 1850, when the *Nation*, under altered circumstances, had to apply itself to what it was possible to hope to accomplish then—the disestablishment of the Irish Church and security of tenant-right for the Irish tenants. One day in that year I had the good fortune to secure the co-operation of three young men—none of them being over twenty years of age, Mr. Hoey being the youngest—as writers for the *Nation*. Mr. Cashel Hoey was one; another was Mr. Edward Butler, who was last week sworn as Her Majesty's Attorney-General in the colony of New South Wales; and the third was Mr. James Doyle, who died in the employment of the identical journal which is now assailing Mr. Cashel Hoey."

This speech was throughout a masterly defence of the policy of the Duffy Ministry. It represents one of the highest flights of political oratory recorded in the pages of any "Hansard." It proved beyond the shadow of a doubt that no Victorian government administered its patronage or conducted the national affairs in a more honest and unexceptionable manner than did the Cabinet presided over by Sir Charles Gavan Duffy. But it was thrown away on the bigoted majority who selected "abuse of patronage" as the most convenient excuse for ejecting an Irish-Australian statesman from power. A subsequent parliament made some amends for this unjust and contemptible conduct, by electing Sir Charles to the high office of Speaker of the Legislative Assembly—a position which he continued to fill with great credit to himself and to the general satisfaction of the House, until he determined to re-cross the equator, and spend the evening of his busy public life in peaceful retirement and the cultivation of that literary leisure which is denied to the active politician.

In any review of Sir Charles Gavan Duffy's Victorian career, it would be an unpardonable oversight to omit some reference to his unique and sparkling lectures, which, after having amused and instructed large audiences in theatres and public halls, continue, in their published form, to amuse and instruct later generations as well. Theirs is not the temporary interest of the superficial address, but the abiding popularity of the thoughtful essay. Hence their happy incorporation in the literature of the colonies. "Why is Ireland poor and discontented?" was a trenchant analysis of those preventible evils that transformed one of the fairest and most fertile spots in God's creation into an island of misery, destitution, and periodical famine. This lecture was eminently serviceable in dissipating the many erroneous impressions concerning Ireland and Irish affairs, that were current in the mixed Australian community of the time. "The National Poetry and Songs of Ireland" was a congenial theme to the early friend and familiar of Thomas Davis, and it is needless to say it was treated with sympathetic force and feeling. "Popular Errors Concerning Australia" was addressed to a London audience, and it was efficacious in dispelling a host of strange delusions that pervaded the British mind with respect to the political and social status of the colonies. "Something To Do" was the suggestive title of a lecture that took a comprehensive and statesmanlike view of the possibilities of future colonial development, and clearly indicated the means by which these possibilities could be turned into potent realities. The sound advice then given has since been partially adopted in several

of the colonies, but much yet remains to be done before Sir
Gavan's ideal can be said to have been realised. "The Birth
and Parentage of Colonial Rights," though delivered as a
popular lecture in all the leading centres of Victoria, is
really a most interesting and instructive chapter in the
history of colonisation in the nineteenth century, and as
such deserves to be as well known and as widely read in the
northern, as it is already in the southern hemisphere.

Though Sir Charles Gavan Duffy is no longer a resident
of Victoria, he is represented there by two worthy sons
of their sire. The eldest, the Hon. John Gavan Duffy, after
a distinguished University career, succeeded Sir Charles in
the representation of the county of Dalhousie, and, having
served a few years' parliamentary apprenticeship, was promoted to the office which his father had filled a quarter of a
century before—that of Minister of Lands. He still retains
his seat in the House, and is one of its most effective and
accomplished speakers. His brother, Mr. Frank Gavan
Duffy, has so far eschewed politics, preferring to devote his
time and attention solely to his extensive practice at the
Victorian bar. Both have gained honours in English literature, the former by carrying off the prize offered by the
Vice-Chancellor of the University of Melbourne for the best
essay on "The Death of Cæsar," and the latter by winning
the first prize presented by Sir George Bowen, Governor of
Victoria, for an essay on "Captain Cook and his Discoveries."

Sir Bryan O'Loghlen, Baronet, the third and last of the
Irish Premiers of Victoria, only entered public life quite
recently, and the rapidity with which he ascended to the top
of the political tree is almost without parallel in colonial
history. For a period of fourteen years—from 1863 to 1877
—he was only known as a most industrious and successful

Crown Prosecutor for the Melbourne district. In the beginning of 1877, on the eve of a general election, he resigned that office, and surprised everybody by offering himself as an ultra-Radical candidate to the electors of North Melbourne, a division of the metropolis in which the Irish vote is particularly strong. Although he polled 1,470 votes, he failed to secure a seat on that occasion, being in a minority of 16. Not long afterwards, however, a vacancy occurring in the representation of the neighbouring electorate of West Melbourne, he was returned after a brisk and exciting contest. He had in the meantime succeeded to the baronetcy on the death of his eldest brother, Sir Colman O'Loghlen, the representative of the County Clare in the House of Commons for fourteen years. The generous men of Clare paid Sir Bryan the high compliment of electing him in his absence to fill the seat that had been vacated by the death of his brother, but he never went home to take the seat, and it remained unoccupied for a lengthened period, until the House of Commons interposed and declared a fresh vacancy. Sir Bryan had the choice between a seat for Clare in the House of Commons and a seat for West Melbourne in the Legislative Assembly of Victoria. He chose the latter, and passed in quick succession from the ministerial office of Attorney-General to that of Acting Chief-Secretary. In the middle of 1881, Sir Bryan received a commission from the Queen's representative, Lord Normanby, to form a government on his own account. Thus, in less than four years of public life, Sir Bryan O'Loghlen had attained the highest office to which any colonist could aspire. In the new Ministry he filled the offices of Prime Minister, Treasurer, and Attorney-General. Two of his colleagues, it may be added, were Irish Catholics like himself, viz., the Hon. Henry

Bolton, Postmaster-General, a native of Galway, and the Hon. Walter Madden, Minister of Lands, whose early days were spent by "the pleasant waters of the river Lee." The O'Loghlen Government ruled Victoria for nearly two years, and its career is now invariably referred to as the era of "peace, progress and prosperity." Sir Bryan's policy was the exclusion of all burning questions calculated to disturb the peace of the community. He sought the progress of the colony at large, the development of its manifold resources, and the prosperity of all its interests. Though he is not now at the head of the State in Victoria, Sir Bryan has the satisfaction of seeing the policy he initiated accepted and maintained by his successors in office.

"When the political history of Australia is written, I believe Moses Wilson Gray, or, as he was familiarly called, Wilson Gray, will occupy no mean position in its pages." These are the opening words of Sir Robert Stout's sympathetic memoir of one of the ablest and most magnanimous Irishmen that have adorned the public life of the antipodes — Wilson Gray, the man to whom Thomas D'Arcy McGee dedicated his "Gallery of Irish Writers." He was the brother of the late Sir John Gray, and the uncle of the present editor and proprietor of the Dublin *Freeman's Journal*, Mr. E. Dwyer Gray. Born in Claremorris in 1813, and educated at Cork, he graduated at Trinity College, Dublin, in company with his friend, Isaac Butt. Soon afterwards he visited America with the object of studying the formation of the new settlements on the western prairies, and the results of his observations are embodied in a thoughtful essay entitled "Self-paying Colonization in North America." In this publication, whilst advocating emigration as beneficial in the main, he was

careful to point out that it was not in his opinion the true
remedy for the evils that afflicted his native land: "In
closing, allow me to say that I am not one of those who look
to systems of emigration as likely *by themselves* to prove in
any considerable degree an efficient corrective of the evils of
this country. Such systems can plainly be made vastly
advantageous to the parties emigrating; and whenever, upon
really overcrowded estates, it is desired to procure larger
accommodation for *men* (and not for *cattle*), emigration can
be made the means of serving the parties who remain behind,
by facilitating such re-arrangement of farms as may be
necessary for the purpose. In the case of an individual proprietor, whose estate is not sufficiently extensive to afford the
means of living to all the population who now occupy it, it
is plainly the only remedy that, as an individual, he can use.
Single-handed, he cannot stimulate general trade or manufactures so as to absorb his people, but he *can* help them to
emigrate. I am anxious that it should not be inferred from
this, that I join in the cry of over-population. Overpopulation was accounted the great source of evil in Ireland
when she numbered little over two millions of inhabitants.
If her present eight millions were reduced back again to
two, it would be a remedy for over-population strong enough
to satisfy the most drastic practitioners; but what would it
do, after all, but put the country back a century? I believe
her disease is constitutional, and that other remedies than
emigration are required for its eradication. I believe, however, that emigration may be made a most effective topical
cure for certain topical sores."

Wilson Gray sailed for Australia almost simultaneously
with Sir Charles Gavan Duffy, and, very soon after his arrival
in Melbourne, he was found in the front rank of the land

reformers—the democratic party that had for its watchword the expressive phrase, "Unlock the lands." When the Victorian Convention met in Melbourne in 1857, with the object of securing a reform of the land laws, Wilson Gray was chosen one of the delegates from the metropolis, in company with three brother Hibernians—Michael Keeley and Stephen Donovan, city councillors, and James Doyle, one of the men of '48. At its first meeting the Convention elected Wilson Gray as its president, and it had no reason to regret its decision, for during a session of three weeks he guided its deliberations with gentlemanly tact and skill. Liberal land legislation was not secured without a protracted struggle with interested wealthy monopolists, but the ultimate success of the people was due in no small degree to the impulse given to the movement by that historical body—the Convention—and to the stirring addresses of its president, Wilson Gray. An agricultural constituency—the county of Rodney—gratefully returned him to Parliament, and he entered that higher sphere with fond hopes of advancing the popular cause. The crooked ways of politics, however, did not accord with his simple honest nature, and it would perhaps have been much better if he had continued to fight outside the Parliamentary arena. The measures on which he had set his heart were not passed into law; politicians on whom he had relied for co-operation proved faithless; and so, with a heavy heart, the popular tribune resigned his seat, bade farewell to Victoria, and made the distant colony of New Zealand his home for the remainder of his life. He never again interfered in politics, but, accepting the position of District Judge of the province of Otago, gave himself up to the conscientious discharge of his official duties until his death on April 4th, 1875. His statue has an honourable place in the Trades' Hall of the capital of Victoria, and his portrait hangs on the walls of the University in the principal city of New Zealand. As illustrating his extreme conscientiousness, it is a fact that he insisted on going circuit whilst almost too ill to walk. At Lawrence, the last town in which he sat, he was carried from his bed to the court, and having performed his last judicial act, was carried back, never to rise again. As a judge he had a great detestation of mere technical defences, of which the following is a humorous instance in point :

There was a case in which a plea of infancy had been put forward. He wanted to know why such a plea had been advanced, and asked if there was no other defence to the action, which was one for goods sold and delivered. The facts were explained to him, showing that the technical defence was set up on the ground that the plaintiff was not morally entitled to recover, if he were legally. The next case on the list was an action for calls due. After hearing the evidence, the defendant's counsel raised a large number of nonsuit points—the company had not been properly registered, the calls not duly made, &c. Turning to the defendant, Judge Gray said: " I want to know why all these technical defences have been raised. Why do you not pay as other shareholders have done ? " The defendant replied: " Well, I have never had any objection to pay with the rest ; but when the secretary of the company called on me, he said I was a puppy, sir ! A puppy ! " " Oh," quietly remarked the judge, " another plea of infancy, I see. I must nonsuit. Call the next case."

Sir Robert Stout, Premier of New Zealand, thus admirably sums up the career of a man, of whom Irishmen all the world over may well be proud : " His distinguishing characteristic was his extreme conscientiousness. This made him doubtful of his own powers and ever prone to underrate himself. He had been offered a seat on the Supreme Court bench of New Zealand, but this he refused. When the Liberal party in Victoria got into power, to their great honour, he was offered a county court judgeship, and this also he declined. Another of his characteristics was his entire unselfishness. At one time, when the business of the court was light, he thought it wrong for the government to keep a district judge for such a small number of cases, and he wrote offering to resign, notwithstanding the fact that, if his resignation had been accepted, he had no means and no business to maintain himself. His benevolence was unbounded. No one in distress who requested aid from him ever met with a refusal. Here then was a politician—radical in his opinions, pure in his life, unsullied in his character, not a self-seeker, and ever modest and humble. Is it not the duty of Australians to cherish his memory? Amidst all the turmoil of party warfare, no one doubted his sincerity. Am I wrong, then, in thinking that, when the impartial historian comes to record the early struggles for Liberalism in Australia, the name of Wilson Gray will stand high amongst the statesmen and politicians of the past? I know of no one's career better fitted to inspire our young colonists with enthusiasm and with a desire so to act that their lives may not be forgotten. Gray strove to so frame the laws and carry on the administration of the government, that the evils which had afflicted European countries might be unknown in these southern lands. He was a Liberal; he was poor; he was conscientious; he was modest; he was able; he was learned. Let our young colonists, remembering him and his life, ask themselves what idea inspires their lives, and what have they done, and what are they doing to elevate their country?"

In the most pathetic and powerful chapter of "New Ireland," the one recording the fate of Glenveigh, the late A. M. Sullivan penned a handsome recognition of the warmhearted, practical patriotism of the Hon. Michael O'Grady, the man who, when scores of poor families in Donegal were evicted from the homes of their fathers, under the most harrowing circumstances, by a landlord of infamous memory, came at once to the rescue, organised the Victorian Donegal Relief Fund, and succeeded in bringing out in a body to the sunny skies and fertile fields of Australia, the unhappy victims of a grievous old-world tyranny. With Michael O'Grady at their head, the Irishmen of the south gave this little band of persecuted emigrants a reception fraternal and cheering in the extreme. Everything that a sympathetic patriotism could suggest was done to efface the memory of the bitter wrongs of the past, to lead the newly-arrived immigrants to look forward to a bright future in Australia, and to settle them in good agricultural holdings on the soil. This policy was successful in every respect, and it is admitted on all hands that no body of immigrants ever gave more satisfaction to the land of their adoption, or reflected greater credit on the land of their nativity, than did these persecuted exiles from Donegal. What Mr. O'Grady reported of them to A. M. Sullivan twenty years ago is just as true to-day of them and their descendants: "They are all doing well, a credit to the old land." But this was far from being the only occasion on which Michael O'Grady exerted himself for the benefit of his emigrant countrymen and their families. Not only in his own colony of Victoria, but, scattered all over Australia, there are thousands of sturdy Irish yeomen, planted firmly and prosperously on the soil, who owe their success primarily to his helping hand and sagacious counsel at the critical moment of their arrival in a strange land. He knew well the dangerous propensity of the average Irishman in a new country to linger about cities and towns, to thoughtlessly cultivate chance acquaintanceships, to give too free a rein to his convivial temperament, and possibly to fall into the terrible gulf of drunkenness, which is the bane of his race. Hence, like the true philanthropist that he was, Mr. O'Grady spared no effort to get his countrymen out of the city as speedily as possible, and to establish them on the 640-acre land selections that were awaiting them in the country. The amount of good and abiding work that he thus achieved in a quiet way will never be known, but it is sufficient to entitle the name of Michael O'Grady to the lasting respect of the Irish in Australia. Though he successively represented South Bourke and the counties of Villiers and Heytesbury in the Legislative Assembly of Victoria, and also held office as Commissioner of Public Works in the Ministries of Sir Charles Sladen and Sir Charles Gavan Duffy, he was never a prominent politician, and never pretended to be such. When his faith or his race was assailed in parliament, he was always ready with a vigorous defence; but his true vocation was outside the political arena altogether, the trusted adviser of his countrymen, the peace-maker in their little differences, the reliever in their distresses, and their best friend in all conditions of life. Springing himself from the people—he was the son of a Roscommon farmer—no one knew better their virtues and their failings, and this knowledge he utilised to the very best advantage for his fellow-countrymen in Australia. An Irishman distinguished for the unblemished integrity of his political life, his sound common-sense, his honest, practical, open-handed charity, his deep attachment to the land of his birth, and loyalty to the faith of his fathers, Michael O'Grady was a typical Celt of the first order, and he died all too early, at the age of fifty-four.

One of the foremost Irish orators of Australia at the present time is the Hon. Nicholas Fitzgerald, the son-in-law of the late Sir John O'Shanassy, whose mantle, it is admitted by colonists of all classes and creeds, has fallen on no unworthy shoulders. For more than twenty years, Mr. Fitzgerald has been an active and leading member of the Legislative Council of Victoria, occupying a place in the front rank of its debaters, and contributing greatly to the promotion of useful legislation by his keen logical insight into the measures devised by successive governments. Gifted with a fine presence and a voice of unusual power and flexibility, he is at his best when addressing a vast gathering of his countrymen and countrywomen on some subject that appeals to their national sympathies. Few will forget it, who witnessed that grand and cheering spectacle on New Year's Day of 1885, when ten thousand Irish-Australian men and women assembled in the heart of the city of Melbourne, to see the first stone laid of a new central Hibernian Hall, and to hear from the eloquent lips of Mr. Fitzgerald such noble sentiments as these : " Yet another object of the Hibernian Society has to be told, and without it our rules, however sound, wise and benevolent, would have their completeness tarnished. I need hardly say I refer to the duty enjoined on our members to cherish the memory of Ireland. We, men of Ireland, claim no monopoly of patriotism, but we do say no country is more loved by its people than our dear old Ireland, whose brave generous children have at all times regarded their country with a loyal love second only to their love of God, and never with greater intensity than at the present time, for assuredly we look forward to a serene and happy future beyond the tearful clouds of this troubled present. We as Australians delighting in the glorious climate of this favoured land, rejoice at, and, with all our energy and all our strength, standing shoulder to shoulder in muscular rivalry with our fellow colonists, assist in every work for the advancement of our adopted country, loyally striving for and proud of its progress, the report of which reads like a chapter of romance. We feel in our hearts that we do not waver in loyal genuine attachment to this our home—the birthplace of our children, the land to which we owe so many and so weighty obligations, when we, as Irishmen, look with eyes of fond loving interest to the land of our birth. To the women of this country— Irishwomen and their descendants—I make a special appeal to nurture and cherish this patriotic sentiment. I ask them to instruct their children never to forget the land that gave their fathers birth, to rejoice in her prosperity and condole in her sorrows, to watch with keen sympathetic eye her struggles, and to pray for her deliverance from her troubles and her woes."

"The Australian Patriot" is the affectionate title which accompanies the name of William Charles Wentworth along the stream of colonial history. And whoever studies the lengthy career of that remarkable man, and estimates at their right value his persistent and eventually successful struggles to rid Australia of a hateful military system of government, and to replace it by one worthy of the confidence and the allegiance of free-born men, will at once admit that the title bestowed upon Wentworth by a grateful people was indeed well deserved. The son of Mr. D'Arcy

Wentworth, an Irish surgeon who received an official appointment in the early days of the colonies, he visited England in the dawn of early manhood, studied at the University of Cambridge, and published in London his " Statistical, Historical and Political Description of New South Wales "—a work that did excellent service in dispelling the ignorance that prevailed in the old world with regard to the actual conditions of life in the newly-settled southern continent. On returning to New South Wales he threw all his efforts into the struggle for the liberty of the press, and, having achieved this first great victory, he established the *Australian* newspaper, and entered with patriotic earnestness and vigour on his career as a reforming journalist. In carrying out his mission of freedom, he necessarily came into collision more than once with the military autocrats of his time, whose sole desire it was to maintain and to perpetuate the gross abuses of irresponsible power and that detestable system of governmental despotism, against which Wentworth directed a galling, unceasing fire of rebuke, denunciation, and sarcasm. As an orator too, the mother-colony of Australasia has never had his equal. The leader of the Patriotic Association, Wentworth, by voice and pen, laboured unceasingly for the recognition of the right of his countrymen to the possession of the self-same privileges as were enjoyed by the subjects of the British Empire in other parts of the world. How he succeeded in his patriotic endeavours is best shown by his own nobly-pathetic summary of his career in a speech to the electors of Sydney towards the close of his public life, when an unprincipled combination made a desperate effort to prevent the return of the veteran statesman to the legislature of which he was the father, the emancipator and the guardian:

"When, five-and-twenty years ago, I devoted myself to public life, I knew full well the vicissitudes of public opinion to which it was exposed, and I was prepared to encounter them. I knew the proverbial inconstancy of the popular gale, that the breeze which filled my flowing sheet to-day might become a head wind to-morrow. I had learned from the unerring history of the past that, whilst the misdeeds of public men are graven on brass, the records of their virtues and services are traced on sand. I had been instructed by the same stern teacher that the lauded patriot of to-day —the benefactor of his country and his kind—might be the despised exile of to-morrow. I foresaw, too, that in a shifting population like this, where circumstances and interests were in a state of rapid transition, I should be particularly subject to events of this description. But with all this knowledge of the fate to which public men are so often subjected, I now fearlessly submit myself a second time to the ordeal of your opinion. From that tribunal I know there is no appeal; but I am content to rely on the merits of my public life. If you consider that that life has been devoted to your service, if you consider that my labours have not been unfruitful of good to this our native and adopted country, you will not on this occasion forsake me. (Cheers and cries of 'No, no.') But whatever your verdict may be with regard to myself, if it be the last public service I am to render you, I charge you never to forget your tried, devoted, indefatigable friend, William Bland. No man has ever served a country in a purer spirit of patriotism; no man ever more deeply deserved the gratitude of a generous people than he has. You may cause it to be written on the tombs of my friend and myself —*Here lie the rejected of Sydney.* But I will venture to prophesy that in juxtaposition with these words posterity will add—*Who gave to those who deserted them the liberty of the press, trial by jury, and the constitutional right of electing their own representatives.* (Tremendous cheers.) You may put it out of my power to serve you again ; you *cannot* erase from memory the services of the past. I can truly say the love of my country has been the master passion of my life. No man's heart has ever beat with a more ardent love of his country than mine, and it is on my native soil that I here stand. From boyhood up to manhood, I have watched over its infant growth as a mother over her cradled child. Its welfare through life has been the object of my devoted love and affection, and now, when my days are in the autumn of their cycle, that welfare is the object of my highest hopes and most hallowed aspirations."

His unscrupulous opponents on the same occasion industriously circulated the report that Wentworth had spoken disparagingly of the land of his forefathers, and this was his indignant reply to that malevolent aspersion :

" It has been said that I have misrepresented and slandered the Irish race. Why, some of the best blood in my veins is Irish, and who will venture to tell me that I am bold enough or base enough to calumniate the land of my fathers ? "

It is a pleasure to place on record the fact that the people of Sydney did not at this juncture exhibit the proverbial ingratitude of the fickle populace towards its noblest and most unselfish benefactors. Wentworth was returned at the head of the poll.

The Australian Patriot's last service to his country was the framing of a constitution based on the British model, and extending to the colonists the amplest measure of political freedom. Though marred considerably in its progress through the legislature of New South Wales, and still further varied from its original purpose by the Imperial Parliament, some of its best features were retained and have worked admirably ever since. The only regret in after times was that Wentworth's statesmanlike proposals were not more closely adhered to. But it was his fate to be systematically thwarted by little-minded men who could not sympathise with his breadth of vision, understand the generosity of his nature, or rise to the loftiness of his aims. The peroration of his final parliamentary speech on the bill for the introduction of the new constitution is well worthy of quotation, as a typical specimen of the Grattanesque character of the eloquence of Wentworth:

"Sir,—I will trouble the House with but a few more observations. This is probably the last occasion—at all events, the last important occasion—upon which this voice may be heard within these walls; and the time cannot be far distant when this tongue will be mute in death. In the short interval which must elapse between me and eternity, on the brink of which I now stand, I would ask what low motives, what ignoble ambition can possibly actuate me? The whole struggles and efforts of my life have been directed to the achievement of the liberties of my country; and it is with this constitution, which I now present for its acceptance, that this achievement will be consummated. Sir, it has not only been my misfortune, but it has been the misfortune of all my countrymen, that we have not lived in troublous times, when it became necessary by force to repress domestic faction or treason, to repel invasion from without, or perhaps to pour out our chivalry to seek glory and distinction in foreign climes. This is a privilege which has been denied to us. It is a privilege which can only belong to our posterity. We cannot, if we would, sacrifice our lives upon the altar of public good. No such opportunity has occurred, or probably will occur, to any of us. Yet, Sir, there is one heroic achievement open to us, and that is to confer upon this country that large measure of freedom, under the protecting shade and influence of which, an ennobling and exalting patriotism may at last arise, which will enable the youth of this colony—the youth of future ages—to emulate the ardour, the zeal and the patriotism of the glorious youth of Sparta and of Rome, and teach and make them feel that ennobling sentiment which is conveyed in the line of the Roman lyric, *Dulce et decorum est pro patriâ mori.* Sir, this is not our destiny, but I trust it will be the destiny of another generation who shall arise with larger feelings and, it may be, purer aims. Sir, this great charter of liberty, which I believe will be pregnant with these results in after ages, I leave now as my latest legacy to my country. It is the most endearing proof of my love to that country, which I can leave behind me. It is also the embodiment of the deep conviction which I feel, that the model, the type, from which this great charter has been drawn is, in the language of the eloquent Canning, the envy of surrounding nations and the admiration of the world. Sir, in the uncertainty which hangs over the destiny of the country—in this awful crisis of our fate—I can only hope that the deliberations of the country may be guided to a safe conclusion upon this vital question, and that by a large, a very large majority of the House, and of the community beyond it, the constitution will be gratefully and thankfully received."

The contemporary records declare that during the delivery of this speech there were enthusiastic bursts of applause from the spectators in the crowded galleries, and, at the orator's pathetic allusions to his past career and the probability of his public life being brought to a speedy termination by the hand of death, many of his fellow-members were moved to tears. When he resumed his seat, the Speaker was unable to suppress the tumult of applause that broke forth from all quarters of the House.

Wentworth lived to the patriarchal age of eighty-one, and his remains were honoured with a public funeral by the decree of the Parliament of New South Wales. A noble statue of the "Australian Patriot" is one of Sydney's proudest possessions. "Wentworth's great public services must never be forgotten. He who obtained for his country trial by jury and other free institutions, including the blessing of Home Rule, which Ireland even now cannot obtain, will ever occupy a prominent position in the history of Australia."*

---

* Sydney *Town and Country Journal*, June 15, 1872.

# CHAPTER XIII.

### NOTABLE IRISH-AUSTRALIANS.

THE RIGHT HON. W. B. DALLEY, P.C.—SIR WILLIAM FOSTER STAWELL—MR. JUSTICE MOLESWORTH—CHIEF JUSTICE HIGINBOTHAM—SIR REDMOND BARRY—THE HON. R. D. IRELAND, Q.C.—THE HON. JOHN HUBERT PLUNKETT, Q.C.—THE HON. EDWARD BUTLER, Q.C.—SIR ROGER THERRY—SIR PATRICK JENNINGS—DR. KEVIN IZOD O'DOHERTY—SIR MAURICE O'CONNELL —SIR ARTHUR PALMER—SIR JOSHUA PETER BELL—HON. J. M. MACROSSAN —IRISH-AUSTRALIAN VICEROYS—SIR RICHARD BOURKE—LORD LISGAR— SIR HERCULES ROBINSON—SIR DOMINICK DALY—SIR RICHARD McDONNELL —SIR GEORGE KINGSTON—SIR GEORGE BOWEN—SIR RICHARD DRY—SIR GEORGE GREY.

IF Australian citizens were asked to name the most popular man on their continent at the present time, William Bede Dalley would assuredly be the reply in ninety-nine cases out of a hundred. He may be said to be the legitimate successor of Wentworth, and to have inherited the choicest gifts of the "Australian Patriot." No public man's speeches are more universally read than his, or have exercised a more ennobling influence on the formation and development of the Australian character. A born orator, he has supplemented his natural gifts with a rare and ripe scholarship, that enables him to draw from many sources a lavish wealth of illustration, a pleasing facility of application, and a command of the choicest and most convincing language. While yet a young man, he attained at a bound a place in the front rank of the public men of the colony, and, amidst the acclamations of thousands, was sent to the first Parliament as a representative of his native city of Sydney. Thirty years have passed since then, but never once has Mr. Dalley lost his hold on the sympathies and affections of his admiring countrymen. Whether valiantly defending his ministerial policy on the floor of the Legislature; or lucidly pointing out the path of progress to his fellow-countrymen in public meeting assembled, or in the hushed silence of a crowded court earnestly addressing a jury on some momentous issue ; or at a great Catholic festival bearing eloquent testimony to the all-pervading truth and traditional grandeur of the Church of his fathers ; or at a national demonstration, now recalling the pristine glories of the historical past, and anon making every one joyous through the instrumentality of his inherited Hibernian humour, Mr. Dalley has ever been an orator with a nation for his audience, and the most interesting figure in the eyes of his countrymen. He enjoys the unique distinction of being the only Australian citizen who has been called to the Privy Council—an honour conferred upon him mainly in recognition of his promptitude in organising and despatching an Australian contingent of soldiers to the seat of war in the Soudan a few years ago. Without expressing any opinion as to the propriety of his policy in this particular, concerning which there has been considerable discussion throughout the colonies, it is unquestionably true that Mr. Dalley's action in despatching a contingent to the Soudan had the effect of bringing Australia very prominently and dramatically before the eyes of the world, and of demonstrating to the older countries that a new nation was beginning to put forth its strength at the antipodes. Mr. Dalley was Acting-Premier of New South Wales at the time, in the absence of the head of the Government, Sir Alexander Stuart. It is related that Sir Alexander was one day last year escorting the Queen

over the Indian and Colonial Exhibition in London. A
large picture of "The Australian Contingent to the Soudan"
attracted Her Majesty's attention, and she paused in front of
it for several minutes. Noticing a portrait affixed to the
frame, Her Majesty inquired the name of the gentleman it
represented. "That, Your Majesty," said Sir Alexander, "is
the portrait of Mr. Dalley, which I have placed here to-day,
because, though I am the Prime Minister, he it was who
actually sent this body of men and officers to the Soudan."
"An Englishman, I presume," remarked the Queen. "No,
Your Majesty; Mr. Dalley is a native of New South Wales,
and a man of Irish parentage, and a Roman Catholic, and
there is not a more loyal subject of Your Majesty in all the
British dominions." The Queen said no more, but Her
Majesty may possibly have thought a little on the causes
that operate to make Irishmen poor and discontented at
home, but loyal and prosperous citizens abroad.

Speaking at the celebration of the national anniversary of
1886, at Sydney, at a time when Mr. Gladstone and his
colleagues were engaged in drafting their scheme of Home
Rule for Ireland, Mr. Dalley, in proposing "The day we
celebrate," observed: "There has been perhaps no period
of Irish history when this festival day of national and
patriotic memories has been celebrated amid circumstances
of such absorbing interest, widespread anxiety, and I
may also say, of reasonable hope of a final and satisfactory
settlement of the Irish question by the Imperial Government, as it has been to-day. That question is at this
moment the one upon the solution of which the genius,
the wisdom, and the liberality of Imperial statesmen are
employed, for the twofold purpose of tranquillising Ireland
and consolidating the Empire. It is admittedly a question

of the supremest importance, and therefore of the greatest difficulty. It can only be determined by men who are prepared to do everything which the situation demands from their courageous statesmanship, and which a conscientious sense of duty requires. Should it be the privilege and, I may say, the blessing of those statesmen to deal with it successfully, their works will unfold a new page in the history of the achievements of modern legislation, and in the glory of the Empire. And in the stupendous work upon which great men are at this moment, while we sit here banqueting, engaged—to which they are devoting the experience of illustrious lives — the statesmanship which has built up the grandeur and protected the renown of the Empire—and to which they are giving the value of services which are a kind of consecration of any cause—I say in this, perhaps of all works of modern times, the greatest in its difficulty, and the vastest in its consequences, they should be supported by our warmest sympathies and our purest prayers. It is under these circumstances that we are here this evening to celebrate a festival which appeals, and ever has appealed, to the emotional sentiment of one large section of the community, and the kindly feeling of all just and gentle men of all parts of the Empire. How different is our fortunate condition here to that of the Imperial statesmen who are called upon to face the situation in England. If this were a political demonstration—which it is not, and never should be—I might properly say that while our immediate duty is to provide for the removal of a paltry pecuniary deficit, which can be instantly effaced by a little self-denial and a slight immediate personal sacrifice, there, at the heart of the Empire, the deficit to be met is one which has gone through centuries of accumulated indebtedness—a deficit which retrenchment cannot help to extinguish nor fresh taxation efface ; which can only be met and removed by heroic justice, and a statesmanship little short of inspiration."

Mr. Dalley was recently offered the high position of Chief Justice of New South Wales, in succession to the late Sir James Martin, but, with characteristic generosity, he declined the honour in favour of the present holder of the office—Sir Frederick Darley, a Dublin man, who followed the Munster circuit for nine years, and afterwards attained considerable distinction at the colonial bar.

" The ability of our countrymen in the administration of government and in the science of politics has been exhibited in our colonies, as well as in numerous instances at home. It was shown by Lords Wellesley, Lawrence and Mayo, in an empire which was founded by Clive and Hastings, and extended by Wellington and Gough. In Canada it was proved by Lords Monck and Lisgar, where also Sir Garnet Wolseley maintained the national reputation. In Australia, under circumstances of almost unparalleled difficulty, similar powers were exercised by several Irishmen in the civil and legal organisation of a new society, notably by the subject of the present sketch."

It is in these words that the *Dublin University Magazine* introduced its illustrated sketch of the colonial career of Sir William Foster Stawell, the recently retired Chief Justice of Victoria, and now the Lieutenant-Governor of that colony. As a junior member of the Irish bar, he thought he saw a quicker way to fame and fortune in a young and rising colony, and he was not disappointed in his anticipations. From his first appearance in Melbourne, he took a leading position at the bar, and on the erection of Victoria into a separate

colony in 1851, his appointment as first Attorney-General of
the newly-born state was only what every one expected. He
had a herculean task before him, for the gold discoveries,
happening at the same time, caused an immense influx of
population, disorganised the whole machinery of government,
and threw the colony at large into dire confusion. But, as
his biographer has truly remarked: "The master mind of
Sir William Stawell rose to the occasion, and it is with
honest pride we record that some of his most efficient colleagues were Irishmen. Perseverance, integrity, and ability
crowned an arduous struggle with success. Light and order
were educed from darkness and chaos, and the prosperous
and magnificent colony of Victoria emerged from the hopeless confusion in which it had its birth. To none was this
more attributable than to Sir William Stawell." Perhaps in
his dealings with the diggers he was somewhat too arbitrary
at times; and it might have been better if he had not
shared in the official impression that the gold-seekers were
an essentially dangerous class, and must be kept in constant
fear of the law. The unhappy collision between the diggers
of Ballarat and the Imperial troops would never have occurred
if this erroneous idea had been dissipated in time, and a
more conciliatory policy adopted towards a large body of
adventurous freemen, the great majority of whom were
untainted by crime. At the same time, it cannot be denied
that there were not a few lawless elements amongst the
heterogeneous crowd that assembled with such marvellous
rapidity on the Victorian gold-fields in 1851; and things
after all, may have been ordered for the best when the helm
of public affairs in the new and suddenly famous colony was
intrusted to the safe and steady hand of Sir William Stawell.
So experienced a judge as Sir Charles Gavan Duffy would

seem to be of the same opinion, for, in one of his historical essays, he says: "It is certain that Mr. Stawell, who, as Attorney-General, long continued to direct the public affairs of the colony, was a man in many respects singularly well qualified for his office. Of a vigorous intellect, indefatigable industry, and clear integrity, he only wanted more sympathy with the mass of the community and less of that love of victory at all costs which is the weakness of strong men, to be an eminent ruler." Soon after this troublous epoch, Victoria received her new constitution, and Sir William Stawell entered the first Parliament as member for Melbourne, in company with his countryman and old opponent in debate, Sir John O'Shanassy. He at once resumed the Attorney-Generalship in the first responsible government that was formed, an office that was soon to be exchanged for the exalted one of Chief Justice, which he filled with honour and credit for well-nigh thirty years. In Mr. Justice Molesworth and Mr. Justice Higinbotham, both Dublin men, he had two accomplished colleagues on the bench of the Supreme Court. The former is a judicial authority of the highest standing, and he is said to be the only judge in the colonies whose decisions have invariably been upheld by the Privy Council. The latter is the idol and the champion of the working classes. As a visible testimony of their gratitude and esteem, they have erected his statue in the Trades' Hall, one of the most unique and extensive buildings in Melbourne, and a striking illustration of what the organisation of labour can accomplish. In the days when Mr. Justice Higinbotham was an active politician, and a democratic leader in parliament during a grave constitutional crisis, the fiery eloquence with which he espoused the popular cause, and resisted what he conceived to be the unjust and tyrannical interference of the Colonial Office in London with the legislative independence of the colonies, secured him the confidence and the attachment of the great bulk of the people to an extraordinary degree. Though no longer in Parliament, and though now hampered with judicial restraints, he is still their leading platform orator whenever the interests of labour are endangered or some new reform has to be gained, and the enthusiastic cheering that greets his appearance at a great public meeting in Melbourne is a pleasing proof that the populace is not invariably fickle. Mr. Higinbotham may be the exception that proves the rule, but here at least is one public man who has never forfeited the favour of a democratic people, and whose popularity has only been mellowed by time. On the recent retirement of Sir W. F. Stawell from the bench, Mr. Higinbotham was at once appointed to the Chief Justiceship.

To the cultivated tastes of Sir Redmond Barry, one of the first of Victorian judges, Melbourne, as is narrated elsewhere, is indebted for the possession of two of its noblest institutions—the public library and the university. A judicial Irishman of lesser degree—Judge Bindon—is to be credited with having established that splendid system of technological training, which has been in successful operation throughout Victoria for years, and which has done so much to elevate the tastes and improve the workmanship of thousands of young colonial artisans. The Hon. R. D. Ireland, Q.C., a member of the Irish Confederation of 1848 (as was also Judge Bindon), was for many years the most famous advocate at the Victorian bar, and one of the wittiest speakers in the Legislative Assembly. Many anecdotes of his readiness at repartee are narrated. On one occasion, when he occupied a seat on the front Opposition bench, a member of the government of the day, who bore a reputation for cunning smartness in political life, began to indulge in some depreciatory personal criticism of his parliamentary opponents. Said he, in pompous style: " On the front Opposition bench, Mr. Speaker, I see neither a Pitt, nor a Burke, nor a Sheridan." "No," quietly retorted Mr. Ireland, looking straight across the table with a twinkle in his eye, " but I see a Fox on the other side of the House." Every one present felt that this happy pun upon a great statesman's name fitted the ministerial speaker's public character like a glove, and he immediately subsided amidst general laughter. As senior law officer of the Crown, Mr. Ireland was the colleague of Sir John O'Shanassy and Sir Gavan Duffy in two Victorian Ministries. Sir Gavan was Minister of Public Works, and in that capacity had occasion to call for tenders for the completion of the Houses of Parliament in Melbourne. The bluestone found in the colony being rather difficult to work, the architect, a staunch Protestant, suggested alternative tenders, with Carrara marble as the material of construction. Some Scotchmen, who were interested in the selection of the local article, set the story afloat that His Holiness the Pope was the secret proprietor of the Carrara quarries, and that Sir Gavan's real object was to try to put Victorian money into the Pope's pocket. A " Papal Aggression " agitation on a small scale sprang up, and when, a few weeks afterwards, tenders were called for the construction of another public building, a no-Popery member rose in the House and gave notice of his intention to ask what material Sir Gavan meant to employ in this particular case. Sir Gavan happened to be absent when the question was formally put, but his colleague, Mr. Ireland— an Irish Protestant—was there, and he gave the honourable and suspicious member an answer that, if it did not remove his doubts, made him look supremely ridiculous, and squelched the stupid anti-Papal agitation amidst universal merriment. "Nothing was yet determined," said Mr. Ireland, "as to the material, but the Minister of Public Works was strongly suspected of meditating the use of Roman cement."

Daniel O'Connell once publicly complimented a young Mr. Plunkett as "the man who had liberated the county of Roscommon," meaning thereby that the young man to whom he referred had been chiefly instrumental in inducing his native county to follow in the footsteps of historic Clare, and send a Catholic representative to the House of Commons. In after years that young man became the Hon. John Hubert Plunkett, Q.C., Attorney-General of New South Wales, a position he filled for a quarter of a century under circumstances that are thus described in the representative organ of the colony, the *Sydney Morning Herald*: "As Attorney-General under the old *régime*, Mr. Plunkett was both grand jury and public prosecutor, and it is something, indeed, to say that in those days of irresponsibility, Mr. Plunkett showed not only great ability, but the highest independence and impartiality. Nothing could have been more high-minded or public-spirited than his official conduct." In one conspicuous instance he vindicated the outraged majesty of the law with a spirit and determination that brought him some temporary odium, but which, when angry passions gave place to quiet thought, won him the respect and admiration of every honest man on the Australian continent. In these early days, the unfortunate aborigines were treated as worse than dogs by the white men who had dispossessed them of their hunting-grounds, and had done them the still deadlier wrong of familiarising them with the worst vices of civilisation. They were indiscriminately shot down on the slightest provocation, and often without any provocation at all. The loss of a white man's sheep or bullock was deemed sufficient justification for murdering in cold blood every black that could be found for miles around. Mr. Plunkett resolved on exercising his authority to check this wholesale destruction of human life, and, by a salutary lesson, to teach all inhuman white scoundrels that the blacks, equally with themselves, were under the protection of the law. An outrage of more than ordinary atrocity soon gave him the opportunity of enforcing this much-needed lesson. A party of ten Europeans, hearing that a number of aborigines were encamped in their neighbourhood, sallied forth with loaded guns to have what they called a "little sport." Stealing on the unsuspecting savages, they opened fire and shot down thirty of the hapless creatures, men, women, and children being included in this frightful and unprovoked massacre. The "sportsmen" returned to their homes well pleased with the success that had attended their shooting excursion. So blunted was their moral sense, that the thought that they had committed a great crime would probably be the last to enter their minds. Hundreds of blacks had been murdered in a similar manner, and the law had called no white man to account. So what reason had they to fear punishment for what they had done? But in this anticipation they were wofully mistaken. The ugly facts somehow leaked out and reached the ears of Mr. Plunkett, whose indignation was fired by the recital. He there and then determined that these horrible offenders should not go unpunished. Setting to work immediately, in spite of the formidable obstacles that were thrown in his way, he succeeded in collecting sufficient evidence to place the whole party on their trial. At every stage he was obstructed by influential friends of the prisoners and numerous sympathisers, who refused to believe that killing the blacks was really murder. Every effort was made to suppress the evidence, but without avail. With invincible courage and determination, Mr. Plunkett prosecuted his self-imposed mission of mercy to a dying race, elicited link by link the whole dreadful story, and awakened the slumbering conscience of the nation to the iniquity that was working in their midst. Truth and justice finally prevailed; seven of the murderers expiated their crime on the scaffold, and the poor blacks were in the future treated more like human beings and less like legitimate game for every white scoundrel in possession of a gun.

When parliamentary government came into operation in New South Wales, Mr. Plunkett sat for some years in the Legislative Assembly, and at a later period he became a member, and was for a time president, of the Legislative Council. Throughout his political career he was distinguished for the same sterling honesty of purpose, strict impartiality, and generous consideration for all classes of citizens, that signalised his official actions as permanent Attorney-General of the colony. "I confess," said Sir Gavan Duffy, in speaking of Mr. Plunkett at a public gathering, "I am proud to see a man of my own creed and nation, who for five-and-twenty years had a power almost uncontrolled over the course of legislation, secure for himself the adherence of the most adverse classes by his systematic liberality and justice. Every clergyman of the Church of England voted for this Irish Catholic; the Wesleyans supported him; the Jews supported him. And why? Because when power was centred in his hands, he protected and secured their religious liberty." To the sorrow of the nation whom he had served so well, John Hubert Plunkett died in Melbourne in 1869. His funeral oration was pronounced by Father Isaac Moore, an eloquent Jesuit then attached to the Australian Church, but who was subsequently recalled to Ireland, and was one of the select preachers on the memorable occasion of the opening of the great cathedral of Armagh. Father Moore truly remarked of the deceased statesman that "his example, his integrity and his blameless life, secured for him, and indirectly for us, the respect of those who by their early associations and early training, had imbibed against Catholics a host of prejudices. Nor during his sway of high office has he been associated with anything questionable. He was esteemed by all, and by all beloved. When he came to these colonies, he found the Church which did not need aid richly endowed, while the Roman Catholics, who were poor, were obliged to provide for the education of their children and for divine service unassisted. Not only this, but in other things they were made to feel that they were not on a footing of equality. Even in such a state of society, one liberal spirit can do a great deal towards a reform. One such spirit alone, so isolated and against such odds, did produce a great effect. It is mainly to him whose memory we honour, to him and his great fellow-champion of liberty in the parent colony, Sir Richard Bourke, that we in common with other denominations, owe the religious freedom we now possess."

The Hon. Edward Butler, Q.C., is another cherished name in the annals of the bar of New South Wales. As a young man fresh from Kilkenny College, he was the coadjutor of Sir Charles Gavan Duffy in reviving the *Nation* after the storm of '48 had passed away. Amongst his contributions were the graceful ballads that appeared in the new *Nation*, over the signature of " Eblana." When he made the parent Australian colony his home, he wrote extensively for the Sydney press, besides occupying a seat in Parliament and appearing as counsel in most of the important cases that came before the higher courts. In 1873, whilst he was holding office as Attorney-General in the Ministry of Sir Henry Parkes, the Chief Justiceship became vacant, and every one expected that Mr. Butler, by virtue of his position as senior law officer of the colony and his acknowledged pre-eminence at the bar, would have received due promotion to the bench of the Supreme Court. But the Premier, Sir Henry Parkes, an unscrupulous politician who, on more than one memorable occasion, has exhibited a rabid anti-Irish and anti-Catholic bias, to the astonishment of all Australia, passed over his gifted Attorney-General and gave the highest of judicial offices to a man who was Mr. Butler's junior at the bar. Naturally after such an unwarrantable reflection, and such a gross violation of the proprieties, Mr. Butler at once severed his connection with the Ministry, and never held office again during the few remaining years of his existence. Sir James Martin, the barrister who was so unjustly promoted to the Chief Justiceship over the head of Mr. Butler, was also an Irishman, but one of a different stamp to the noble-minded, unselfish, and patriotic Edward Butler. Sir James delivered many able addresses from time to time, but there is little in any of them to suggest that their author was a native of Cork. In this respect he differed very much from his colleague, Mr. Justice Faucett, a Dublin man, who is frequently the chosen mouthpiece of his countrymen and fellow-Catholics. In the early autocratic days of the colony the Irish Catholics were fortunate in having a valiant defender on the judicial bench in the person of Sir Roger Therry, whose vigorous addresses and well-reasoned pamphlets did much to stem the tide of intolerance that at one time threatened to flood the country. For kindred services to the faith of his fathers in subsequent days, Sir Patrick Jennings, the Prime Minister of New South Wales last year, was highly honoured by the late Sovereign Pontiff. Besides being in the front rank of the politicians of the parent Australian colony, Sir Patrick continues to sturdily champion the interests of Catholicity, when assailed from time to time for political or party purposes. At the present time (April, 1887) he is attending the Imperial Conference in London as the representative delegate of the senior colony of Australasia.

Queensland, though the youngest of the colonies, is not without its roll of distinguished Irishmen. At the head of its list of honour stands the valued name of the Hon. Kevin Izod O'Doherty, M.D. The doctor's first exile to Australia, as most people know, was the reverse of voluntary, for he was sent out by the British Government in a convict ship, in company with honest John Martin, under a sentence of ten years' transportation for his connection with the events of '48. The year 1854 brought a conditional pardon to such of the Irish exiles as had not escaped to the "land of the free and the home of the brave." Liberty was given them to reside anywhere "out of the United Kingdom." Dr. O'Doherty then took up his residence in Paris, and very justifiably ignored the condition attached to the Queen's pardon, in snatching a stolen visit to his native city of Dublin, and returning to the continent with a faithful and gifted bride—"Eva," the poetess of the *Nation*—who had promised the young medical student when he was going into captivity, that she would wait for him, and who had devotedly kept her word. Two years later the pardon was made wholly unconditional, and Dr O'Doherty, after spending some time in Ireland, resolved to establish his home in the new colony of Queensland, which had just been called into existence. Brisbane, the capital of the infant state, presented him with a seat in the Legislative Assembly, where for years he showed in a marked manner the innate capacity of the Irishman to work with perfect harmony a complete system of local self-government in a mixed community. The doctor has himself given an interesting and humorous account of his first entry into colonial political life. " When I had been only a short time in the colony, and before I had connected myself in any way with public affairs, I was bodily laid hold of and forced into public life, simply because I was known as an Irish exile. I warned my friends who had invited me to take part in public affairs that I was no orator, and that all I could do was to give them an honest vote, but they replied that that was all they wanted, an honest vote being a great deal better than a glib tongue with no honesty in it. A stalwart Irish Orangeman went round and got signatures to the requisition inviting me to stand, and another Protestant, a wealthy native of the colony, insisted on proposing my election, not only on that, but on every subsequent occasion, during the six years that I represented the constituency of Brisbane. It must not, however, be imagined that all the Orangemen in the colony were like my friend. I had rather a comical experience to the contrary. On the day of the first election, before the result of the poll was declared, I had to attend a meeting at some distance from Brisbane, and on my way back that night, meeting on the road a car coming from the town, I shouted to one of the occupants, 'Pray tell me how the election has gone on?' 'Oh,' said the person addressed, with a fine North of Ireland brogue, 'bad enough. That b——y Papist, O'Doherty, has got in.' This story, however, would not be complete if I did not add that this same man, black Northern as he was, voted for me at the next election, and, moreover, became a very good patient of mine." The doctor was subsequently invited by the Governor of Queensland and the Executive Council to take a seat in the Legislative Council, and he continued to be a member of that chamber up to the date of his departure from the colony. From the beginning of his Australian career Dr. O'Doherty has been an avowed Irish Nationalist, and the acknowledged leader of his countrymen in Queensland; but, though he never concealed the strength of his convictions on the great question that lay nearest to his heart, he at the same time never forfeited the goodwill and esteem of his fellow-citizens of other nationalities. They, in fact, admired him all the more for his life-long consistency in being, to quote the phrase of one of themselves, "as ardent in the cause of his youth as though his head were still untouched by the snows of time." The crowning honour conferred by the Irish in Australia on this true and tried champion of the liberties of their race, was on the occasion of the great Irish-Australian Convention held in Melbourne towards the close of 1883, when delegates from all parts of the southern continent and the adjacent islands assembled in force, and enthusiastically elected the aged "Young Irelander" to the presidential chair.

Other Irishmen, whose names are prominent in the history of Queensland, are Sir Maurice O'Connell, a relative of the Liberator, and a European soldier of distinction, who was on four occasions the acting-governor of the colony, and one of the first presidents of its Legislative Council; Sir Arthur Palmer, Prime Minister for five years, and one of the most successful pioneer colonists; Sir Joshua Peter Bell, a Kildare man, who, after holding office in the lower house as colonial treasurer, was called to the presidency of the upper chamber; the Hon. H. E. King, a Limerick man, who for years was the Speaker of the Legislative Assembly; the Hon. John Murtagh Macrossan, a working miner, who, by force of character and natural gifts, rose to the position of political head of the Mining department; the Hon. Patrick Perkins, the ministerial colleague of Mr. Macrossan and administrator of the department of Lands; and Denis O'Donovan, parliamentary librarian, and the accomplished author of "Memories of Rome."

Oftentimes has it been remarked how Irishmen are so singularly successful in governing the Greater Britain that occupies so large a share of the world's surface; whilst they, themselves, have been systematically denied the privilege of ruling in the land of their birth. It is a strange and striking anomaly that Ireland should be the only place on the face of the earth where Irishmen are not permitted to govern. History shows how Irish governors have been mainly instrumental in building up and consolidating the colonial empire of Britain, and yet, during the currency of the nineteenth century, Ireland has never had a viceroy chosen from her own distinguished sons. Englishmen and Scotchmen have been regularly sent to govern a nation that supplied rulers to every quarter of the civilised globe. Carrying coals to Newcastle were wisdom in comparison with this, and it is no small satisfaction to know, that such a ridiculous and exasperating state of things is visibly coming to an inglorious end. It is a matter of absolute certainty that the Irishmen who have manifested the highest qualities of government in distant colonies, and gained the esteem and affection of the mixed communities whom they were appointed to rule, would have been equally successful in the land of their birth, if only the opportunity had been given them at home for the exercise of their commanding abilities. Foremost in the list of those Irish-Australian viceroys stands the honoured name of Sir Richard Bourke, the most able and the most popular of all the Sydney governors. "He had," says Mr. Sutherland, in his "History of Australia," "the talent and energy of Macquarie (one of the early governors of New South Wales), but he had in addition a frank and hearty manner, which insensibly won the hearts of the colonists, who, for years after his departure, used to talk affectionately of him as 'good old Governor Bourke.' During his term of office, the colony continued in a sober way to make steady progress. Governor Bourke, on his landing, found that much discontent existed with reference to the land question. It was understood that any one who applied for land to the Government, and showed that he could make a good use of it, would receive a suitable area as a free grant. But many abuses crept in under this system. In theory, all men had an equal right to obtain the land they required; but in practice it was seldom possible for one who had no friends among the officials at Sydney to obtain a grant. An immigrant had often to wait for months and see his application unheeded; while in the meantime a few favoured individuals were calling day after day at the Land Office, and receiving grant after grant of the choicest parts of the colony. "Governor Bourke made a new arrangement

21

There were to be no more free grants. In the settled districts, all land was to be put up for auction; if less than five shillings an acre was offered, it was not to be sold; when the offers rose above that price, it was to be given to the highest bidder. This was regarded as a very fair arrangement; and, as a large sum of money was annually received from the sale of land, the government was able to resume the practice — discontinued in 1818—of assisting poor people in Europe to emigrate to the colony. Beyond the surveyed districts, the land was occupied by squatters, who settled down where they pleased, but had no legal right to their 'runs,' as they were called. With regard to these lands, new regulations were urgently required, for the squatters, who were liable to be turned off at a moment's notice, felt themselves in a very precarious position. Besides, as their sheep increased rapidly and the flocks of neighbouring squatters interfered with one another, violent feuds sprang up and were carried on with much bitterness. To put an end to these evils, Governor Bourke ordered the squatters to apply for the land they required. He promised to have boundaries marked out; but gave notice that he would in future charge a small rent, proportioned to the number of sheep the land could support. In return he would secure to each squatter the peaceable occupation of his run, until the time came when it should be required for sale. This regulation did much to secure the stability of squatting interests in New South Wales. After ruling well and wisely for six years, Governor Bourke retired, in the year 1837, amid the sincere regrets of the whole colony."

A contemporary eye-witness, Mr. Marjoribanks, speaks of Sir Richard Bourke as being "extremely popular amongst all classes. He was a man that scorned oppression of any kind, but he was remarkably conscientious in endeavouring to do justice to all. Whatever he considered right, he carried into effect boldly and fearlessly, disregarding equally threats and flattery. He was so much beloved, indeed, and his character for the conscientious discharge of his duty is still held in such veneration, that I have seen tears come to the eyes of many of the people in that country whenever his name was mentioned. They collected several thousand pounds for a monument to him, which was on the eve of being erected when I left Sydney, and he will be the first governor to whom that honour has been paid. He returned home by way of Chili, on the west coast of South America, and his fame had gone before him, as, when he landed in Valparaiso, the authorities there turned out to pay him every respect in their power."

The monument here referred to assumed the form of a splendid statue, erected in the Sydney Domain, and bearing an inscription which is an apt summary of the good work achieved by this great Irish-Australian governor: "This statue of Lieutenant-General Sir Richard Bourke, K.C.B., is erected by the people of New South Wales, to record his able, honest, and benevolent administration from 1831 to 1837. Selected for the government at a period of singular difficulty, his judgment, urbanity, and firmness justified the choice. Comprehending at once the vast resources peculiar to this colony, he applied them for the first time systematically to its benefit. He voluntarily divested himself of the prodigious influence arising from the assignment of penal labour, and enacted just and salutary laws for the amelioration of penal discipline. He was the first governor who published satisfactory accounts of the public receipts and expenditure. Without oppression or detriment to any interest, he raised the revenue to a vast amount, and from its surplus realised extensive plans of immigration. He established religious equality on a just and firm basis, and sought to provide for all, without distinction of sect, a sound and adequate system of national education. He constructed various works of permanent utility. He founded the flourishing settlement of Port Phillip, and threw open the wilds of Australia to pastoral enterprise. He established savings banks, and was the patron of the first mechanics' institute. He created an equitable tribunal for determining upon claims to grants of lands. He was the warm friend of the liberty of the press. He extended trial by jury after its almost total suspension for many years. By these and numerous other measures for the moral, religious and general improvement of all classes, he raised the colony to unexampled prosperity, and retired amid the reverent and affectionate regrets of the people, having won their confidence by his integrity, their gratitude by his services, their admiration by his public talents, and their esteem by his private worth."

Amongst the successors of Sir Richard Bourke in the governorship of New South Wales, Sir John Young (afterwards Lord Lisgar), a County Cavan man; and Sir Hercules Robinson, a son of Westmeath, were perhaps the most conspicuous for their executive ability and the widespread popularity they acquired. A ripe scholar and a gifted speaker, the public addresses of Sir Hercules Robinson were invariably of a high order of excellence, and well merited the honour of collection and republication in permanent form that has since been paid to them. His brother, Sir William Robinson, who now rules over the extensive colony of South Australia, has attained distinction in another field as a musician and a composer. South Australia was governed for a number of years previously by a genial Galway man, in the person of Sir Dominick Daly, "a thorough Irish gentleman, who during his term of office endeared himself to the people of South Australia by his courtesy and affability, and by the great interest he always manifested in everything affecting the welfare of the colony." Even Mr. G. W. Rusden, who, in his voluminous "History of Australia," has but too frequently allowed his anti-Irish and anti-Catholic bias to warp his calm and critical judgment, admits that "the urbanity of Sir Dominick Daly won golden opinions, and his death at the close of the customary term of government, elicited such earnest feeling as to prove the hold he had gained upon the people by his genuine sympathy with their interests."

Another authority declares: "Of all the different governors of South Australia, none had been more generally esteemed than Sir Dominick. Combining the most genial manners with the greatest tact—thoroughly comprehending the nature of a constitutional government, and having no political prejudices, he managed in a remarkable degree to gain the sincere good-will of all classes in the colony."

Sir Dominick's immediate predecessor, Sir Richard M'Donnell, was an Irishman of the most active and energetic type. Not content with governing the settled districts of South Australia, he engaged personally in several exploring tours through the unknown regions to the northward, and thus added a large extent of valuable pastoral territory to his colony. It was during Sir Richard's administration that responsible government was inaugurated in South Australia, and, by his wise guidance and conspicuous tact, the system soon worked as smoothly and as successfully in South Australia as in the other colonies. The first parliament elected under responsible government appointed as its Speaker the foremost Irish colonist of his time, Sir George Kingston, who presided in that capacity over the House of Assembly for many years. Both Sir Richard McDonnell and Sir George Kingston rejoiced in their nationality, and, during their residence in the colony, invariably took a leading part in the Hibernian festivals on St. Patrick's Day. It was another Irish governor—Sir George Bowen—who, as has been remarked by Dr. O'Doherty, "well and duly laid the foundation of a free government in the colony of Queensland," and who in after times was a popular ruler in New Zealand and Victoria. More than one Irishman has been placed over the little island colony of Tasmania, but the greatest name in her history belongs to the son of a United Irishman, who was expatriated by the British Government during the early years of the century. The infant son accompanied his exiled father to the antipodes, and took a glorious revenge on the Imperial authorities by becoming in course of time Sir Richard Dry, first Speaker of the Tasmanian House of Assembly, and Prime Minister at the time of his lamented death. Mr. Fenton, the historian of the colony, describes Sir Richard as the "most popular statesman Tasmania ever possessed. He was known and beloved by all. He inherited a magnificent estate from his father, and possessed ample means wherewith to indulge the generous impulses of his warm-hearted nature. His liberality knew no bounds. Indeed, at one time it had well-nigh crippled his resources."

In New Zealand, Irishmen have always been well to the front, and in consequence the Hibernian roll of eminence in this enterprising State would occupy a large amount of printed space if given in full. Sir George Grey, son of an

Irish mother and one of the most ardent of antipodean advocates for home rule, has a unique record, extending over half-a-century, as a fearless explorer, a versatile author, a successful governor and a distinguished statesman. He is the Gladstone of the south, the "grand old man" of New Zealand. Sir James Prendergast, Chief Justice; Sir G. Maurice O'Rorke, Speaker of the House of Representatives; the Hon. P. A. Buckley, Colonial Secretary; the Hon. John Ballance, Native Minister; the Hon. Alfred Tole, Minister of Justice; and the Hon. J. E. Fitzgerald, first Superintendent of the Province of Canterbury, and an orator of great power and pathos, worthily uphold the reputation of the old land amongst the public men of New Zealand.

## CHAPTER XIV.

### LITERATURE, SCIENCE AND ART.

MARCUS CLARKE, AUSTRALIA'S PREMIER NOVELIST—EDWARD WHITTY—DANIEL HENRY DENIEHY—DR. HEARN—PROFESSOR McCOY—EDMUND HAYES—HIS COLLECTION OF IRISH BALLAD POETRY—"THE DREAM OF DAMPIER"—WILLIAM CARLETON, JUN.—JOHN FINNAMORE—RODERICK FLANAGAN—WILLIAM VINCENT WALLACE—COMPOSITION OF "MARITANA"—CHEQUERED CAREER OF A MUSICAL GENIUS.

COLONEL SIR ANDREW CLARKE, the son of the first Irish governor of Western Australia, was a man who rendered very efficient service to the young colony of Victoria as its first Surveyor-General and Chief Commissioner of Crown Lands. To him was delegated the herculean task of organising municipal government throughout the country amongst a promiscuous population drawn by the golden magnet from all points of the compass. How well he succeeded is shown by the host of cities, towns, boroughs and shires, that are spread over the face of the land, each locally self-governed, each raising its own revenue, and controlling the expenditure of its own funds. Science also owes him a debt of gratitude, for he was the founder of the Philosophical Society of Victoria—the earliest organisation for the collection of scientific data on all matters connected with the colonies. Under the title of the Royal Society of Victoria, the institution continues to flourish and to publish a yearly volume of its "Transactions." Sir Andrew's near relative, Marcus Clarke, is the only novelist of the first rank that Australia has yet produced, and it will be many years before the colonies cease to mourn the early death of that gifted son of genius. Though born in a London suburb, Marcus Clarke was always proud of his Irish lineage, and, at the outset of his literary career, he had the good fortune to secure the friendship and patronage of Sir Redmond Barry and Sir Charles Gavan Duffy, who were instrumental in procuring for him a congenial appointment in the Melbourne Public Library.

It was to Sir Charles Gavan Duffy that he dedicated his most powerful and thrilling work of fiction—"His Natural Life"—a book familiar as a household word throughout Australia, and almost as widely known in America, where it was republished by the Harpers. Three editions were issued in London, and the story was also translated into several European languages. It is a tale told with a purpose, and that purpose was to unveil before the eyes of the world the horrors of the English transportation system. Seeing that Marcus Clarke had not been born into the world when these horrors were in full blast, and that he had to search through a multiplicity of old newspapers, prison records, and blue-books, for the facts that formed the groundwork of his story, the realism of the narrative and the enthralling interest it excites in the mind of every reader, are calculated to excite a feeling of wonder at such a brilliant performance on the part of a young man of five-and-twenty, coupled with a feeling of deep sorrow that a life so rich in promise and possibilities, should have been extinguished so soon after the threshold of fame was passed. But, if it was impossible for him to witness the fiendish cruelties, by which the hapless convicts were in bygone days systematically goaded to madness or murder by inhuman military tyrants, he could at least visit the scenes of those dismal tragedies of a terrible past, and this he did by spending some time on the sites—physically beautiful but morally detestable—once occupied by two of the most infamous of the "convict hells" of Van Diemen's Land, viz., Port Arthur and Macquarie Harbour. He thus acquired valuable local knowledge, and assimilated all the local traditions, besides ensuring that topographical accuracy of description which characterises the premier novel of Australia. All who have read "His Natural Life" will have no difficulty in agreeing with the dictum of Lord Rosebery that: "There can indeed be no two opinions as to the horrible fascination of the book. The reader who takes it up and gets beyond the prologue, though he cannot but be harrowed by the long agony of the story and the human anguish of every page, is unable to lay it down: almost in spite of himself, he has to read and to suffer to the bitter end. To me, I confess, it is the most terrible of all novels, more terrible than 'Oliver Twist' or Victor Hugo's most startling effects, for the simple reason that it is more real. It has all the solemn ghastliness of truth." And Mrs. Cashel Hoey, than whom there is no more competent judge, published this high estimate of the deceased young author in her "Lady's Letter from London," which has for years formed one of the most attractive features of a leading weekly journal of Melbourne:* "His tales of the early days of the colonies, and his very striking novel, 'His Natural Life,' made a deep impression here. We were always expecting another powerful fiction from his pen. I fear he has not left any finished work, and I regret the fact all the more deeply that I have been allowed the privilege of reading a few chapters of a novel begun by Mr. Marcus Clarke, under the title of

* The *Australasian*.

'Felix and Felicitas.' The promise of those chapters is quite exceptional ; they equal in brilliancy and vivacity the best writing of Edward Whitty, and they surpass that vivid writer in construction. It is difficult to believe, while reading the opening chapters of this, I fear, unfinished work, that the author lived at the other side of the world from the scenes and the society which he depicts with such accuracy, lightness, grace and humour." Though it is on " His Natural Life " that the literary reputation of Marcus Clarke will permanently rest, he is perhaps seen at his best in those thirty shorter tales and sketches which he wrote during his brief but industrious lifetime. In these minor efforts, the versatility of his genius is strikingly displayed. Some of them are tenderly pathetic, whilst others are grotesquely humorous, and several may be described as wildly imaginative, but all are essentially Australian in their character, and each of them happily illustrates some particular type or phase of colonial life. They afford abundant evidence that if the life of their talented author had been prolonged, he would, with matured powers of study and observation, have diligently explored the virgin fields of fiction at the antipodes, and enriched Australian literature with more than one book racy of the soil.

Edward Whitty, the "vivid writer" with whom Mrs. Cashel Hoey compares Marcus Clarke in the foregoing extract, also lies in a Melbourne cemetery, where his last resting-place is pointed out by a column of white marble that was placed over his grave by the well-known, warm-hearted, sympathetic Irish actor, Barry Sullivan. Like Marcus Clarke, Edward Whitty was born of Irish parents in London, and, by a strange coincidence, both died in Melbourne at precisely the same premature age of thirty-four. Whitty's father was a journalist who did good service in the cause of Catholic emancipation, and Whitty the younger adopted the paternal profession at an early age. When he was nineteen, he joined the staff of the *Times*, " the youngest man that the Thunderer ever entrusted with literary functions of any kind." He was successively editor of that most outspoken of journals, the *Leader*, and the radical Irish organ known as the *Northern Whig*. A sad domestic calamity, the death of his wife and two children within a short period of each other, made the old scenes unbearable to his sight, and he wandered away to the antipodes, only to find an early grave awaiting him. The book by which Whitty is best known is his "Friends of Bohemia," a series of powerful and graphic sketches of adventurers in politics and literature. "The Governing Classes" is another work of his that attracted some notice. Montalembert speaks of it in the highest terms in his "Constitutional Government in England," and describes its author as "the most original and accomplished journalist of the day." Just as in the case of Marcus Clarke, poor Whitty's fruitful mind was full of ambitious literary undertakings in the new land of his adoption, when he was suddenly struck down in the flower of early manhood. A brilliant Irish-Australian friend and contemporary has placed on record this by no means exaggerated estimate of his abilities: "There is no story in the whole melancholy chronicle of misfortunes of men of genius so sad as this of Edward Whitty. That he was something more and something higher than a man of genius, that his nature was moulded of the profoundest sensibilities, and that he altogether lived upon deep and passionate affections, is evinced by the utter shattering and subversion of health, hopes, and interests in the world, which followed the loss of his dear ones. Others, and men of fine mind and fine feeling too, would perhaps have come out of the typhoon dismasted and with broken timbers, but eventually to regain and to ride quietly for years on the world's waters. So young, too—so gifted—so abounding and ebullient with the life-blood of intellectual power, not the mere faculty of writing graceful verses or beautiful trifles of any kind, but with that power, disciplined by learned experiences of the ways of life, to deal with men and things, hard and cold and clear, and bright, warm and joyous, just as they are. His creation of Nea in 'Friends of Bohemia'—the poor girl-wife that her father, a selfish peer, deeply in debt to an old commercial speculator, had given to the latter's Bohemian son—though but a sketch, is a creation of the very highest beauty and a positive contribution to imaginative English literature."

The hand that penned this fraternal criticism belonged to Daniel Henry Deniehy, and the mention of that honoured name, in conjunction with those of Marcus Clarke and Edward Whitty, completes an ill-fated trinity of Irish-Australian genius. Born in the capital of the parent Australian colony, he mastered several European languages at an early age, and, in his twenty-fifth year, gave his countrymen the first glimpse of his oratorical powers in a striking course of lectures on "Modern Literature." His fresh and vigorous eloquence made him, at the outset of his career, the idol of the people, and, unfortunately for himself, he was triumphantly elected to a seat in the first representative assembly of New South Wales. Mr. Frank Fowler, in his "Southern Lights and Shadows," passes in review the leading politicians of New South Wales, and describes Deniehy as the "most accomplished man in the popular chamber. Brought up under the care of the best of guides, philosophers and friends, his sweet home, overlooking the waters of Port Jackson, is the happy refuge of all poor workers in the field of art or letters. Mr. Deniehy has attained the subtle critical faculty of a De Quincey, with conversational powers as brilliant as they are profound. His grasp of subjects is wonderfully extensive, while his rare and highly cultured intellectual faculties dart into every nook and cranny of a topic, convexing its hidden recesses into sharp and vivid relief." His future would perhaps have been far brighter and happier, had he eschewed politics and devoted his splendid abilities to his practice at the bar. Retiring after a few years from public life, he took up his versatile pen, established the *Southern Cross*, and in its pages, and those of other Sydney journals, poured forth that graceful, scholarly series of critical, historical, descriptive, and satirical papers, the perusal of which induced an English author-statesman* to exclaim : " Had Deniehy lived, he would have become the Macaulay of Australia, the first of critics and essayists." But fate had willed it otherwise; the once bright and powerful intellect went out in deepest gloom, and the once favourite pet of the populace was found one morning in the streets of an inland city, and carried, like another Edgar Allan Poe, to a public hospital to die, in his thirty-fifth year. Truly a sad ending to a career that opened with such exceptional sunshine and promise.

    Deniehy, then a young man of twenty, spent the opening months of 1848 in the land of his forefathers, and became acquainted with the leaders of the Young Ireland party, with whose views he was in enthusiastic sympathy. In one of his most interesting sketches, he describes John Mitchel as *le*

---

\* The late Lord Lytton.

*beau sabreur*—the Murat of the movement; Charles Gavan Duffy as showing a literary character, broad, abundant, luminous as a river, and yet chequered with soft, sad autumnal hues; and Thomas Davis as the archetype of Young Ireland culture, and of the masculine purity of genius hallowed to lofty purposes—the scholar and the poet of his party. He thus admirably hits off the leading characteristics of John Mitchel's energetic journalism in 1848 : " Splendid sarcasm, vitriolic in its specific quality as a destructive ; argument close and conclusive, couched in eloquent execration, taunt and curse and defiance, jest and jeer, as grim in their way as attainders or excommunications ; but above all, history —Irish history—pointed out week after week in such a light as, from the flames of a burning church, one might see the inscriptions on mural tablets a minute ere the slabs crack, and drop into the blazing chaos. Compared to them, the thunderers of the *Times* were weak rum-and-water to Russian quass or the Tartar distillation from equine milk. The denunciations of Junius, whose flimsy pretensions to power as political literature De Quincey has, among a host of similar services, shown the world, were as lemonade, and inferior lemonade, too, beside the arrack of the Mitchellian diatribes."

And in his elaborate review of the journal kept by John Mitchel during his detention as a prisoner of state, he soliloquises :

" Even to me, an Australian, who spent but a swallow's season in Ireland, there are passages in Mitchel's ' Jail Journal' that set my memory retouching Irish landscapes. They conjure up the places I know best in Erin—the brimming Lee with a midnight flash of the mill-wheels at Dripsey ; Gougane Barra, with its ' pomp of waters unwithstood,' sung by Callanan in strains where, as often in martial music, the victorious mingles with the plaintive ; the black waters shimmering by the home of Raleigh, and those sacred shades, the wizard woods of Kilcolman, that, with useful and shadowed beauty, closed in about the visions of the dying Spenser."

Contemplating in another essay the extent of the unexplored regions of Irish literature, he exclaims:

"What a tract of imaginative grandeur, lying away dim, sublime and gloomy, like the isle O' Brazil of popular legend, Irish writers of poetry have left untouched in portions of the early religious history of Ireland! Lough Dearg, with so much of what is mightiest and most lasting in relation to the heart and soul floating dimly about it, is an instance. Calderon, the Catholic, soars into this region for the poetic; but the *Purgatorio del San Patricio*, though Shelley dug the finest image in the 'Cenci' from it, is only a scratch on the surface of an auriferous soil."

In the ranks of Australian scholarship no name stands higher than that of Dr. W. E. Hearn, a county Cavan man, and a distinguished alumnus of Trinity College, Dublin. Selected at the age of twenty-eight, by a committee presided over by Sir John Herschel, to fill the chair of history and political economy in the newly-founded University of Melbourne, Dr. Hearn has for more than thirty years been one of the chief bulwarks of that institution, and one of the great intellectual forces of the southern continent. "The Government of England," "Plutology," and "The Aryan Household," are three works from his pen, displaying an erudition which has won for them a recognised position as text-books on the subjects of which they treat, in European seats of learning. His colleague, Professor McCoy, is a Dublin man, and was chosen at the same time by Sir John Herschel to occupy the chair of natural science. The scientific attainments of Professor McCoy are widely known, and the splendid Australasian museum which has been established in Melbourne under his fostering care, whilst being a source of delight and instruction to thousands, is a standing monument to his painstaking industry and his scientific enthusiasm. It is to a Victorian citizen that the Irish race is indebted for the best and most complete collection of national poetry in existence, viz., "The Ballad Poetry of Ireland," in two volumes, compiled by Edmund Hayes, a long-time resident of Melbourne. Conversely, the native-born Australian race is under an obligation to an Irishman resident in their midst—Gerald Henry Supple—for the only national poem of the first order of merit they possess. "The Dream of Dampier" is styled by its author "An Australasian Foreshadowing," and, in its full and flowing verse, there seems to throb the ardent life-blood of the youngest of the nations; the vision of the future rises before the dreamy gaze of the hardy buccaneer as he skirts the shores of Australia, and he sees in wondrous anticipation the golden glories that were destined to remain hidden for two centuries before being revealed to mortal eyes.

William Carleton, jun., and John Finnamore are two Irish-Australians who have also attained distinction in the field of colonial poetry. The former is the son of the great Irish novelist of the same name. His chief work is entitled "The Warden of Galway." It is a metrical romance founded on a remarkable incident in Irish history—the execution of his own son by an inexorable father, who sacrifices all the feelings of nature in order to vindicate the law. Mr. Finnamore's two well-constructed tragedies, "Francesca Vasari" and "Carpio," have a circle of admirers that increases in circumference with the progress of the colonies, and the extension of the higher education. In the realm of Australian history, "there is no more reliable chronicler," to quote the words of a literary critic in the *Argus* newspaper, "than Roderick Flanagan, whose two well packed volumes," he adds, "will always be treated with respect by reason of their honesty, their modesty, and their simple dignity." Flanagan's "Hitsory" is, in fact, a mine of information on colonial subjects, from which many valuable pieces of rough gold have been extracted, and briskly polished, and brightened up by a later generation of literary artists, and made to appear as much as possible like original discoveries.

It is something to be proud of that the two most popular English operas of the century—"The Bohemian Girl," by Michael William Balfe, and "Maritana," by William Vincent Wallace—are the products of Irish musical genius; and it is a fact not generally known that it was in an Australian city, Sydney, that the delightful music of "Maritana" was mainly composed. Wallace seems to have caught a happy inspiration from the serene and sunny skies of Australia, and the lovely surroundings of Sydney, which are reflected in the airiness, the brightness, and the vivacity that distinguish his *magnum opus*. Though he achieved distinction as a young violinist in Dublin, Wallace seems to have emigrated to Australia in 1835, with the fixed determination of abandoning a musical career, and turning himself into a hard-working pioneer colonist. Anyhow, it is certain that he buried himself for some time in the bush country to the west of Sydney, and it was whilst paying a brief visit to this metropolis that a lucky accident revealed his secret, and opened the eyes of his fellow-colonists to the fact that they had a musical genius of the first order in their midst. The discovery was the turning-point of his life. Under the patronage of Sir Richard Bourke, the reigning governor and an admiring compatriot, he gave a concert in Sydney that was so successful from every point of view, as to convince the young Irish emigrant that he had been allowing a God-given talent to lie unproductive. As if to make up for lost time, Wallace now applied himself with much industry to the work of composition in private and violin-playing in public. He travelled professionally through the Australian colonies, and he more than once placed his life in jeopardy by a reckless disregard of necessary precautions, when passing through districts where the natives happened to be in a belligerent humour at the time. On one of those occasions, he was on the point of being sacrificed by a party of Maories who had made him prisoner, and it was only the opportune intercession of the chief's daughter that saved him from a horrible death. After this, his Bohemian temperament prompted him into the eccentricity of embarking on a whaling voyage, and this also was very nearly ending fatally for him. The native crew mutinied in mid-ocean and seized the vessel, and Wallace was one of the four white men who barely escaped with their lives. We next have a glimpse of the wandering minstrel crossing the Andes on the back of a mule, and traversing the whole distance from Valparaiso to Buenos Ayres in this primitive fashion. Other romantic episodes in the chequered career of this erratic genius might be narrated, but, to turn from the man to the music, it is a safe prophecy to assert that many a year will elapse before the works that he has given to the modern lyric stage will cease to charm the popular ear. Such widely-known and such favourite airs as "Let me like a soldier fall," "There is a flower that bloometh," "In happy moments, day by day," "Alas, those chimes," "No, my courage," and "Sainted mother, guide his footsteps," throb with the life-blood of humanity, and will long perpetuate the name and fame of William Vincent Wallace.

# CHAPTER XV.

### IRISH-AUSTRALIAN CHARACTERISTICS.

THE COLONIES A FAIR AND OPEN FIELD—GOOD RESULTS OF HONOURABLE COMPETITION — HOW IRISHMEN COME TO THE FRONT — TESTIMONY OF DION BOUCICAULT—REPRESENTATIVE IRISHMEN AT THE INDIAN AND COLONIAL EXHIBITION—THEIR WELCOME TO DUBLIN — SPEECH OF MR. T. D. SULLIVAN, M.P., LORD MAYOR — JOINT ALLEGIANCE OF IRISH-AUSTRALIANS TO THEIR NATIVE AND ADOPTED LANDS—WHAT SMITH O'BRIEN THOUGHT OF IT—LOCAL AND GENERAL GOVERNMENT IN THE COLONIES — IRISHMEN PECULIARLY ADAPTED FOR ADMINISTRATIVE FUNCTIONS—THEIR HARMONIOUS RELATIONS WITH PEOPLE OF OTHER NATIONALITIES — LADY WILDE ON THE COMING GREATNESS OF THE AUSTRALIAN IRISH—THE FUTURE OF THE COLONIES.

MR. DION BOUCICAULT, the world-renowned reformer and delineator of the Irish character on the modern stage, in one of the many speeches he recently made in the principal cities of the colonies in response to addresses of welcome, pithily summarised the success of the Irish in Australia in a sentence, "They get a chance here." That is to say, our countrymen find in the colonies a fair and open field for the exercise of their abilities and their industry; their onward march is not obstructed by racial or religious prejudices; they are not unfairly or unjustly handicapped in the race with men of other nationalities; and thus, in the honourable competition for colonial honours in various departments of life, they always secure a goodly share of the prizes and distinctions in which young countries are proverbially fruitful. "I asked myself," said Mr. Boucicault, at a picnic given in his honour at Sydney, "as I came here and saw around me the evidences of such prosperity—such level prosperity, such level comfort; no great heapings of wealth, but then no great poverty—I asked what share Irishmen could fairly claim in the development of this great continent, in the discovery of its hidden wealth, in the enterprises of commerce, and in maintaining its peace and prosperity; and I found on inquiry that foremost amongst the explorers who opened up the central regions of Australia were Irishmen— I found that many of the wisest heads and most respected members of the legislative assemblies were Irishmen, that they were luminaries on the bench and leaders at the bar, and that men for places of trust and positions of responsibility were chosen from the ranks of the Irish. These Irishmen— why do they come here? They come from our native country. And in what spirit do they leave it? They leave it because they have no home in the land of their birth, because they have no scope for the exercise of their mental and physical energies. And it is for a home and a livelihood that they cross the Atlantic and the Pacific Oceans, and enter the Heads of Sydney, where they see, as though inscribed above their rocky portals, the words, 'Ye who enter leave despair behind.' They were poor and unappreciated at home; but they come here, and what is the result? They prove themselves to be most valuable citizens—good, loyal, hard-working members of your great progressive communities."

These reflections of a shrewd and much-travelled observer received ample corroboration at the recent Indian and Colonial Exhibition in London, in which Irish art and industry in the colonies formed no inconsiderable portion of a brilliant and effective display, and at which representative Irishmen from the various divisions of the colonial empire attended officially on behalf of their respective states. In welcoming to Ireland a large contingent of these colonial visitors, Mr. T. D. Sullivan, M.P., Lord Mayor of Dublin, referred to the many reasons that actuated the Irish race at home in giving the heartiest of greetings to their colonial guests. " We know," he said, " that crowds of our expatriated countrymen have found freedom and happiness in these distant lands. Our exiled people have been kindly and well received in these countries, and I am proud to-night to hear it said that they have given good and honourable services in the lands where they have made their homes. Yes, gentlemen, they form a large portion of the working population of these countries, and have formed no inconsiderable portion of the brain and intellect that have helped to make these countries free and great and prosperous. We have here to-night amongst our visitors Irishmen who have rendered good service in these countries, and who have won distinction there. We are glad to know and to hear from themselves that they do not forget, and that they do not ignore, the little island of their birth. Gentlemen, it befits a man, whatever his nationality, to remember his own country, and to call it by its own name, not to ignore it, not to seem to think that no such geographical entity exists on the face of the earth. You are citizens of the British Empire, subjects of the British Crown, but, I ask you, are you not proud to be self-governing communities? Gentlemen, your connection with the British Empire is a link of love and affection; that is the bond which unites you to the Crown, and to the Empire of which you form a part. The bond is not one of force, not one of compulsion, but it is one of good-will, and the good-will is there because you get fair-play, fair treatment, and freedom to develop the resources of your own country according to the power within yourselves. May such be the lot of every portion of the British Empire. May we see the day when it can truly be said that no portion of the Empire is held within its bounds by any other tie but the tie of good-will and affection. (Cheers.) Gentlemen, in many of the dark and troubled periods through which we have passed in Ireland, our sufferings would have been far harder, were it not for the large and abundant gifts that were poured in upon us in our day of distress with generous hands by our kindred and sympathisers, and friends abroad. From Australia, from New Zealand, from Canada, and from the great free republic of America, have come to this country generous gifts, and largely have they come from our own people—from the sons and daughters of exiled Irishmen."

One of the chief characteristics of the Irish in Australia is felicitously indicated in the foregoing remarks by the Lord Mayor of Dublin—the remarkable manner in which they have succeeded in rendering full and satisfactory allegiance to the land of their adoption and all its local institutions, whilst never forgetting the filial loyalty they owed to the land of their fathers and all its cherished traditions. Whilst bravely doing their part in building up new states in faraway lands, founding fresh cities, taming the wild bush, and developing all the natural resources of the fifth division of the globe, they have at the same time religiously preserved a deep and abiding interest in all that pertained to the old land of their affections, in every national movement, in every patriotic undertaking, in every successive advance towards the goal of legislative freedom. If any proof of this assertion were wanting, it is abundantly supplied by the active and continuous interest that has been manifested by the Irish race throughout the colonies in the present national movement ever since the first day of its inception, and by the thousands of pounds that have been remitted from time to time in support of that movement to the parent National League in Dublin by its scores of colonial children. When Mr. J. E. Redmond, M.P. and Mr. W. H. K. Redmond, M.P., visited the colonies a few years ago, as the delegated representatives of the Irish National League, they were everywhere received with a generous welcome and a rousing enthusiasm, that were the most eloquent of testimonies to the depth and the strength of the sympathy and the affection, subsisting between the Irish in Australia and their brethren in the old land. The recent intercolonial tour of the Earl and the Countess of Aberdeen affords another evidence of the solidarity of the race. The knowledge that Lord Aberdeen was the first Irish Viceroy, for many long years, who had honestly striven to rule Ireland in accordance with Irish ideas, secured him a princely reception at the hands of grateful Irish-Australians in all the colonial cities that were visited by the Countess and himself. The moment a patriotic note is sounded in the home country, it immediately finds a responsive echo in the hearts and deeds of the Irish in Australia showing how thorough is the sympathy, and how magnetic the influence, that bind together the "sea-divided Gael." The same fraternal feeling finds expression in the loving conservatism which has led to so many distinctively Irish customs and festivals being transplanted to the antipodes, and taking deep and lasting root in the soil. This striking characteristic of colonial Irishmen—this measure of equal justice meted out to the land of their birth and the land of their adoption—did not escape the notice of Smith O'Brien during his tour in Victoria after his recall from a five years' exile. "It has caused me intense satisfaction," said the leader of '48, "to find that in this colony the Irish have distinguished themselves by their industry, intelligence, enterprise, and good conduct, as well as that their exertions have for the most part been rewarded with success ; but the satisfaction is greatly enhanced when I perceive that they retain in this hemisphere those features of the national character—those noble impulses, those generous emotions, those genial susceptibilities—which I have been elsewhere accustomed with loving pride to extol as the attributes of our race."

A second conspicuous feature in the character of the typical Irish-Australian is the remarkable facility, and the pronounced success, with which he has adapted himself to the administration of municipal and parliamentary forms of government in these newly-created states. Coming from a country in which the fewest possible governing privileges are grudgingly granted to the people, the signal all-round ability displayed by the Irish settlers in Australasia, in the work of both local and general government, is little less than marvellous, considering the previous absence of any adequate training for such positions of authority and responsibility. They seem to possess an intuitive acquaintance with the rules and forms of popular government, and a ready tact by which this invaluable knowledge becomes easily translated into action for the benefit of their fellow citizens. Special references have been made in preceding pages to the number of Irish-Australians who have distinguished themselves in the parliamentary arena, but it must not be forgotten that there are hundreds of their brother Celts all over the colonies doing equally good and useful work on a less lofty platform as mayors, presidents and councillors of cities, towns and shires. Many a business Irishman in Australian

centres works hard all day for himself and his family, and
gives his evenings to the service of the community that has
called him to a foremost place in its Town Hall; and many an
Irish farmer in thinly-settled districts travels twelve or fifteen
miles at periodical intervals to take his seat in the shire
council, of which he is an elected member. Facts like these
are the strongest possible condemnation of the traditional
policy, which has so long and so unwisely refused to Irishmen
in their own native land, those legislative and municipal
rights, which they have proved themselves fully competent to
exercise in all other English-speaking dominions. As Sir
Charles Gavan Duffy once told a Melbourne audience, " the
history of the Irish race in Australia was one they might
fairly be proud of. They exercised a large influence in public
affairs, and he challenged any man to say it was not a beneficial and a salutary one. Every enlargement of Australian
liberty had them for zealous friends ; every enemy of Australian rights had them for uncompromising antagonists."

One further characteristic of the Irish in Australia must
not be overlooked, and that is the general good-will, the
prevailing amity of their social relations with their fellow-
citizens of other nationalities. It is unfortunately true that,
in times of exceptional political excitement, it is possible for
unscrupulous agitators to raise and profit by an anti-Irish
or anti-Catholic cry, but, viewing the colonies in their
normal condition, the harmony that subsists between the
inhabitants of Irish birth or parentage and the other com-
ponent parts of the population, is one of the most noticeable
and gratifying features of Australian life. In every colonial
centre, Irishmen are found associated on the most amicable
terms with their fellow-citizens of other nationalities in the
management of public and charitable institutions, and in

every movement devised for the furtherance of the common weal. Not a few Irish-Catholic charities in the principal Australasian cities number Protestant ladies and gentlemen amongst their most generous patrons and subscribers. This well-known and pleasing fact was once felicitously referred to by Mr. Dalley, in addressing a Sydney audience, as " a proof of their enjoyment of a civilisation which made the efforts of the intolerant and the fanatical mere exhibitions of impotent malignity, which could have no effect whatever upon the actions of the good and the gentle."

Lady Wilde ("Speranza"), writing a few years ago in a London magazine, prophesied that "the Australian Irish will in time be as powerful a people as their American kindred," and expressed her conviction that "the chances of wealth are even greater in Australia" than in the republic of the west. The famed poetess of the Young Ireland era went further, and anticipated a day when the Australian Irish would "return to green Erin and buy up the estates of the pauperised landlords." This would certainly be a sensational dramatic revenge—the evicted coming back with well-filled purses to enter into possession of the properties of the once harsh but now humble evictors—but it is by no means beyond the range of probability, in view of the remarkable rapidity with which large fortunes have been accumulated in Australia by Irishmen who landed there with nothing to bless themselves with, save the clothes on their backs and the few shillings in their dilapidated pockets.

When it is remembered that the marvellous progress detailed in the foregoing pages, to which Irish brains, courage, and enterprise contributed so much, has taken place within the lifetime of a single generation, no one will be surprised at the glowing anticipations in which many writers

have indulged, regarding what the future has in store for
these great southern lands. There is, it must needs be
admitted, a substantial foundation on which the prophet
is at liberty to build. Abounding in vast and still undeveloped resources, possessing large areas of unoccupied
territory, blessed with many safe and commodious harbours,
and enjoying the freest of free constitutions, there is nothing
to prevent the Australian colonies becoming, at no distant
date, a second America, a national safety-valve, a home for
millions. Manhood suffrage is the almost universal law, and
no restriction whatever is placed, nor would it be tolerated
for an instant, on the free and untrammelled exercise of the
franchise. Practically, every man who can sign his name,
and is not suffering under any legal disability, has a
potential voice in the making of the laws by which he is
governed. It is to the operation of this grand principle,
that the Irishmen of the antipodes have been enabled to
exert their due influence on the conduct of public affairs;
to send, as representatives to their local parliaments, men
of ability chosen from their own ranks; and, on occasions,
by the weight of their united sentiment and generous
indignation, have succeeded in keeping off the colonial
statute-book some of those legislative enactments that have
been productive of lamentable evils in the land of their birth.

The Celtic element of the Australian population has,
in fine, proved a valuable factor in the work of building up
new states, and founding free, intelligent and enlightened
communities beneath the Southern Cross.

THE END.

PRINTED BY
KELLY AND CO., GATE STREET, LINCOLN'S INN FIELDS, W.C.;
AND MIDDLE MILL, KINGSTON-ON-THAMES.

www.ingramcontent.com/pod-product-compliance
Lightning Source LLC
Chambersburg PA
CBHW020244240426
43672CB00006B/635